MARRIAGE COUNSELING

PRENTICE-HALL INTERNATIONAL, INC., *London*
PRENTICE-HALL OF AUSTRALIA, PTY., LTD., *Sydney*
PRENTICE-HALL OF CANADA, LTD., *Toronto*
PRENTICE-HALL OF INDIA (PRIVATE) LTD., *New Delhi*
PRENTICE-HALL OF JAPAN, INC., *Tokyo*

Marriage Counseling

A MANUAL FOR MINISTERS

J. KENNETH MORRIS

PRENTICE-HALL, INC. *Englewood Cliffs, N.J.*

Library of Congress Catalog Card No.: 65-17575

Printed in the United States of America
C-55914

Dedicated to Elizabeth, Kenneth, Jr., and Robert,
their beloved mates John, Harriet, and Mary
and their children

Foreword

In September 1959, Prentice-Hall asked me if I would read a manuscript of premarital counseling for ministers. Aware of a chronic shortage of good material in this field, I readily agreed. I was gratified to find that it was an excellent manuscript, and strongly recommended its publication. It has fully justified its early promise, and is still, in my opinion, the best book available on the subject.

At that time J. Kenneth Morris was to me no more than a name. But in the intervening years, the man who bears that name has become a personal friend who has won my deepest admiration and respect. I have also come to know him, through our professional association in the American Association of Marriage Counselors, as a highly skilled practitioner in the complex art of dealing with marital problems.

When I learned that he was working on a companion volume for guiding ministers in helping parishioners in marital trouble, I was delighted. Being invited to introduce this book to its readers was a great honor. I was sure that such a task would be a very pleasant one because I knew the caliber of the writer, and was confident that the book would prove to be a good one. I was not disappointed. This volume is as good as was the other—and as badly needed.

The changing patterns of marriage in our contemporary urban-industrial culture and the often unrealistic expectations that men and women bring to the task of interpersonal adjustment between man and wife have created many marital problems. No task calling for attention in our time is more urgent than providing remedial services to the unhappy men and women confronted with the prospect that their marriages, upon which they had placed such high and fervent hopes, are daily sinking deeper in a sea of trouble.

Therapeutic intervention in a disturbed marriage is a difficult and delicate task, and some of us are devoting our lives to making increasingly competent services available to the public in this field. No professional person is more deeply involved in providing such services than the minister, who enjoys a day-to-day contact with the families in his parish, and is esteemed and trusted as a man to whom one can confidently turn in a desperate emergency. The result is that ministers, priests, and rabbis are called upon, to an extent that often alarms and disconcerts them, to perform a complex operation for which they know themselves to be poorly equipped.

Slowly the churches are coming to realize the need to provide better training in this field, and some of the younger clergymen, just out from the seminaries, are able to handle these delicate human crises with a sure touch. However, the vast majority of ministers must still do the best they can with very limited competence; and I know well from my experience in leading a few institutes and workshops for groups of clergy how eager they are to improve their skills.

We now have a growing literature in the field of marriage counseling, but some of it is too technical for the minister who has had little orientation to the behavioral sciences. There is therefore great need for written material which will give ordinary parish ministers enough self-confidence to do a creditable job, yet not enough to lure them out of their depth.

That is exactly what this book does, and does very well. J. Kenneth Morris is a highly skilled marriage counselor, but he is a humble man and a man of keen discernment. In his book he has avoided the very common human weakness of trying to impress his readers with his own knowledge. Instead he has concentrated on communicating, with a minimum of technicalities, the essential facts to do marriage counseling at the beginning level.

Moreover, he has carried out his task in a way that cannot fail to arouse and to sustain interest. It is a highly commendable feature of the book that it is based not primarily on theory, but on practice. After the necessary basic explanations in the early chapters, our author, like a good guide, takes us on a conducted tour, explaining and commenting as he goes. The main substance of the book is case histories from his own counseling experience. But he has gone further in the use of this case material than any similar book that I can recall. His cases are not merely used as illustrations; they are the very substance of his teaching.

The reader, therefore, has the rewarding experience of seeing a good marriage counselor at work and of learning from him first-hand. And whether we like it or not, in this kind of field, this experience often proves to be a better way of learning than listening to a systematized course of lectures.

Another very welcome feature of the book is that J. Kenneth Morris never forgets that he speaks as a minister-counselor. There are a few clergymen today who have become such devotees of the behavioral sciences that they seem almost apologetic about bringing in religion at all. Not so with our author. He neither drags religion in nor leaves it out. He introduces it exactly where it is relevant, and it is seen in wholesome perspective as an integral element in human life. His treatments of sin, of confession and absolution, and of redemption and forgiveness are realistic, convincing, and wholly free from cant. One sees real religion as an added dimension in good counseling, which is what it is and should be.

The reading of this book will not turn the average parish minister into a professional marriage counselor, but it will certainly clarify for him what he can do and cannot do when confronted with a marital crisis. It will help to deliver him from presumption on the one hand and from despair on the other. In short, it will make him a more effective minister to human need, aware of his limitations and yet also aware of the resources he has to offer.

The book probably will be read by only a fraction of the 247,000 clergymen who, the author tells us, are actively engaged in pastoral work in the United States, but those clergymen who do read it will be able to face more comfortably and confidently the next married couple in trouble who say—"Pastor, can you help us?"

David R. Mace
Executive Director,
American Association of Marriage Counseling

Preface

This book on marriage counseling is a sequel to my book, *Premarital Counseling—A Manual for Ministers*. *Marriage Counseling* is written for the average minister who is looking for help in his efforts to counsel those couples who are considering a dissolution of the marital bonds or those who wish to improve the marital relationship and make their marriage a happy and successful one.

A friend who has been in the ministry for many years remarked that his most frustrating experiences were in trying to help couples with marital problems. Many times I have heard other ministers express the same thought. Generally speaking, those who have consulted me (regarding couples they were counseling) revealed a lack of training, knowledge, and skills in dealing with marriages near the point of dissolution. This book is an attempt to help ministers constructively counsel such couples and thereby save and reestablish many families. Ministers can assist especially those marriages begun with the Church's blessing and consummated in Christian love.

Every broken marriage of Church-related couples leaves a divided family in the Church and weakens the Church's witness to a divided world. But it is equally disastrous to the Church and society for a family in which there are children to continue creating an atmosphere of distrust, hostility, and hate. Such marriages offer the children no stable environment in which to grow up to be well-adjusted adults capable of forming wholesome creative relationships with their fellows. This is one of the far-reaching effects of unhappy marriages, for they are continually dumping maladjusted people into society.

There is no way to determine the number of unhappy marriages. There are couples who do not believe in divorce and live together by mutual agreement to tolerate each other. There are others who love each other and could not live happily if separated, yet no longer communicate, no longer express their love in the many little intimate ways used by those whose love is more mature. Much can be done for these couples through marriage counseling with a minister who understands something of the sociological and psychological factors involved in the marital relationship.

In counseling Church families, the minister has a great advantage over the secular counselor, because he can combine the theological and psychological approaches to marital problems. The minister as a father-confessor can deal with moral problems in such a way as to bring the assurance of God's love and forgiveness to those burdened with guilt. And often it is guilt that stands in the way of a good marital adjustment.

Also, to counsel effectively, the minister must know the rudiments of psychology. Many ministers depend almost entirely upon "natural" psychology, or common-sense psychology, rather than make the effort to study psychology either by private reading or by taking courses in a university. And there are, unfortunately, some ministers who show disdain for psychology and sociology, even in their sermons. Psychology, as the study of human behavior, cannot be neglected by the minister who is genuinely interested in helping his people with their personal and marital problems. Psychology can be one of his most effective aids, not only in improving his own personal adjustments which all of us have to make, but also in counseling, which every minister must do, and in his sermons, for all ministers preach. Practically all seminaries, recognizing the importance of psychology, now have courses in pastoral counseling, and some require their students to spend a summer in Pastoral Clinical Training.

In all cases presented in this book the anonymity and confidence of counselees have been carefully protected by disguising names, locations, ages, and other information.

All biblical quotations are from the Revised Standard Version of the Bible, copyrighted 1946 and 1952 by the Division of Christian Education of the National Council of Churches, and are used by permission.

I am deeply grateful to the following who have given generously of their time and thought in criticizing the manuscript and offering valuable suggestions: Carl A. Bramlette, Jr., coordinator of planning, State Department of Mental Health; Elmore A. Martin, chief psychologist, South Carolina State Hospital; Erland N. P. Nelson, professor of psychology, University of South Carolina; and M. Kershaw Walsh, head of the department of psychology, University of South Carolina. I am especially grateful to David R. Mace, executive director, American Assocation of Marriage Counselors, for reading the manuscript and writing the foreword. I wish to express my appreciation also to Judith Steinberg for the painstaking care with which the manuscript was edited; to my wife for her encouragement throughout the years of preparation and for her assistance in proofreading; and to my daughter, Elizabeth, and Mrs. T. Clark Shuler for typing the manuscript. For errors of omission and commission which may be discovered, I am solely responsible.

J. K. M.

Contents

MARRIAGE COUNSELING

The Scope
of Marriage Counseling

1

First of all, let us consider the general scope of
marriage counseling.

This is not a new field for the minister. He has
always been a pastoral counselor, seeking to help
couples and individuals experience abundant living. That is his job.

A report of the National Conference on Family Relations
concluded that

> Marriage Counseling is an inescapable function of the pastor since
> he maintains standards of marriage, administers the sacraments, is called
> during family crises, and is involved in the attitudes and responsibilities
> of the members of the family throughout their total life-span.[1]

THE MINISTER'S UNIQUE RELATIONSHIP
TO THE FAMILY

This unique relationship of the minister to the
family cannot be equaled by the professional marriage counselor.
Also, the minister's orientation is different from that of the professional in that the minister's frame of reference is always Christian
marriage. He sees the abundant life as centered in Jesus Christ. He
is the Way, the Truth, and the Life for individuals and families.
Therefore, the minister takes a different position from other counselors.[2] The marriages that concern the minister are usually those

---

[1] "Marriage and Family Living," *Marriage Counseling and the Ministry*,
Journal of the National Council on Family Relations, VI, No. 3 (Autumn 1944),
74.

[2] Daniel Day Williams, *The Minister and the Cure of Souls* (New York:
Harper & Row, Publishers, 1961), pp. i, ii.

in his congregation. They may involve people he knows well and loves deeply. He may know their children and the couple's own parents. There may be many family connections in the parish which place upon the minister a personal emotional burden the professional marriage counselor does not experience.

Often the couple whose marriage is threatened were united in holy matrimony by the same minister who now is called upon to help them with some marital problem. The very couple who so blissfully and hopefully pledged their vows to each other now stand apart quarreling, accusing, and suspicious of each other. Any minister who truly loves and cares for his people is saddened at such a turn of events.

This does happen to some very devoted church members, for nothing is perfect in life, and men and women, whether Christian or not, are all subject to various strains and stresses. Disagreements arise in the best of families. Selfishness can rear its ugly head and destroy love and confidence. Alcoholism can enter any home and make it a shambles, materially and spiritually. Our Lord was right when He said to his devoted disciples, "Watch and pray that you may not enter into temptation." [3] When devoted church members disclose serious marital problems to the minister, he cannot but carry a heavy burden on his heart.

THE REALITY OF THE NEED
FOR MARRIAGE COUNSELING

One of the gravest social problems the Church faces today is the deterioration of family life. Families live under severe stress due to the complications of both parents working, the father often traveling and away from home several days a week; the demoralizing effect on our young people of some television programs and movies, the automobile, and unchaperoned and often unrestricted dating; and the vicious struggle for obtaining status symbols beyond the financial reach of many people.

Young marriages are on the increase, along with illegitimacy, criminal abortion, and divorce. The only remedy lies in Christian family-life education, adequate preparation for Christian marriage, and thorough premarital counseling. Unless the Church takes a

---

[3] Mark 14:38.

strong stand for the Christian ideals of marriage through educational material and group discussions with parents and young people, and unless the clergy preach sermons which speak plainly to the people, there is little hope of saving our own church families, engulfed as they are in the sea of an un-Christian and morally unhealthy society. The Christian family finds itself today, as in the time of Christ, in the world, but it must not be of the world.

For several years divorces in the United States have been approaching 400,000 a year, and legal separations are estimated to number more than 2,000,000 a year. But these figures tell us nothing about the large number of unhappy couples separated by mutual consent, some living under the same roof while occupying separate bedrooms. Nor do any of these conditions describe the loneliness of such couples or the unhappy influence upon the children in these families.[4]

The dire need for adequate preparation for marriage begins early in the school years. The need for thorough premarital counseling is emphasized by several studies made on the duration of marriage to separation and to divorce where public records carry the information required. In all of these studies it was found that the greatest number of marriage breakups come in the first 12 months in terms of separation duration and in terms of number of petitions for divorce filed.[5] This supports the popular belief that the first year of marriage is the hardest. If young people are to weather this first year, they must be prepared to meet the strain of adjustment, and there must be available to them persons trained in marriage counseling.

The accelerating degree with which people are seeking marriage counseling is evidence of the reality of an unmet need. One evidence of this is the large number of "marriage counselors" who advertise in large city newspapers. Ministers should warn their people against going to any professional marriage counselor who is not listed by the American Association of Marriage Counselors, the National Council on Family Relations, the Family Service Associa-

---

4 Rex A. Skidmore, Hulda Van Streeter Garrett, and C. Jay Skidmore, *Marriage Consulting* (New York: Harper & Row, Publishers, 1956), pp. 4, 5.

5 Thomas C. Monahan, "When Married Couples Part: Statistical Trends and Relationships in American Divorce," *American Sociological Review*, XXVII, No. 5 (1962), 625–33. This article lists a large number of references for further study.

tion, or some other reputable organization interested in marriage and the family.

Scarcely a magazine comes out today which does not have an article on marriage or sex. That people's minds are being focused upon these subjects is good, but sometimes one would think that all the world's problems are sexual. People are becoming more and more aware of what a successful marriage should hold for them in happiness, love, and companionship and are realizing that somehow their marriage has missed the boat. They read avidly the various columnists who write on love and marriage. The average person contracting a marriage anticipates happiness; however, that a large percentage do not find it is evidenced by letters to columnists, records of counseling services, and the sale of literature on marriage.

The constructive way to marriage success and happiness lies in thorough preparation for marriage. This is where many of our ministers are failing those couples who come to them for the marriage instruction now required by the Protestant Episcopal Church, the Methodist Church, the United Lutheran Church, and others. That marriage should never "be entered into inadvisedly or lightly, but reverently, discreetly, soberly and in the fear of God" [6] is the teaching of the Church, but how many young people understand what this means? Who is to help them form the kind of marriage in which they shall find happiness and the highest development of their personalities, unless they and their partners are prepared and willing to do this through premarital counseling?

Because of the lack of training of ministers in counseling couples for marriage, it is the author's experience that the premarital counseling, if given, was of little value when maladjustments appeared.

The increase in divorce is further evidence of the need for marriage counseling by ministers who by their calling should be most concerned about the success of the marriages and the stability of the homes of their own people. The rise in divorce rate can be checked only by education, preparation for marriage, and providing services capable of giving marriage counseling when needed.

Whenever there is a vacuum, something is going to fill it. The reality of the need for marriage counseling reveals a vacuum in the Church's program for helping her people, with the result that

---

[6] *The Book of Common Prayer*, p. 300.

unless the ministers assume their responsibility in this field, it will be taken over by other professions, and the minister will lose one of the most cherished opportunities to serve his people in his role as pastor.

It is good that marriage counseling is developing into a profession, however, for there will always be a vast number of marriages unrelated to the Church.

THE CONCERN OF THE CHURCHES
REGARDING DIVORCE

The churches are deeply concerned about the increasing divorce rate. Some have passed laws either requiring or advising couples facing serious marital problems to consult their ministers. The Protestant Episcopal Church makes it obligatory:

When marital unity is imperiled by dissension, it shall be the duty of either or both parties, before contemplating legal action, to lay the matter before a Minister of this Church; and it shall be the duty of such Minister to labor that the parties may be reconciled.[7]

The Methodist Church has this statement:

Divorce is not the answer to the problems that cause it. It is symptomatic of deeper difficulties. The church must stand ready to point out these basic problems to couples contemplating divorce, and help them to discover, and, if possible, to overcome such difficulties.[8]

The Presbyterian Church in the United States points out that every

. . . Christian minister will view as a vital pastoral responsibility the duty of preventing, so far as he can, by wise and prayerful counsel, the hasty or ill-considered separation or divorce of any couple committed to his care.[9]

---

[7] Canon 16, Sec. 3(c).

[8] *Doctrines and Discipline of the Methodist Church* (Nashville, Tenn.: The Methodist Publishing House, 1960), p. 693. Copyright © 1960 by Board of Publication of the Methodist Church, Inc.

[9] *The Book of Church Order of the Presbyterian Church in the United States* (Richmond: John Knox Press, 1945), Chap. 15, Sec. 215–5.

The United Lutheran Church in America adopted the following statement in 1956:

The church should extend its counseling services in an effort to maintain and strengthen families when they face difficulties threatening their unity.[10]

THE NEED TO PUBLICIZE CHURCH LAWS

It is the author's experience that very few church members are aware of church laws regarding marriage, indicating that ministers are not using a very valuable aid in getting couples to consult them about their marital difficulties. Church members who are faithful in their church duties generally want to obey the church laws, provided they understand them. It is quite possible that some couples would not wish to take their problems to their own minister, but would gladly consult another minister in whom they have confidence. There are many excellent statements on marriage expressed in the canons and resolutions of some of the churches.[11] These should be put in the church bulletins and papers frequently.

THE MINISTER NOT CONSULTED

All of these regulations acknowledge the reality of marital discord. Maladjustments in the marital relationship can and do arise among members of all churches. But the fact is that too many Church couples think first of seeing a lawyer instead of going to their own or some other minister.

Why do they not think of going first to the minister? The author's observations from counseling with many couples substantiate the following statements, which are not complimentary to our profession:

---

[10] *Minutes of the Twentieth Biennial Convention, 1956,* The United Lutheran Church in America (Philadelphia: The United Lutheran Publication House, 1956), p. 1145.

[11] For statements by the Anglican, United Lutheran, Methodist, and Presbyterian Churches, see the Appendix in the author's book, *Premarital Counseling—A Manual for Ministers* (Englewood Cliffs, N.J.: Prentice-Hall, Inc., 1960).

(1) My minister would not understand our problem. He is not qualified.

(2) I tried to talk with my minister, but he would not listen—instead he began talking about ideals of marriage. How can you talk about ideals when there is no foundation left on which to build them?

(3) Four times we consulted our pastor but he seemed too busy and hurried. He was no help at all.

(4) My minister is too innocent and other-worldly. We could not discuss our sexual problems with him.

(5) My parents told me to go to a good lawyer, that some of them are able to bring about a reconciliation.

(6) I went to a lawyer because I felt he would understand our problem better than a minister and at the same time would tell me how to protect my interests in case of a divorce.

(7) My marriage was so far gone that I felt my minister would scold and condemn me. He is so opposed to divorce that I doubt if he could possibly understand the difficulties we have in our marriage.

(8) We could not talk with our pastor because we do not feel that he would be interested in us and our problems. He is a very scholarly man!

Results of a survey conducted at Harvard Divinity School in cooperation with the Joint Commission on Mental Illness and Health found that the major reservation offered by those persons who had never gone to a clergyman for help were:

> Ministers are too moralistic and I couldn't talk to them; you'd get more hell than help; ministers don't know anything about counseling people; I just wouldn't want anyone to find out I had those kinds of problems.[12]

Where have we ministers failed our people that they should feel this way about consulting us concerning so vital a matter as their marital unity when we, generically speaking, pronounced them man and wife? So the Church laws are disregarded. Instead of the minister's counseling, legal advice is sought first.

---

[12] Richard V. McCann, *The Churches and Mental Health* (New York: Basic Books, Inc., 1962), p. 79.

CHURCH LAW AND THE MINISTER'S RESPONSIBILITY

The second requirement of these Church laws is that the minister shall "labor that the parties may be reconciled."

Of course, if the couple does not consult the minister, there is little he can do. In some cases he may be able to enter the situation, but often legal advice has already been sought and the machinery put in motion for a legal separation or divorce.

Some lawyers welcome the minister's help. Many cases have been referred to the author by lawyers who were more interested in reconciliation than in continuing the legal procedure. Whenever asked by a lawyer, physician, or friend to counsel with a couple, the author always requests that during the period of counseling the other party withdraw from the case, for if he continues to counsel with the couple, the couple is apt to be torn between the counselors. Furthermore, the lawyer, physician, or friend often takes sides and pronounces judgment, which helps not one bit. Unless they work together in close consultation as a team, two people cannot counsel the same person successfully.

Where there are two counselors available who work together, good results may be obtained by one of them counseling with the husband, the other with the wife, and consulting together. As we shall see later, a team may be composed of the minister-counselor, the family physician, legal counsel, and a psychiatrist or psychologist. Or there may be a cooperative effort including social agencies. The writer has dealt with all of these combinations.

It is not easy for the minister to initiate counseling with a couple, for they are apt to consider him as interfering. However, if he is very close to a couple and aware of their marital difficulties, he may tactfully suggest that they talk with him. If they will not do this, and there is no referral to him by lawyer, physician, or friend, then the minister is helpless to intervene.

If the couple does consult the minister, then a marriage counseling procedure is in order.

Should he always labor that the parties be reconciled? This question cannot be answered categorically, for, in the first place, the marriage may never have been of God's will and planning. The question can be answered only after an analysis of many factors involved in the marriage and its present difficulties. It is the minister's duty to explore with the couple all factors that may lead to a reconciliation. One of the minister's first questions to himself should be, Can this marriage be saved?

Some marriage counselors would disagree with this, saying that saving the marriage is not most important, but rather, what is important is helping the individuals find happiness in or out of marriage. Some seem to make light of the institution of marriage, claiming that they are not interested in preserving the institution. As a prominent professional marriage counselor said, "I do not intend to be an ambulance chaser to save the institution of marriage. My concern is only with the happiness of the individuals involved." Up to the present time, however, no substitute for marriage has been found. Individual happiness and welfare are contingent upon belongingness and the stability of the relationship in a basic institution. All disciplines recognize the family as the basic institution of society. No other institution has been found capable of providing an adequate substitute for character building and personality enhancement in children and adults. In addition to this, the frame of reference for the minister-counselor is that marriage is "instituted of God" as a means of procreation, of stabilizing the family, and of helping the individuals involved achieve their greatest happiness in their completion of each other and the realization of the potentials in their personalities.

A DEFINITION OF CHRISTIAN MARRIAGE

The Declaration of Intention (see Appendix I), required to be signed by all who marry in the Protestant Episcopal Church, substantiates this view. From it may be formulated the following definition of Christian marriage: Christian marriage is a lifelong union of a man and woman with the complete sharing of body, mind, and spirit as it is set forth in the Bible. It is for the purpose of mutual fellowship, encouragement, and understanding; for the procreation (if it may be) of children, and their physical and spiritual nurture, for the safeguarding and benefit of society.

MARRIAGE COUNSELING DEFINED

Marriage counseling may be defined as that form of counseling which (a) prepares a couple or individual for marriage,[13] (b) seeks to help couples resolve such marital problems as they may be unable to resolve without the assistance of a counselor, and (c) includes counseling of a general nature regarding any problem disturbing to the peace and welfare of the family.

Gladys Gaylord offers this definition:

Marriage counseling is the process of helping men and women, before and after marriage, to consider objectively their roles in marriage and their responsibilities for the atmosphere of the home.[14]

Marriage counseling involves (a) instructing the couple before marriage—premarital counseling; (b) helping couples to make adjustments in their marital relationship when difficulties arise; and (c) helping families enhance all the interpersonal relationships within the family constellation.

According to Skidmore, Garrett, and Skidmore:

Marriage counseling, then, is the process of helping persons, mainly through interviewing, to help themselves in regard to problems and plans involving courtship, marriage, or family living. Its main objective, according to Burgess, is to promote human happiness and personality development.[15]

PREPARATION FOR COUNSELING ESSENTIAL

Every factor in a marriage imperiled by dissension should be carefully analyzed in the hope of finding a basis on which to reconstruct the marital relationship.

This is one of the most important jobs the minister has. He must not fail his people here. They have a right to expect him by

---

[13] Fully discussed in Morris, *Premarital Counseling—A Manual for Ministers,* and will not be dealt with in this book.

[14] Gladys Gaylord, "Marriage Counseling in Wartime," *Annals of the American Academy of Political and Social Science,* September, 1943, p. 39.

[15] Skidmore, Garrett, and Skidmore, *Marriage Consulting,* pp. 12–13.

his reading, studying, and clinical experience to be able to do what the Church lays upon him as a duty and tells him he must do: ". . . labor that the parties may be reconciled." Obviously he cannot do this unless he prepares himself for it.

This book is an attempt to enable the minister to catch a glimpse of this phase of the great work to which God has called him. To meet the needs of his families the minister must study marital problems and become proficient in marriage counseling. The Church allows him no alternative; nor should he seek one; for when his people are in marital difficulties, his heart should go out to them in prayer and earnest endeavor to help them, by the grace of God, to rebuild their marriage on a solid foundation.

It is not expected that every minister should prepare himself to become a professional marriage counselor, although some ministers are undergoing training to this end. In fact, the counseling phase of the minister's work is becoming more and more important to the parish program, and some parishes have on their staff a minister-counselor. Pastoral clinical training is also helping ministers to become good counselors.

Some understanding of the dynamics of personality development, the art of human relations, and the techniques of counseling, supplemented by continued reading, study, and clinical experience, will enable the minister to be of help to those couples who bring him their problems. He will be able also to detect such defects of personality in the individuals as may require referral for psychiatric treatment. If he is to do effective marriage counseling, the minister must prepare himself along minimal lines of study.

The American Association of Marriage Counselors, Inc., recognizing that marriage counseling as a profession is still in the process of being established and that those engaging in it today are working in other fields, such as religion, education, psychology, and social work, has set up certain basic requirements for membership.

The AAMC defines its standard of training in this field as requiring a minimum of one academic year of supervised clinical internship in marriage counseling as such, following the attainment of all credentials and the appropriate graduate degree required for the practice of one of the established helping professions, such as medicine, psychiatry, psychology, education, theology, or sociology. Marriage counseling is thus seen as an advanced professional operation requiring special training and representing perhaps the most complex therapy in the entire field of personal adjustment. The AAMC feels that its membership should be confined to those who represent a high level of clinical excellence.[16] The Association does not use terms such as "licensing," "certification," or "accreditation." Those who hold membership have had their clinical competence investigated; they are under obligation to observe the AAMC Code of Professional Ethics; referrals are made to them with confidence in their professional ability. These requirements may also be a guide in the preparation of ministers who are especially concerned in counseling people with marital problems. A most important qualification for any counselor is that he loves people, gets along well himself with people, and sincerely desires to help those who come to him.

THE MINISTER'S EMOTIONAL MATURITY ESSENTIAL

Ministers who have not resolved their own personal and marital problems may be in the position of the blind leading the blind. Maladjusted ministers may do harm to those who consult them by contributing to a client's emotional instability, thus accelerating a pathological mental condition and causing increased family disturbance.[17]

Personal emotional maturity is essential to pastoral counseling in any area, and self-understanding is a prime requisite in understanding others.

Ministers are not immune from marital difficulties; those same problems which plague other humans plague them also. I have counseled ministers' sons and daughters who described their unhappy home background due to quarreling between parents, oversevere parental authority, in-law problems, friction over spending the family income, unwanted children, and lack of mutual consideration between members of the family. There are couples in the min-

---

[16] Since requirements for membership in the American Association of Marriage Counselors, Inc., change with the advance and development of marriage counseling, any interested persons should write to the Executive Director, 27 Woodcliff Drive, Madison, New Jersey.

[17] David O. Moberg, *The Church as a Social Institution* (Englewood Cliffs, N.J.: Prentice-Hall, Inc., 1962), p. 364.

istry who because of their position in the community endure an unhappy marriage and seek no help from a marriage counselor.

If the minister is struggling with some unresolved problem between himself and his wife and a couple present to him the same kind of problem, he will very likely become subjective in his attitude toward the couple and may even try to use them for the therapeutic help he and his wife failed to seek. But if the minister has resolved his own marital problems, or at least has talked them out with a counselor, then he can see more objectively the problems presented to him by a couple, thus helping them also to see them objectively and to work toward a solution.

Before a psychiatrist is permitted to practice psychoanalysis, he must first be psychoanalyzed. It is the writer's opinion that before the minister can do his most effective marriage counseling, he should also be counseled regarding his own marriage and his own personality problems, so that by being more objective with those who come to him for counseling, he will be better able to avoid countertransference.

Countertransference as defined by Colby

. . . refers to all the therapist's feelings and reactions regarding the patient. But in its limited and more accurate sense, it concerns those moments when one unconsciously reacts to a patient [counselee] as if he were some important figure in one's own psychological past.[18]

For example, a minister who as a child had not gotten along well with his father might feel toward an older man consulting him much the same way he had felt toward his father and show hostility toward the counselee. Or, again, a minister who does not get along well with his wife may be consulted by a wife who raises some of the same problems his own wife raises with him, resulting in his adopting an attitude toward the counselee similar to his attitude toward his wife. The minister who is willing to recognize his marital difficulties and seek counseling himself will avoid such pitfalls as these which may affect adversely his ability to help those who come to him.

---

[18] Kenneth M. Colby, *A Primer for Psychotherapists* (New York: The Ronald Press Company, 1951), p. 25. Copyright 1951 by The Ronald Press Company.

COUNSELING—A PASTORAL FUNCTION

Richard V. McCann [19] reports on a survey made by mail of parish clergymen. The directors of 212 state and city councils of churches in the United States were asked to send names and addresses of 10 to 15 clergymen in each council with little as well as much experience in counseling, from rural and urban parishes, and representing a variety of denominations. Of 480 clergymen sent the questionnaire, 166 replied. In addition, 45 Roman Catholic priests who were attending a workshop on mental health were contacted, and from a list provided by rabbinical associations, 80 replies were received. Fourteen Protestant denominations and 24 states were represented in the replies.

The respondents were asked to state what they thought was the most important aspect of their ministry in contributing to the emotional and spiritual growth of their parishioners. They were not asked to choose from a list but "were given complete freedom in answering the questions." Preaching, given first place, was followed in close second place by counseling. Other significant aspects of their ministry in decreasing frequency were pastoral visiting, worship, church fellowship, teaching, and the personality attributes of the clergyman.

Although counseling was selected by the second largest number as most effective in applying spiritual answers to their parishioners' problems, many of the respondents reflected concern over their own adequacy to deal with parishioners' emotional conflicts and other related matters. Their self-criticism, and in some cases self-doubts, centered around two focal points: their own capacity and adequacy as persons, and their training and experience.

Most of the problems brought to these clergymen were concerned with marriage and the family. Another wide area of parishioner problems with which these ministers expressed concern was "the whole domain of personality development." This in turn also involves the family, home environment, and parent-child relationships.

---

[19] McCann, *The Churches and Mental Health*, pp. 173ff.

It may be concluded from this survey that the average clergy-man is a pastoral counselor who does a considerable amount of marriage counseling.

Nameche [20] conducted structured interviews with a stratified random sample of 100 Protestant ministers. He found that urban and suburban ministers counsel an average of 2.2 hours a week; rural ministers slightly less. This amounts to approximately 112 hours per year. Other data indicates that the average number of counseling sessions for each counselee is four. Therefore a minister might counsel with 28 different persons during the year. The ministers were divided into three theological categories based on their responses: conservative, moderate, and liberal. The moderate Protestant group did by far the most counseling; the liberals were second; the conservatives (including fundamentalist) third.

About 60 per cent of the clergymen interviewed counsel less than two hours per week, depending on a kind of common-sense psychology. These men may have had one or two general psychology courses, usually in college rather than in the seminary, but they are usually unfamiliar with abnormal and counseling psychology. (It is estimated that less than 10 per cent of the country's clergymen have received clinical pastoral training or its equivalent in psychology or counseling.)

A third of the clergymen counsel between two and nine hours per week; many of these have received their training in psychology at the seminary level.

The last 7 per cent of the clergymen, mostly theologically "moderate," spend from ten to twenty-two hours a week doing counseling, and usually have had graduate training in clinical or social (not pastoral) psychology. Many are trained at least to the Master's Degree level in psychology; some have doctorates in psychology; others in pastoral psychology. The greater part of pastoral counseling, it would appear, is done by a comparatively small number of clergymen.[21]

Nameche found that twice as many women as men had sought help from the clergy.

---

[20] Gene F. Nameche, *Pastoral Counseling in Protestant Churches,* Part I: "The Minister as Counselor." (Unpublished manuscript, 1958.) Research project at Harvard Divinity School. Results of survey reported in McCann, *The Churches and Mental Health,* pp. 75ff.

[21] McCann, *The Churches and Mental Health,* p. 76. In these paragraphs McCann has summarized Nameche's findings.

Where marital discord is the cause of seeking pastoral counseling, it is more likely the wife who comes to the clergyman, and only after considerable persuasion does the husband enter a counseling relationship.

. . . . .

Individuals who had been to their clergyman for counseling were no more active in church affairs than the average parishioner. Thus, contrary to many church members' expectations, it would appear that one does not need a long record of church activity, involvement, and "faithfulness" to call on his pastor for personal help in time of distress. In fact, in terms of daily religious activity, the counselees interviewed were considerably *less* active than the average noncounseled parishioner. Counselees of ministers seemed to be no more "pious" than laymen who don't go for counseling. Whether persons who are less active in church affairs, less involved with church, less "faithful," less "pious," need—and receive—more pastoral counseling cannot, of course be established from these data.[22]

It was also found that those who sought help from the minister did not select one on the basis of any special training he might have but because they felt that he was concerned. Nameche distinguished seven broad categories of counseling problems brought to the clergymen. These were in order of frequency:

(1) Marriage and family
(2) Psychological distress
(3) Youth behavior
(4) Illness and aging
(5) Alcoholism
(6) Religious and spiritual
(7) Vocational-occupational

Only between 6 and 9 per cent of all counseling problems were directly concerned with "religious or spiritual" matters.

PASTORAL FUNCTION AND COMMUNITY SERVICE

Personality growth and creativity are not limited to church or religious activities. A counselee's spiritual concern should be expanded to include the whole community. Many latent potentialities lie dormant because no one guided them into fields of service through which their potentialities could develop. Mem-

---

[22] McCann, *The Churches and Mental Health*, p. 77.

bership on agency boards and volunteer work in hospitals and other institutions can open up great avenues of service and promote mental health, a sense of being needed, and a feeling of accomplishment.

OUT OF A PARISH MINISTRY

The author's parish ministry substantiates generally the findings presented in *The Churches and Mental Illness*. It was proven in his case that as his training and proficiency increased, the case load increased. People come to have more confidence in taking their problems to a clergyman known to have training and experience in counseling.

During the last decade of his parish ministry,[23] problems brought by counselees were classified under several broad categories: marriage, premarital, personal, and family. Problems relating to marriage involved such personal problems as alcoholism, sex, and infidelity in about 75 per cent (estimated) of the couples. Family finances were also high on the list, followed by social activities, in-law relationships, religious activities, mutual friends, and problems involving job analysis and vocational guidance.[24]

In the category of family problems, the predominant areas of discord involved child training; teenage behavior, especially relating to dating and going steady; and premarital pregnancy.

Personal problems involved alcoholism, sexual promiscuity, homosexuality, and dishonesty. These counselees were disturbed enough about their personality adjustment problems to seek help. Referral for psychiatric treatment was made when indicated.

Those who came with specific religious problems were very few. Their problems included lack of faith and questions about the Bible, the Church, and the sacraments. Of course, because many of the problems mentioned above involved guilt, the need for a new religious orientation was frequently expressed. This was sometimes given as the reason for coming to a minister-counselor. People generally do want a religious orientation provided it is intelligent,

---

[23] In 1961 the author left the parish ministry to become the Director and Counselor of the Marriage Counseling Service under the auspices of the Bishop of the Diocese of Upper South Carolina of the Protestant Episcopal Church.

[24] Compare Judson T. Landis and Mary G. Landis, *Building a Successful Marriage* (4th ed.; Englewood Cliffs, N.J.: Prentice-Hall, Inc., 1963), p. 361.

allows freedom for creative development, and is relevant to modern life.

Without thorough preparation and training the minister-counselor can no more deal with people concerned with such a variety of problems than a physician can treat his patients without adequate knowledge and training. The minister today is faced with unparalleled opportunities to be of help to his people in personality enhancement, religious growth, and mental health, but he must be prepared and trained to do it.

Fairchild and Wynn [25] report a survey begun in 1956 in which questionnaires were sent to 3,541 Presbyterian ministers serving churches; from that number, 74.7 per cent were returned, and from these, 1,000 questionnaires were selected for tabulation. The largest number, 38.1 per cent, were serving churches having 100 to 299 members. In three age groupings (under thirty-five, thirty-five to forty-nine, fifty or over) they were fairly evenly divided; the largest, 36 per cent, were in the thirty-five- to forty-nine-year-old age group. The ministers were asked to rank in order the ten functions they would most like to improve through special training if given the opportunity and time. Counseling headed the list. The ministers felt that this feature of their pastoral care was one of their two greatest contributions to family stability (the other being preaching and worship). From counseling they revealed that "they gain more sense of satisfaction and accomplishment than from any other ministry they perform." The authors draw this conclusion:

> Whatever their situation, urban, suburban, or rural, pastors everywhere are seeking additional help in their counseling because these problems (marriage and family living) are growing more complicated and difficult as our culture grows more complex and unfathomable.[26]

CHURCH COUNSELING CENTERS

The churches are establishing pastoral counseling centers as trained personnel becomes available. Clergymen, whether trained or not, have always counseled, and still do, with

---

[25] Roy W. Fairchild and John Charles Wynn, *Families in the Church: A Protestant Survey* (New York: Association Press, 1961), pp. 205–7, 234, 235.

[26] Fairchild and Wynn, *Families in the Church: A Protestant Survey*, p. 235.

their church members. This has been recognized as a function of the ministry since its founding. There are 246,600 active clergymen with charges in the United States.[27] It is estimated that only 8,000 have had some form of clinical pastoral education in their seminaries or since ordination.[28]

Berkeley Hathorne [29] made a listing in 1960 of 73 pastoral counseling centers [30] sponsored by the church, denomination, or council of churches located in 24 states and the District of Columbia. Detailed reports were received from 48 centers. Of these 48, 15 are located in the northeast, 14 in the north central section, 6 in the southeast, 5 in the south central section, and 8 in the southwest. The majority are located primarily in the larger urban communities; only one center is in a town with fewer than 10,000 inhabitants. Forty-three are located in cities with a population of over 50,000, and 20 are in cities with a population larger than 500,000.

A summary of the survey follows:

A majority of the centers have been established under the auspices of a single church or denominational organization, with individual churches accounting for over a third of the total. Local interdenominational councils of churches have taken responsibility for nine of the centers; an equal number have been sponsored privately. Six of the centers studied operate under the auspices of hospitals and schools. One was set up by a major tobacco company.

The measure of competence of counselors is difficult to ascertain; however, academic preparation, clinical training, and professional experience are valid indications of qualifications. Thirty-six centers reported in detail the qualifications of the counselors, including degrees, clinical training, professional affiliations, and experience. A total of 153 counselors are associated with the 36 centers: 101 ordained clergymen, 17 psychiatrists, 16 clinical and educational psychologists, 18 social workers (mostly psychiatrically trained), and one gynecologist. Thirty-seven of the centers are directed by clergymen, three by psychiatrists, and two by social work-

27 Benson Y. Landis, ed., *Yearbook of American Churches* (Office of Publication and Distribution, National Council of Churches of Christ in the U.S.A., 1964), p. 266.

28 McCann, *The Churches and Mental Health*, p. 81.

29 McCann, *The Churches and Mental Health*, pp. 86ff.

30 Since this survey, this number has increased to 161 as listed in the 1964 *Directory of the American Association of Pastoral Counselors.*

ers. Seven of the directors are or have been hospital chaplains. Six are or have been professors of pastoral psychology and counseling.[31]

The above survey indicates the concern of the churches to meet the needs of their people through a well-organized scientific approach in cooperation with other disciplines.

PERSONAL QUALIFICATIONS FOR THE MINISTER-COUNSELOR

Listed below are some of the personal qualifications for the minister-counselor: He should

(1)   Love people for what they are, not for what they do
(2)   Understand his own emotional drives and problems
(3)   Be patient with human frailty
(4)   Be a good listener
(5)   Display warmth and friendliness
(6)   Manifest his desire to be of help
(7)   Cultivate the mind of Christ that he may see through the failures of people to their real potentialities when touched by the Spirit of God
(8)   Have Christian marriage as his frame of reference
(9)   Have a broad background of training in the allied disciplines of psychology, sociology, and anthropology
(10) Have a sense of humor
(11) Be able to take a professional stance in his counseling
(12) Be objective, able to carry his "problem" people in prayer, but not be emotionally involved and upset by them
(13) Be relatively free from annoying traits and habits
(14) Limit himself to his own area of competence
(15) Possess humility
(16) Realize that there is a solution to every problem in the mind of God and seek together with the counselee to find that solution
(17) Have self-understanding
(18) Recognize the need for the individual to direct his own life and to participate in plans concerning his life

---

[31] McCann, *The Churches and Mental Health*, p. 88.

(19)   Understand that people do not like to be stereotyped; that each individual has a right to be different from every other individual

(20)   Be able to accept hostility and aggression, as well as love and affection, as normal reactions of human beings toward one another

(21)   Be able to feel with individuals, without feeling like them

(22)   Understand that all behavior is purposive for the individual concerned

(23)   Be able to keep confidences

FOUR ATTRIBUTES OF THE THERAPIST

Dollard and Miller [32] name four attributes of the therapist that apply to a large degree to the minister-counselor, who functions also as a teacher in the counseling situation. They suggest that he should be mentally free, empathic, restrained, and positive.

Mental freedom

The counselor must be able to hear and restate, without anxiety, whatever the counselee may say. The minister must not censor what he hears or thinks but must accept objectively what is told him as part of a real life situation. To quote Dollard and Miller:

In listening without criticizing, the therapist is not saying that "anything goes." He is merely affirming that the past is past and cannot be changed. The conditions of the past must be identified and the habits they produced be recognized. Only in this way can patients gain some faith that the conditions of the present are different and that the habits learned under past conditions are not appropriate to present conditions. Naturally if the therapist shows fear or avoidance when the patient fearfully communicates his thoughts, the therapist will strengthen rather than weaken repressive tendencies in the patient. The therapist will then be unable to learn what he needs to know to help the patient reconstruct his life.[33]

---

[32] John Dollard and Neal E. Miller, *Personality and Psychotherapy* (New York: McGraw-Hill Book Company, 1950), pp. 411 ff.

[33] Dollard and Miller, *Personality and Psychotherapy*, p. 411.

Empathy

The counselor should be able to respond to the counselee's emotional feeling with understanding and appropriate feelings of his own, except, of course, in the case of excessive fear expressed by the counselee.

One can agree with Rogers that the counselor's function is not emotional identification, "but rather an empathic identification, where the counselor is perceiving the hates and hopes and fears of the client through immersion in an empathic process, but without himself, as counselor, experiencing those hates and hopes and fears." [34]

Restraint

The counselor should not allow the counseling session to become a mere conversation. He must restrain himself from the give and take and argument characteristic of conversation. He is responsible for the control of the session and to see that it moves constructively toward helping the counselee reach an objective understanding of his problems in order to work toward solving them. "The therapist should restrain himself from giving any verbal cue which the patient can hit upon by himself and should allow good time for the patient to try." [35]

Positive outlook

The counselor must believe in the counselee's ability to adjust to real life situations in keeping with his capabilities, mental and physical. He must convey this attitude to the counselee. As we shall see in the cases presented later, many of those who come for counseling have failed to make satisfactory adjustments to the environment—be it marriage, children, relatives, friends, business associates, or what not—and feel frustrated, inadequate, and defeated. The counselee's greatest need may be to have the counselor believe in him and in his ability to learn new skills either in adjusting to or in changing his environment.

---

[34] Carl R. Rogers, *Client-centered Therapy* (Boston: Houghton Mifflin Company, 1959), p. 29.

[35] Dollard and Miller, *Personality and Psychotherapy*, p. 409.

Of course the counselor must be careful not to hold on to the counselee. The aim of counseling is to enable the counselee to learn skills with which he can deal successfully or adequately with his problems and life situations so that he has confidence in himself to go it alone, independent of further support by the counselor. The minister-counselor's task is not to seek "disciples" who cling to his ecclesiastical robes, looking always to him for guidance. We should seek, instead, to help those who come to us to become independent persons in their own right, free to develop their personalities and to grow into "mature manhood, to the measure of the stature of the fullness of Christ." [36] And we must believe positively that this can be achieved. Many a counselee has said to me, "I don't believe he (she) can possibly change." My reply is, "If I believed people could not change, I would have no gospel to preach and my work as a counselor would be of little value. I am in this work because I believe he (she) and you can change and learn new and better skills in dealing creatively with life situations."

When the minister-counselor goes into an interview with that conviction, he conveys strength and encouragement to the counselee, and they are soon on their way toward good rapport, mutual confidence, and learning experiences.[37]

SUMMARY

This chapter has presented the scope of marriage counseling as it involves the minister because of his unique relationship to families in the Church. This relationship cannot be equaled by the professional marriage counselor. The minister views marriage as a part of the Christian way of life and understands that if marriages in the Church break down, then those affected are left without a full representation of Christian living. Therefore, the minister will strive to help his people build such marriages as will result in the abundant life for all members of the family.

It is a part of the minister's job to prepare himself to do counseling by a reading program, study, and clinical experience.

---

[36] Ephesians 3:13.

[37] A. H. Maslow, *Motivation and Personality* (New York: Harper & Row, Publishers, 1954), pp. 312–13.

To meet the needs of his families he must understand marital problems and the techniques of counseling.

The minister's own degree of emotional maturity and the success of his own marriage are requisites for good counseling. Some may require counseling in order to guard against countertransference.

Marriage counseling can be a very humbling experience for the minister. There are times when he may feel that he stands on holy ground and has no right to be there, that what he is witnessing is something only God should see. Many a time in counseling he will need to pray silently as he listens that the Holy Spirit will enable him to perceive reality as the counselee sees it; will guide the counselee into new avenues of progress, opening new vistas of growth; and will ultimately illuminate both their minds to see reality as it really is. It is remarkable how effectively this silent prayer to the Holy Spirit opens up new approaches to problems and makes clearer what objectives should be sought. One cannot go through a counseling session without being deeply affected by it; indeed, to quote Rogers again, one finds oneself "compellingly influenced by the therapeutic experience of which one has been a part." [38]

SUGGESTED READING

Brammer, Lawrence M. and Everett L. Shostrom, *Therapeutic Psychology*, Chaps. 1, 4, 12. Englewood Cliffs, N.J.: Prentice-Hall, Inc., 1960.

Carrington, William L., M.D., *The Healing of Marriage*, Chaps. 1, 3. Great Neck, N.Y.: Channel Press, 1961.

Cryer, Newman S., Jr. and John Monroe Vayhinger, eds., *Casebook in Pastoral Counseling*, Introduction. Nashville: Abingdon Press, 1962.

Moser, Leslie E., *Counseling: A Modern Emphasis in Religion*, Chap. 1. Englewood Cliffs, N.J.: Prentice-Hall, Inc., 1962.

Oates, Wayne E., *Protestant Pastoral Counseling*, Chaps. 1, 6. Philadelphia: The Westminster Press, 1962.

Wise, Carroll, *Pastoral Counseling in Theory and Practice*. New York: Harper & Row, Publishers, 1951.

---

[38] Rogers, *Client-centered Therapy*, p. xi.

Factors Involved
in Marriage Counseling

2   In this chapter we will consider some of the basic factors involved in marriage counseling which will help the minister make a good beginning in this rather new field of pastoral theology—new in the sense that the modern day minister must be oriented toward marriage counseling as a prime function of his ministry.

Counseling with individuals about life's deepest problems brings into the minister's office the hopes, fears, and anxieties of persons desperately striving to find for themselves full and more satisfying lives. As the individual struggles to express himself, the counselor tries to identify with him and to perceive reality as he sees it. He tries to open a way for the counselee to move toward the realization of his potentialities as a human being created in the moral and spiritual image of God—to see himself as a worthwhile person, thereby gaining hope and the courage to improve his relationships with others. As Carl Rogers says,

> I rejoice at the privilege of being a midwife to a new personality—as I stand by with awe at the emergence of a self, a person, as I see a birth process in which I have had an important and facilitating part.[1]

THE ATTITUDE OF THE COUNSELOR

The counselor must above all else believe in the worth of the individual and in the ability of the individual both

---

[1] Carl R. Rogers, *Client-centered Therapy* (Boston: Houghton Mifflin Company, 1959), p. x.

to make decisions regarding his life plan and to carry them out. As Rogers [2] points out, to have a deep respect for and acceptance for another is most likely to be the philosophy held by a person who has a basic respect for the worth and significance of himself. He cannot, in all likelihood, accept others unless he has first accepted himself.

To speak of the worth of the individual is not new to the Christian minister. He has been taught that nothing is of greater value than the individual. Jesus said, "For what does it profit a man, to gain the whole world and forfeit his life?" [3] which may be interpreted to mean that one's real self, one's personality, is something of infinite value to be greatly treasured. Therefore, anything which cheapens, belittles, or injures the real self must be avoided. Moreover, the self like any other organism has a natural power to enhance itself in accord with its ideals and goals. For the counselor this means that he must show great respect for every individual who consults him.

It means also that whatever deviation in behavior and morals the counselee describes must be seen against the background of the counselee's version of the life situation as it appears real to him. In no case should the counselor be shocked, ashamed, or embarrassed. If he is, then he increases the shame and guilt of the counselee, but if he is not, then the counselee feels free to move ahead in coping with his problems. When attitudes of guilt, shame, and disgust expressed by the counselee are accepted without emotion by the counselor, then those attitudes become objectified and subject to control and organization. This means, to quote Rogers:

. . . that it is the counselor's function to assume, in so far as he is able, the internal frame of reference of the client, to perceive the world as the client sees it, to perceive the client himself as he is seen by himself, to lay aside all perceptions from the external frame of reference while doing so, and to communicate something of this empathic understanding to the client. [4]

This is by no means easy to accomplish. It requires considerable concentration. Even the most experienced counselor will at

---

[2] Rogers, *Client-centered Therapy*, p. 22, fn.

[3] Matthew 16:26.

[4] Rogers, *Client-centered Therapy*, p. 29.

times find himself "standing outside the client's frame of reference and looking as an external perceiver at the client."

In psychological terms, it is the counselor's aim to perceive as sensitively and accurately as possible all of the perceptual field as it is being experienced by the client, with the same figure and ground relationships, to the full degree that the client is willing to communicate that perceptual field; and having thus perceived this internal frame of reference of the other as completely as possible, to indicate to the client the extent to which he is seeing through the client's eyes.

Suppose that we attempt a description somewhat more in terms of the counselor's attitudes. The counselor says in effect, "To be of assistance to you I will put aside myself—the self of ordinary interaction—and enter into your world of perception as completely as I am able. I will become, in a sense, another self for you—an alter ego of your own attitudes and feelings—a safe opportunity for you to discern yourself more clearly, to experience yourself, more truly and deeply, to choose more significantly." [5]

. . . . .

We might say then, that for many therapists functioning from a client-centered orientation, the sincere aim of getting "within" the attitudes of the client, of entering the client's internal frame of reference, is the most complete implementation which has thus far been formulated, for the central hypothesis of respect for the reliance upon the capacity of the person.[6]

AN ILLUSTRATION FROM ROGERS

Rogers gives an example:

. . . from a report written by a young woman who had been, at the time she came in for counseling, rather deeply disturbed. She had some slight knowledge about client-centered therapy before coming for help. The report from which this material is taken was written spontaneously and voluntarily some six weeks after the conclusion of the counseling interviews.

In the earlier interviews, I kept saying such things as "I am not acting like myself." "I never acted this way before." What I meant was that this withdrawn, untidy, and apathetic person was not myself. I was trying to say that this was a different person from the one who had previously functioned with what seemed to be satisfactory adjustment. It

---

[5] Rogers, *Client-centered Therapy*, pp. 34–35.
[6] Rogers, *Client-centered Therapy*, p. 36.

seemed to me that must be true. Then I began to realize that I was the same person, seriously withdrawn, etc., now, as I had been before. That did not happen until after I had talked out my self-rejection, shame, despair, and doubt, in the accepting situation of the interview. The counselor was not startled or shocked. I was telling him all these things about myself which did not fit into my picture of a graduate student, a teacher, a sound person. He responded with complete acceptance and warm interest without heavy emotional overtones. Here was a sane, intelligent person wholeheartedly accepting this behavior that seemed so shameful to me. I can remember an organic feeling of relaxation. I did not have to keep up the struggle to cover up and hide this shameful person.

Retrospectively, it seems to me that what I felt as "warm acceptance with(out) emotional overtones" was what I needed to work through my difficulties. One of the things I was struggling with was the character of my relationships with others. I was enmeshed in dependence, yet fighting against it. My mother, knowing that something was wrong, had come to see me. Her love was so powerful, I could feel it enveloping me. Her suffering was so real that I could touch it. But I could not talk to her. Even when out of her insight, she said, while she talking of my relationships with the family, "You can be as dependent or as independent as you like," I still resisted her. The counselor's impersonality with interest allowed me to talk out my feelings. The clarification in the interview situation presented the attitude to me as a *ding an sich* which I could look at, manipulate, and put in place. In organizing my attitudes, I was beginning to organize me.

I can remember sitting in my room and thinking about the components of infantile needs and dependence in maladjustment, and strongly resisting the idea that there was any element of dependence in my behavior. I think I reacted the way I might have if a therapist in an interview situation had interpreted this for me before I was ready for it. I kept thinking about it, though, and began to see that, although I kept insistently telling myself I wanted to be independent, there was plenty of evidence that I was also wanting protection and dependence. This was a shameful situation, I felt. I did not come to accept this indecision in myself until I had guiltily brought it up in the interviews, had it accepted, and then stated it again myself with less anxiety. In this situation, the counselor's reflection of feeling with complete acceptance let me see the attitude with some objectivity. In this case, the insight was structured rationally before I went to the interview. However, it was not internalized until the attitude had been reflected back to me free of shame and guilt, a thing in itself which I could look at and accept. My restatements and further exposition of feeling after the counselor's reflection were my own acceptance and internalization of the insight.[7]

The people who come for counseling are those who are disturbed and anxious about some life situation with which they feel inadequate to cope. If it is a threatening marriage relationship, and especially if children are involved, they may have a deep sense of failure. They need to talk with someone whom they can trust and who will give them an emotionally warm relationship in which they will experience a feeling of safety in expressing any attitude, assured that the counselor perceives and accepts the relationship in the same way that the counselee does, but unemotionally.

The therapist perceives the client's self as the client has known it, and accepts it; he perceives the contradictory aspects which have been denied to awareness and accepts those too as being a part of the client; and both of these acceptances have in them the same warmth and respect. Thus it is that the client, experiencing in another an acceptance of both these aspects of himself, can take toward himself the same attitude. He finds that he too can accept himself even with the additions and alterations that are necessitated by these new perceptions of himself as hostile. He can experience himself as a person having hostile as well as other types of feelings, and can experience himself in this way without guilt. He has been enabled to do this (if our theory is correct) because another person has been able to adopt his frame of reference, to perceive with him, yet to perceive with acceptance and respect.[8]

It should be emphasized that in all counseling the minister need only remind himself of New Testament instances in which Jesus showed His love, concern, and respect for the individual; in each case He was able so to relate himself to them and their problems that they were freed from shame, guilt, fears, and anxieties and were thus able to acquire new attitudes toward themselves and accept themselves as forgiven and accepted by God. St. Paul calls this rising from the dead to a new life in Christ. Theologically, a resurrection takes place in every successful counseling process as an end result. It comes when the counselee can look upon his former life (the old self) objectively, can accept it, with self-forgiveness, as a part of himself, and, looking to the future, can see himself as a new self able to achieve the ideals and goals he cherishes.

---

[7] Rogers, *Client-centered Therapy*, pp. 38–39.
[8] Rogers, *Client-centered Therapy*, p. 41.

THE COUNSELOR'S IDENTIFICATION
WITH THE COUNSELEE

The minister-counselor may find it difficult to dissociate himself from the moral problems that arouse resentment and condemnation in a counselee whose spouse has been unfaithful. Although the minister-counselor is not called on to condone immorality, neither is he expected to prejudge or condemn the spouse whom he may not have counseled. The counselor must not allow himself to be biased by one spouse against the other. In counseling cases involving what the minister-counselor may feel is "obviously immoral," he must remain objective and accepting toward both spouses.

In a case involving a wife's adultery which led to pregnancy and then to criminal abortion, the writer found in his notes summarizing the first interview, which was with the husband, that he had unconsciously written, "Does not know whether we can accept her." He should have written, ". . . whether *he* can accept her." This was discovered as he was preparing for his first interview with the wife. As soon as he noticed the "we," he began some self-analysis of his own: Was he rejecting her sight unseen? Was he prejudging her, and had he already condemned her?

The writer had to admit, as he recalled the interview with the husband, that he had felt strong feelings toward the wife, not only because of her adultery in the light of her husband's professed faithfulness, but also because of her agreeing to the abortion which he demanded, then blaming him for her adultery and the abortion. The writer's feelings toward him were mixed. He could not go along with the abortion, but he was understanding in regard to the husband's feeling about the adultery.

Morally, the writer could condone neither. But as a counselor, and therefore a catalyst, he could not judge, condemn, or sympathize. He needed to refresh himself on his own need and ability to understand empathically both of them.

Every counselor needs to watch out for indications in his discussions and notes of evidence of his own psychological involvements in the client's problems. Because he must remain objective, he must not be afraid to face up to any betraying evidence in his notes indicating his bias. Indeed, he must be scrupulously severe with himself to see that his prejudices do not influence his attitudes toward the counselee.

OPENING THE CLOSED MIND

One of the counselor's main jobs is to open closed minds so that creative thinking may be brought to bear upon the problems. The old cliché, "My mind is made up; do not confuse me with the facts," must be circumvented. Allowing a client to express fully even his unsubstantiated opinions without opposition or argument relieves the client of considerable anxiety. When the anxiety is reduced, the counselor then can, because of his seeming agreement, ask for the factual evidence that may lead to a reevaluation of the whole problem.

A woman who had made up her mind that divorce was the only practical solution to her unhappy marriage came to ask the counselor's opinion. (Of course, this in itself was evidence that she had some question about her decision.) The counselor heard her out for some 30 minutes. He then agreed, asking why she did not go ahead and get her divorce; then, as though an afterthought, he said, "Let us write on the greenboard the incontrovertible facts which you will present to the court." She had none. She then asked, "Do you think our marriage can be saved?" This led to a discussion of the positive values in the marriage. Her mind was now open for creative thinking. Her husband also came for counseling, and the marriage was saved.

Closed minds are a block to creative thinking and to progress in any kind of interpersonal relationship, be it family, social club, business, or politics.

UNDERSTANDING

No qualification of the counselor excels understanding. Sometimes the minister can do nothing to help solve the problems brought to him. They are too complicated. Their ramifications are too complex. But he can always try to understand.

Even though she had two small children, a woman whose husband was overseas allowed herself to fall in love with a man several years younger. She and her lover worked in the same establishment. Both of them were from families of good reputation. She came for counseling. Later the author received this note from her:

> May I thank you for your time, your advice, your understanding. I felt your time was a sort of special commodity, and I expected your advice to be certainly sound; but your understanding was an unexpected gift. Thank you.

One may ask, why did this woman come to a minister-counselor in the first place? What kind of help was she seeking? She was neurotic due to a conflict between her conscience and her natural passions. She knew she was doing wrong and knew that the counselor could not approve of her behavior, but she may have hoped as many counselees do that he would save her from the objectionable consequences of her immoral behavior. As Mowrer would say, she did not want relief from her behavior pattern or personal weaknesses, but from the results. She was really not seeking help in changing her personal values and general life style; instead she was looking for symptom relief—"obliterating the objectionable *consequences* of her deception and dissociative strategies." [9]

Another counselee who had said that he realized his extramarital relations with a young woman were morally wrong sought help in resolving his marital problems as a result of his affair. But he became angry when the interview moved into a constructive plan for breaking off relations with the woman, indicating that he wanted the counselor on the one hand to approve of the relationship and to help it continue, and on the other hand to help him keep his marriage. Even understanding cannot resolve a conflict in a closed mind.

In another, similar case the man expressed his love for his paramour, and also for his wife. He realized that he had sinned, but did not want to hurt the woman. He also would have liked to keep both. But he continued in the counseling with the result

---

[9] O. Hobart Mowrer, *Psychotherapy, Theory, and Research* (New York: The Ronald Press Company, 1953), p. 554. Copyright 1953 by The Ronald Press Company.

that he gave up the woman and began to rebuild his marriage. Mowrer's explanation of this result would be that as the picture unfolded to the counselee, despite the frustrations and resentment he felt when he found that the counselor was unwilling to "help" him in the originally hoped for way, he succeeded in modifying his objectives and accepted a painful but a more workable approach —an approach for which the minister-counselor must stand because of his vocation.

While the author feels very strongly that the minister-counselor cannot compromise his moral convictions in order to enable the counselee to continue a deceptive and immoral life style, at the same time he does not mean that the minister should assume a condemnatory attitude; rather, that he should strive for empathic understanding. People in trouble look for understanding, not criticism. They are often overcritical with themselves. They need understanding in order to correct their behavior—not only the understanding of the counselor, but understanding of themselves, for self-understanding is a wonderful stimulus in enabling one to find hope and motivation for a new and better way of life.

A mental health leaflet received read:

> The most precious gift you can give to the 16 million or more emotionally disturbed or mentally ill is *understanding*. For as your help grows—their hope of recovery increases.
> Let us cultivate *understanding*.

What is meant by understanding as a tool in good counseling? Understanding does not mean agreement. By understanding we mean that the counselor is able to visualize the environmental situation in which the counselee finds himself, however unreal or immoral that situation may be. As the counselor then enters empathically into the emotional situation of the counselee, he carries with him certain facts of which the counselee may be unaware, but as they communicate, the counselee begins to reevaluate the situation in the light of these facts communicated to him by the counselor. This enables the counselee to orient himself toward decision making in keeping with reality, e.g., either to decide to continue an illicit relationship as in one of the above illustrations or to change to a more mature decision as in the following illustration.

This man, whom we shall call Pete, was separated from his wife because of his adultery and excessive drinking. His behavior had also caused him to leave the fraternal order in which he had occupied a very high position. "My behavior would not permit me to continue in the order." As he went over his life and expressed his pride in his achievement in the order, the counselor entered into the whole situation with empathic understanding. As the man saw his present life, his loneliness without his family and without his friends in the order, the counselor said, "It would be great to be there again, wouldn't it?" The man was thoughtful for a moment, then looking up said, "Yes. I see it all now. I've been in the wrong course. I can go back. I can be again what I once was."

Understanding helps the counselee to see for himself what he can and should do in the light of facts and possibilities set before him by the counselor. But the decision is the counselee's.

Empathic understanding [10] is to enter into the counselee's world and to look at his hopes, fears, and indecisions as though they were one's own without experiencing the emotional reactions of the counselee. Because he is not emotionally disturbed by what he finds in the counselee's relationships, the counselor can point out facets undetected by the counselee. In this way the counselor, by his comments and questions, by the tone of his voice and gestures, reveals to the counselee that he is going along with him in his search for the most constructive solution to his problems.

CLIENT-CENTERED THERAPY

Client-centered therapy is perhaps the best for the minister-counselor—at least for those beginning counseling. This type of therapy has been developed by Carl R. Rogers. Simply stated, it means allowing the client or counselee to discuss whatever he wishes and to discover for himself the decisions he should make.

A measure of good counseling is the permissiveness which allows an interpersonal situation to be structured by the counselee, not by the counselor. It is based upon "confidence in the potentiality of the individual for constructive change and develop-

---

[10] Carl R. Robers, *On Becoming a Person* (Cambridge, Mass.: The Riverside Press, 1961), Chaps. 1, 3, 14.

ment in the direction of a more full and satisfying life." [11] For the minister-counselor this means confidence in the potentiality of the individual to move in the direction of the abundant life in Christ.

After one has become familiar with other methods, he should be flexible and eclectic in their use. All counselees differ, and some respond to one method and some to another.

Along with the qualifications named above, the minister should know some of the common techniques of counseling: giving attention to what the person is saying, being a good listener, creating a permissive atmosphere for the counselee to talk freely without fear of censure, refraining from condemnation or judgment, reacting with empathic understanding and emotional objectivity. He does not take sides in marital disputes nor tell the couple what to do. He tries to help them work out for themselves what is best for them to do. In marriage counseling, the counselor believes that individuals can change their attitudes and behavior patterns as they learn better ways of dealing with their spouses. The minister's role is a helping one to this end.

CLASSIFICATION OF COUPLES

A survey made by Landis and Landis [12] reveals six areas of major difficulties among married couples. In order of difficulty in making a satisfactory adjustment, beginning with the greatest, these are, sexual relations, spending the family income, social activities, in-law relationships, religious activities, and mutual friends.

People who come for marriage counseling seem to fall into the following classifications:

Couples with relatively minor problems

Such problems may be resolved in two or three counseling sessions. A couple, very much in love, married for several years, began having trouble when the husband's mother came to live

---

[11] Robers, *Client-centered Therapy*, p. 35.

[12] Judson T. Landis and Mary G. Landis, *Building a Successful Marriage* (4th ed.; Englewood Cliffs, N.J.: Prentice-Hall, Inc., 1963), p. 288.

with them. At first it seemed like a good arrangement, and the wife agreed. But now, three years had passed, and friction had developed between the wife and her mother-in-law. The wife, husband, and mother-in-law were continually wrangling. Finally, the wife left. She and her husband came for counseling. It did not take long for the husband to realize that his mother would have to leave and spend some of her time with his sister. This was arranged. The wife returned, and peace settled over the home.

A couple, having friction over the family finances, were spending many unhappy days every month when the bills came in. Two or three counseling sessions helped them in setting up a budget, and an allowance was set up for the wife who was to pay the small regular bills. The husband was relieved, and harmony returned.

Couples who seem basically incompatible

Their incompatibility may be due to several causes.

Sexual incompatibility. This is a frequent complaint of husbands and wives who come for marriage counseling. Often it is only a matter of ignorance. The minister should be well informed himself on factual sex knowledge and well adjusted in the area in his own marriage. The average couple can be helped greatly by an understanding counselor, frank discussion, and good books.

Perverted sex practices with one's spouse, if not mutually agreeable, can lead to great unhappiness and divorce. A spouse who insists on such practices should be referred to a psychiatrist.

The homosexual who has been overt in his practices finds it difficult to be content with heterosexual relations. Many wives of homosexuals are frustrated and bewildered. Some do not know their husbands are homosexual and suspect them of heterosexual affairs. The homosexual should also be referred for psychiatric treatment.

Neurotic spouse(s). Everyone is neurotic to some extent. But the so-called normal people are able to handle their neuroticism so that it does not impair human relationships. Some people are able to understand, analyze, and accept their neuroticism and learn to live with it.

Also, there are those who can understand and accept the neuroticism of their spouses and learn to react to their peculiarities with a minimum of friction. Love, security, and understanding are essential to the happiness of everyone, but the neurotic spouse is particularly dependent upon these qualities.

The neurotic spouse complains over trivialities. An incident that would pass unnoticed by the average person is picked up by the neurotic as being of grave importance. The tone of the voice, a normal reaction to a simple question, failure to clean every inch of a room, or any slight disorder is enough to set the neurotic playing over again the same old record of quibbling, fussing, nagging, and complaining.

Neurotics seem to have an affinity for neurotics. Although many marry each other, they do not complement each other; consequently, the home is in a constant turmoil. Children in such a home are likely to become neurotic also.

Many neurotics can be helped through marriage counseling. The minister should not despair of them, though he often will. There are those who can come to understand themselves and their anxieties and make good adjustments. Often they need someone like the minister-counselor to give them support by reinforcing their superego and by showing them with examples how they may be more objective and build better relationships with their spouses and children.

Psychotic spouse. A psychotic individual is sure to come into the minister's office at some time. Often, it is the spouse who brings him or her. The minister may detect such psychotic personalities by their apprehensiveness, suspiciousness, inappropriate verbal responses, hallucinations, hearing of voices, inattentiveness, emotional responses inappropriate to the situation, depression, and staring—all of which are symptoms. Needless to say, such persons should be referred for psychiatric treatment.

The minister should know the address of the local psychiatrist, or the nearest one available. Sometimes he may be asked to arrange an appointment. The minister should also be familiar with the state laws regarding the commitment of persons to the state hospital for treatment; also, he should know how to make arrangements for persons to visit the mental health clinic, if there be one, in his community.

Alcoholic spouse. The alcoholic may also be placed in this category. Much time can be wasted by the minister in counseling with alcoholics. Some success may be achieved, but my experience has led me to refer the alcoholic to some rehabilitation center. I have sent many men and women to such centers, and with few exceptions all have found sobriety. I also recommend Alcoholics Anonymous, and when requested by the alcoholic, I arrange for him to be visited by a member of a nearby group.

While the alcoholic spouse is receiving treatment, it is important that the other spouse enter counseling so he or she will be able to correct any environmental factors that may have an influence on the drinking habits of the other. This counseling helps the couple greatly in making a new start. Sometimes the older children also require counseling during this period.

Couples in which one or both spouses have been unfaithful

The unfaithful spouse is the cause of many marital problems—more, perhaps, than we realize—because of the shame attached to admitting this problem to anyone. This leads many couples simply to continue their marriage, but under trying conditions, sometimes occupying separate rooms.

Couples in conflict over child training

Disagreement between parents arise over methods of child training, disciplinary problems, degree of latitude in selecting playmates, and later, teenage dating, study regulations and going out, and manner of dress. For example, husbands who travel and are away from home several days a week, upon returning, may seek to take over the home, complain about the wife's disciplinary measures —too lenient or too severe—thereby confusing the children and upsetting the mother-child relationship when the father is absent.

Couples in which one or both spouses desire remarriage

There are those individuals who come for counseling because they have failed in their marriage, are divorced, and seek another marriage; or individuals who may even still be married but, having fallen in love with someone else, wish to dissolve the marriage in order to form a new contract. Several such cases have come to the author and, sad as they were, several said that when they went to their minister for counseling, they were rejected and sent away. How can a minister reject anyone who comes to him for help? Why would such people, some living in adultery, seek out a minister? Does the minister who rejects them realize that these people may need his help more than the "good" people who come to church every Sunday? Our Lord said that he "came to seek and to save the lost." [13]

A woman whose marriage had failed, and who had been divorced for several years, sought help from a minister in another city. As soon as she stated her problem, he closed the interview abruptly by saying he had no interest in discussing her marriage. She spent only about 10 minutes with him. How could he know her need in 10 minutes?

This woman had been a loyal member of her church. She was about twenty-eight at the time her husband deserted her. After the divorce he remarried. It had never been a happy marriage, and after the divorce she felt that she had failed. She was also very lonely. About three years later she met a man who seemed to have what the other had lacked. Since her divorce she had not received Communion, erroneously thinking that she was prima facie excommunicated. This had made her feel even more lonely. With the prospect of a new marriage and a desire to rectify her communicant status, she went to her minister, and he "threw me out." She and the author spent several sessions together. The man she wished to marry came a distance of 800 miles to be counseled. She came to Communion. Application under the canon was made to the bishop, who granted permission for her marriage. The man was baptized, and the marriage solemnized.

If this case were rare, it would not be mentioned, but it has happened too many times to the author's limited knowledge to think it is unusual. A young priest said, "I break off these neurotic people quick." How can he? Archbishop Temple said, "The unlovely members of our congregations need us more than the self-confident ones."

Thus we see that a great variety of cases are brought to the marriage counselor. Some are cases of sexual promiscuity, some-

---

[13] Luke 19:10.

times on the part of both husband and wife. Once one gets into marriage counseling, one will sooner or later hear related every form of sexual perversity.

The minister-counselor meets with many disappointments in people. The novice will be astonished at the things the "best people" do. He will grieve if not weep over the failures and sins of his own people. But he must never give up trying to help them. He must never turn a deaf ear. He must never be shocked. He must never show by any change of expression or posture that what he hears is unusual.

COMMUNITY RESOURCES

Every minister should be familiar with the community resources for helping people in trouble. A person's problems may be too complex to be solved by any one discipline. And problems brought to the minister may be enough beyond his training for him to be of much help. Some family problems may be diversified, calling for help from employment agencies, social agencies, or the medical or legal professions.

Skidmore, Garrett, and Skidmore [14] point out that today the leaders in marriage counseling recognize a variety of approaches to the many complex marital and family problems. No one discipline has all the answers. Since marriage counselors work with many types of personal and social adjustments, all the sciences dealing with human behavior should be actively tapped in the counseling process. However, areas of specialization are recognized wherein the family doctor, the psychiatrist, the sociologist, the psychologist, the home economist, the clergyman, the social worker, the judge, and the educator may effectively serve. No one of these professional persons or fields has a monopoly on marriage counseling; each makes a significant contribution. Often teamwork is needed to achieve the goals of marriage counseling.

Mace groups under four main headings services presently being offered to men and women as means of increasing their happiness and usefulness:

---

[14] Rex A. Skidmore, Hulda Van Streeter Garrett and C. Jay Skidmore, *Marriage Consulting* (New York: Harper & Row, Publishers, 1956), Chap. 14.

(1)   Services which aim to relieve tensions in the individual, and in the relationships between individuals, created by the pressure of a hostile environment. This is in the main the task of the social worker of the traditional type, of the sociologist, and perhaps also of the lawyer.

(2)   Services which help the individual to attain his maximum level of physical health and efficiency. This is the province of medicine and of its satellites.

(3)   Services designed to resolve the unconscious conflicts which undermine the integration of the personality. This is at present the exclusive province of psychiatry and psychotherapy.

(4)   Services which help the individual, at the conscious level, to achieve a better understanding of himself and of his destiny. This broad category includes all functionally directed education—teaching, preaching, and propaganda. It also includes all counseling in the generally understood meaning of the word.[15]

Besides the medical profession, including psychiatry, many communities have the Family Service Association of America, an employment agency, the Traveler's Aid Society, the Red Cross, a mental health clinic, a department of public welfare, etc. The minister-counselor will often turn to one or more of these services for special aid for the couples he counsels.

MARRIAGE COUNSELING IS INTERDISCIPLINARY

Anyone who has interviewed even a few couples with marital problems realizes that marriage counseling is interdisciplinary. By its very nature marriage, although primarily an emotional relationship, involves all aspects of life: cultural, legal, psychological, social, medical, and economic, as well as religious. The family is a community in itself.

A minister is not expected to be an expert in all these matters, but in many congregations there are experts trained in these various disciplines whom the minister may form into a team so that he can call on them for advice and to whom he may refer clients

---

15 David R. Mace, "What is a Marriage Counselor?" *Marriage and Family Living*, XVI (May 1954), 136.

who need legal, medical, or psychiatric help. The layman is happy to be of service to his pastor and to those to whom his pastor ministers. The minister-counselor, however, should increase his knowledge of other disciplines besides those of his major interest, for the greater his store of knowledge gathered from other disciplines, together with his skill in using it, the greater his effectiveness as a pastor and preacher. Since one finds a use at some time for practically everything one has learned, the minister-counselor will be more effective through his reading in many fields. Skidmore, Garrett, and Skidmore suggest basic understandings which should be considered a minimum for the marriage counselor.[16]

The influence of culture [17]

Human beings grow up in various and sometimes quite different environments which reflect the way of life of the people with whom they live and work. Cultural differences are social, economic, and racial. Many marital conflicts have followed in the wake of World War II because of interracial and international marriages. In the case of an international marriage, the German husband and his American wife were in constant conflict because neither understood that the other brought into the marriage very different concepts of the role of husband and wife. The minister-counselor should be able to understand cultural differences and how they affect interpersonal relationships in marriage.

Legal information

The average minister will probably have available to him the assistance of one or more attorneys who will be glad to advise him regarding legal questions that often arise in counseling, e.g., the rights of a spouse in a separation or divorce action, legal protection from a spouse who becomes dangerous when drinking, problems relating to adoption laws, etc. The minister-counselor should have at hand a copy of the laws of his state regarding marriage and divorce even though he is not always qualified to interpret the law; however, in some cases, a telephone call to an attorney friend without divulging names may bring the interpretation and

---

[16] Skidmore, Garrett, and Skidmore, *Marriage Consulting*, pp. 237–54.
[17] Landis and Landis, *Building a Successful Marriage*, pp. 281ff.

determine whether or not the counselee should seek further legal advice. Of course, when indicated, referral should be made to a reputable attorney.

Medical information

The minister-counselor needs some knowledge of psychosomatic medicine, effects of tranquilizers, female disorders, use of contraceptives, and the principles of planned parenthood. It will be necessary at times for him to phone, with the counselee's permission, a physician to discuss the physical and medical aspects of a problem. The author's experience has been that physicians are more than willing to cooperate with the counselor in helping their patients. In some cases a personal conference between the counselor and the physician may result in much benefit to the counselee. In other cases a written request to the physician by the counselee that he send the counselor information on his physical condition will bring a medical report from the physician.

Psychological and psychiatric knowledge

As pointed out elsewhere, both in *Premarital Counseling* and in this book, the minister must acquaint himself with the principles of psychology and elementary psychiatry in order to understand the dynamics of human behavior. If he lives near a college, he may have the opportunity of taking courses in psychology. It will be of inestimable value to him in his preaching, teaching, and counseling.

Only a few communities have psychologists and psychiatrists among the professional group, but where they are present, the minister-counselor should know them and consult with them when it may be helpful to his counseling. He should never hesitate to refer to them those who may be helped by more extensive therapy. In fact, the minister may be the first to detect evidences of a mental illness.

Economic practices

One of the greatest sources of marital conflict is in spending the family income.[18] The minister-counselor should familiarize him-

---

[18] Landis and Landis, *Building a Successful Marriage*, Chap. 20, pp. 361ff.

self in family budget planning, insurance, savings, and install-
ment buying.

CONFIDENTIALITY ESSENTIAL

A person who cannot keep in confidence what
is told to him has no business counseling anyone. The minister-
counselor must be extremely cautious in what he says to those
who ask about family situations. There are "nosey" people in every
parish who will use clever questions to "pry out" of the minister
some lead as to family problems. They will also try to find out from
the minister's wife. The wise counselor will tell his wife nothing
that would identify those who consult him on confidential matters.

It is surprising how people expect the minister's wife to know
about those who consult her husband. They may even open a
conversation with her on the assumption that she knows what
has been told him. Sometimes the people who consult him also
assume this. The minister's wife should be able to say to anyone,
"My husband never tells me what goes on in his counseling sessions.
I have no idea to what you are referring."

Woe to the minister who uses in his sermon illustrations from
his counseling involving identifiable persons. Illustrations may be
used, but they should be in the past, disguised, changed as to
time, location, sex, etc. To say, "The other day a man brought
this problem . . ." may immediately enable someone to identify
the person. One might say, "Here is a problem common to many
people . . ." If the minister is thinking of a specific problem brought
to him, he should change everything in it so that no one could
possibly identify the person who presented it. Once a congregation feels that what someone tells the minister in confidence will
be the subject or the main illustration in next Sunday's sermon,
his effectiveness as a counselor is over—no one will come to him.

Nor should the minister reveal identities when discussing his
counseling problems with other ministers or even when he seeks
help from a psychologist, psychiatrist, or some other professional
worker as he sometimes needs to do, unless, of course, he has the
consent of the counselee.

In the cases referred to in this book, the details have been changed so that no one could possibly identify the individuals concerned.

PHYSICAL ARRANGEMENTS FOR COUNSELING [19]

Privacy is most important. If the minister has to hold his interviews in his home, he should arrange for some sound such as that of a radio or television to conflict with the voices from the study.

Counseling is becoming such an important part of the modern minister's program that he should give thought and spend money to provide an adequate counseling room, which should be well ventilated, comfortably heated in winter, and with a fan or air-conditioning unit in summer. When the new parish house at St. John's Episcopal Church, Columbia, S.C., was constructed, the author's counseling program was considered in the planning. The rector's office is very nearly sound proof. It has double walls, an acoustical ceiling, and a double door. In his present office he has walnut-paneled, hollow tile walls, an acoustical ceiling, a heavy solid core tightly fitting door, and a carpet which makes for privacy and low-tone conversation. Drapes further deaden the sound.

If a church understands that counseling is an important pastoral function, the vestry or board should be glad to furnish the minister an adequate study or office in which to do it. Imagine a doctor examining his patients in an old room in a parish house without adequate light, heat, chairs, desk, or privacy. The minister is just as much a professional as the physician. He should insist upon adequate facilities for his work. Most laymen have high regard for the professional man. They will regard their minister in the same way if the minister makes the demand upon them.

The furniture in the counseling room is also important. The room should have a desk or table and two or three chairs or a sofa. Comfortable chairs should be provided both for the minister and counselee. If the minister is not comfortably seated, he will become very tired and restless before the interview is over. It is not easy to sit for an hour to an hour and a half giving careful attention to what is being said by another. The minister must be relaxed and

---

[19] J. Kenneth Morris, *Premarital Counseling—A Manual for Ministers* (Englewood Cliffs, N.J.: Prentice-Hall, Inc., 1960).

at ease, but not indifferent, for he must remain alert throughout the interview. A comfortable chair is a big help.

The counselee should also be comfortably seated. He or she may pace the floor, but a good chair helps to add dignity to the interview as well as to allow the counselee to relax if he so desires. Some do. Some will lean back, sigh and talk with their eyes closed. Some will express anger; a chair with arms to hold on to may help the person to express himself. The counselee's chair should face the light, but the light should not glare. The window facing the counselee should be properly shaded.

Where should the counselor sit, behind the desk or to one side? Some feel that to sit behind the desk facing the counselee places a barrier between them, and that it is better for the counselor to sit at the corner of the desk or entirely away from it. Others feel that sitting behind the desk presents a more formal or professional atmosphere and puts the counselee at ease. The author has used both arrangements and finds that there is really no choice between them. The counselor should experiment and use the arrangement which he feels is best suited for his counseling.

Good counseling can be done anywhere in an emergency, just as a doctor may operate in a kitchen if necessary. But adequate thought should be given to the counseling setting wherever it may take place regularly.

The counselor should allow no interruptions. If there is a telephone in the study or office, it should be an extension which does not ring. An arrangement can be made for someone else to answer the main phone. It should be understood by whoever answers it that the minister must not be disturbed during his counseling. Interruptions in a counseling process may break a chain of thought which may never be recovered and which may be the key to the whole marriage relationship. Furthermore, if the counselee was on the verge of saying something of which he might be ashamed, he might never have the courage to bring it up in the future. Interruptions can spoil a good counseling session.

The counselor should be prepared to take notes or to write up the case when the counselee has left. A file should be kept of all interviews, but it should be in a steel cabinet under lock and key. Notes enable the counselor to refresh his memory of the interview when he studies the case and is planning for the next interview. As cases multiply, notes become more and more necessary. When the case is closed and if the counselor wishes to keep the file, all names may be erased and a private code symbol attached to the file for future reference. This is also important in case of the death of the minister to protect those involved. In the author's case he has it arranged in his will that all records in his filing cabinet in his office are to be destroyed by court order. Nothing is kept in the cabinet except material connected with his counseling service, and he alone always carries the key!

In the author's present office, where the counseling takes place, he has a small chalkboard, 2 feet by 3 feet, mounted on the wall facing the large, comfortable chair in which the counselee sits. The chalkboard is green. It is so placed that a person sitting in the chair can see it while talking with the counselor at his desk without changing position. Also, the chalkboard is at a convenient elevation for him to stand when writing and drawing on it.

The author finds simple drawings of great advantage and uses them in lectures, discussions, and television programs. They are simple line sketches requiring no skill or training. Anyone can do them. They hold the attention of an individual or group. He has used them successfully, also, with audiences of several hundred students.

Visual aids are of great value in the instructional part of marriage counseling. The use of a greenboard makes it possible to outline, pinpoint, and clarify particular ideas. There are many excellent short films which may be used effectively with couples and groups. Every minister should become acquainted with his state's mental health commission: its personnel, educational program, and film and book lending library.

SUMMARY

In this chapter we have considered many of the factors involved in marriage counseling.

The minister-counselor has the unique privilege of witnessing the renascence of those who come to him as they become increasingly aware of their own potentialities and appropriate the spiritual and Christian significance of marriage. But this is dependent upon the counselor's own beliefs both in the worth of the individual and in the ability of the individual to plan and direct his own life. The counselor must never show shock or embarrassment at what is told him. He must be able to enter the counselee's internal frame of reference and show respect for his capacity as a person. Theologically, a resurrection takes place in every successful counseling process.

The counselor will find it difficult at times to identify with the counselee and at the same time not prejudge the other spouse because of his (the counselor's) prejudices. His psychological involvement in the counselee's problems may vitiate his own objectivity. When this happens, he losses his opportunity to open a closed mind and initiate creative thinking.

The minister cannot expect to help resolve all the problems brought up in counseling, but he must always try to be understanding. Even in situations which may be repulsive to his sense of righteous conduct, he must seek to be understanding. This does not mean compromising his moral standards—that he cannot do, but he must not assume a condemnatory position. He must cultivate emphatic understanding. People want understanding, not criticism.

Client-centered therapy as developed by Carl R. Rogers is recommended to the minister-counselor as not only "safe" from a therapeutic standpoint, but also as a reliable method of allowing the counselee to discuss whatever he wishes and to discover for himself the decisions he should make. As one becomes familiar with other methods, he can be eclectic in the use of them. Of course, this implies that the counselor should know the common techniques of counseling. It is not his role to give advice but to work with the counselee to an acceptable resolution of his problem—personal and marital.

In every community except some rural areas, there are resources which the minister may call upon to help him in his work with individuals and couples. Many approaches to complex marital problems exist. All the sciences dealing with human behavior should be utilized as available locally through the physician, psychiatrist, sociologist, psychologist, home economist, social worker, judge, attorney, and educator.

SUGGESTED READING

James, E. O., *Marriage and Society*. London: Hutchinson's University Library, 1952; New York: John de Graff, Inc., 1955.

Johnson, Dean, *Marriage Counseling: Theory and Practice*, Chaps. 11, 12, 13. Englewood Cliffs, N.J.: Prentice-Hall, Inc., 1961.

Masserman, Jules H. and J. L. Moreno, eds., *Progress in Psychotherapy*, Vol. III, *Techniques of Psychotherapy*. New York: Grune & Stratton, Inc., 1958.

May, Rollo, "Historical and Philosophical Presuppositions for Understanding Therapy," in *Psychotherapy Theory and Research*, ed. O. H. Mowrer, New York: The Ronald Press Company, 1953.

Moser, Leslie E., *Counseling: A Modern Emphasis in Religion*, Chap. 8. Englewood Cliffs, N.J.: Prentice-Hall, Inc., 1962.

Oates, Wayne E., ed., *An Introduction to Pastoral Counseling*, Chaps. 3, 5, 8, 13. Nashville: Broadman Press, 1959.

Patterson, Cecil H., *Counseling the Emotionally Disturbed*, Chaps. 3, 7, 8. New York: Harper & Row, Publishers, 1958.

Roberts, David E., *Psychotherapy and a Christian View of Man*, pp. 1–84. New York: Charles Scribner's Sons, 1951.

Skidmore, Rex A., Hulda Van Streeter Garrett, and C. Jay Skidmore, *Marriage Consulting*. New York: Harper & Row, Publishers, 1956.

Wynn, John Charles, *Pastoral Ministry and Families*, Chap. 6. Philadelphia: The Westminster Press, 1957.

Interview Procedure

3   How does one get started in an interview? How is contact made in the first place to have an interview? There are ministers whose counseling sessions with parishioners are at a minimum of almost none. Sometimes their sessions are limited to casual talks while fishing, hunting, or playing golf, or to a chance meeting on the street. No serious counseling regarding fundamental psychological problems of marital adjustment is possible under such conditions. There are better and professional ways of counseling which result in closer ties with pastor and church, and gratifying improvement in the personal Christian life of the parishioner.

Since World War II more and more people have sought help from their pastors, believing that their pastors would be able to understand and help them with their emotional disturbances. This has given the pastor a renewed challenge to assume his role in the cure of souls. But often he misses or overlooks opportunities to help people because of his reluctance to enter into the deepest and often tragic conflicts of human life. Yet by God's grace here is his real call to minister.

MAKING THE APPOINTMENT

It is advisable that the interviews be arranged by appointment. This enables the minister to plan his schedule so that he will not be hurried; also, it makes the same possible for the interviewee. Telephone interviews should be avoided. Sometimes a person will call over the phone and begin with a question and a statement about the marriage. This may be a "feel out" to find out the reaction of the minister—a sort of testing to see how understanding the minister may be. It is not easy to admit marital failure, or to discuss its unpleasant aspects. It is wise to listen patiently over the phone and then say something like, "Wouldn't you like to come to the study or office where we can talk this over privately and without interruptions?" This sort of suggestion carries several points:

(1) Wouldn't you like to come—leaving the person free to make a choice.

(2) To the study or office—a professional touch. Like one goes to the doctor's office.

(3) Where we can talk privately—suggests confidence. No one will hear what is said.

(4) Without interruptions. At the interviewee's home the phone will ring or children will run in and out or a neighbor will call. At the study or office you more or less promise there will be no interruptions.

(5) It indicates that the minister has plenty of time to give to this person, that this person and his problem is so important that the minister will provide the time and place for the interview.

THE USE OF SCHEDULES AND TESTS

Many schedules and tests are available to the minister-counselor who is trained in their use. Those with psychological training are familiar with the various tests now being used in clinics. Since this book is primarily for the minister who may not have a degree in psychology, no comment will be made on these tests. However, there are schedules which the minister may find very helpful. The Marriage Council of Philadelphia [1] puts out several including the Background Schedule discussed in the author's book, *Premarital Counseling*.[2] Schedule 1A [3] (see Appendix

---

[1] Address: 3828 Locust Street, Philadelphia, Pa.

[2] J. Kenneth Morris, *Premarital Counseling—A Manual for Ministers* (Englewood Cliffs, N.J.: Prentice-Hall, Inc., 1960), pp. 67ff.

[3] Sample copies of other schedules will be sent on request to the Marriage Council of Philadelphia.

II) is valuable in indicating areas of conflict. The Sex Knowledge Inventory [4] discussed in *Premarital Counseling* [5] is also helpful.

Many counselors prefer to rely entirely upon the interview for information on the sources of friction. It is my feeling that the counseling should be flexible and the counselor free to follow the method which he can handle most effectively.

INTERVIEWING SPOUSES SEPARATELY

It is the experience of most, if not all, marriage counselors that it is best to see husband and wife separately at first. This is especially advisable for the minister-counselor who may not have special training in marriage counseling. When they are seen together, they are apt to begin accusing each other, using the minister as an audience, each trying to prove his or her case and thus gain the counselor's sympathy.

When they come to the office together, it is advisable to ask which one would like to come in first for an interview. They usually look at each other and one defers to the other. I always insist on their own decision, which is usually made without argument.

It is helpful and time-saving in the number of interviews to make a two-hour appointment with the couple for the first interview. Under this plan, each one would be seen separately for about 45 minutes and then together for about 30 minutes. In some cases, however, it is not wise to see both together at this time. Of course, there are many cases in which only one spouse can or will come for the initial interview. But when both do come together and are seen separately, the intense feelings of animosity, disappointment, and discouragement are ventilated and relieved individually so that when the couple are seen together at this time there is more objectivity and relaxation between them, and they rarely argue. In this interview, after seeing each one separately, the counselor may sum up the salient factors in the marriage relationship as he sees them, give the couple reassurance, and make a few suggestions for them to follow until the next interview.

After several personal interviews with each one it is helpful

----

[4] May be ordered from Family Life Publications, Inc., 6725 College Station, Durham, N.C.

[5] Morris, *Premarital Counseling—A Manual for Ministers,* Chap. 7.

to see the couple together for an hour to evaluate the situation, pull together some of the points made in the individual interviews, and discuss further improvement in the relationship. In this connection the greenboard is very useful for listing positive and negative factors in the marriage and improvements accomplished, and for outlining subjects having a bearing on the relationship.

When a joint interview for discussion with husband and wife is planned, it should be agreeable to both parties. This joint interview should take place only after the minister has established a good rapport with each one for the counselor must not take sides. In his presence each now may be able to express thoughts to the other that he had not been able to before. Each may see the other more objectively. Also, this gives the counselor an opportunity to explain to both of them together matters which must be considered if the marriage is to be reconstructed on a more permanent and stable basis.

AMPLE TIME FOR THE FIRST INTERVIEW

The first interview may be the most important one. It must not be rushed. The counselee has come to talk. It may have taken him months or even years to come to the point of baring to another his deepest problems and sharing his deepest regrets. The counselee must be allowed to talk freely and at length. This is called ventilating. Persons with disturbed feelings are like a kettle with a weight on the lid. The more the pressure builds up inside, the more they are likely to explode. When some people sit down to talk, their words fall from their lips like water over a dam. The counselor must let them flow. He must let the pent-up feeling be fully, freely expressed. Tears may flow also. That is good. The counselor should never stop them; rather, he should reassure the person that it is good to cry. Men as well as women need to cry. Persons while ventilating, may hit the desk, walk the floor, and curse. They may sigh frequently and heavily, and their lips may tremble, but all this reduces tension and hostility and brings great relief. It has a cathartic effect. That is why the first interview is so important. One should allow plenty of time for it.

Many first interviews may last an hour or more. In making appointments always allow at least 45 minutes to an hour. A client should never be stopped when he is in the midst of or about to bring up a crucial matter.

A counselee related that he had been in therapy in another city. He said that it took him almost the entire 45 minutes (which was the schedule on which appointments were made) to feel that he could bring up the main problem for which he was in the therapist's office. But abruptly he was told that his time was up. The therapist lost a good patient, for he never went back, and he failed to get the help he needed. In telling about this the counselee remarked, "That man was not interested in me—he was interested in how many clients he could see in a day!"

The person who comes for counseling should feel that while he is there, he is the most important person in the world to you and that you have plenty of time to counsel with him.

Now, of course, the first interview does have to end. Usually after an hour a terminating place may appear. One might say, "I think I understand now. You have given me a good picture of the situation. Let us consider it further in our next interview."

THE COUNSELING PROCEDURE

In the first interview it should be explained that counseling takes time and that the problems which caused the couple to seek counseling cannot be resolved in one or two interviews. It is impossible to predetermine the number of interviews which may be required to reach a satisfactory solution which, of course, may be either to reconstruct the marriage or to dissolve it. Generally, the spouses are seen alternately once a week.

After several interviews and if progress is being made, the counselor brings up the question of terminating the counseling. If each one feels that the time has come when he can confidently face the future and continue to rebuild the marriage into a strong, stable one, then the terminal interview is set. This may be held within a week or it may be held two or three weeks after the last personal interview depending on the circumstances, e.g., the seriousness of the problems of adjustment, insight gained, and success in reality testing.

The important point in setting the terminal interview is that it not be done without due warning and that each partner feels ready to terminate the counseling.

BEGINNING THE INTERVIEW

An interview on marital problems begins itself. Usually the person who has asked for the interview is ready to talk. But the progress of the interview depends on how good a rapport is established.

A good or bad rapport may be set up at the first meeting with the interviewee: "When their eyes first meet," as one counselor writes. The minister's handshake, if limp or formal, may convey to the other person the feeling that he is a cold, indifferent person. The manner of greeting, showing a person into the office or study, indicating a concern when the person has been seated and begins to talk, leaning forward, concentrating on what the person is saying, and listening patiently, and the tone of voice—all these tend to give the interviewee assurance that the counselor wishes to be of help and is trying to identify himself with the person and his problems. A good rapport usually follows naturally.

After the counselee and minister have been seated, the latter should wait quietly for the other to begin.

Generally the counselee asks, "Where shall I begin?" The counselor may reply, "Well, why not at the beginning?" or "Just tell me why you have come."

If the counselee shows apprehension lest someone overhear, point out the precautions taken for privacy mentioned above. Also, reassure the person that what is said will be kept in strict confidence, perhaps adding, "Not even my wife knows what is discussed here; nor does my secretary have access to any information you may tell me. No one will ever know without your permission." That generally relieves any anxiety.

Once the interview gets under way, a pertinent question here and there for clarification keeps it going.

The test of good counseling lies in the large amount of talking done by the counselee and the small amount done by the counselor.

All who counsel should be careful not to use the counselee for their own therapy. Everyone has problems, and it is a temptation for the inexperienced counselor to use the counselee to unburden himself. That is one reason why those who do counseling should themselves be counseled. The author has consulted a friend who is a psychiatrist, and also one who is a minister. Both helped him greatly in understanding himself and in resolving his own problems of personality adjustment and marriage. Just because one is a minister does not mean that he has no problems and that once married he will "live happily ever after." It is no admission of failure for the minister to seek counseling for himself and his wife or children if need be.

When the counselor finds himself doing most of the talking, he should stop and let the counselee take over again. The interview is no time to lecture, preach, or moralize. Nor should the counselor fall into the trap of saying, "So and so had this problem, and he did such and such." The counselee is not interested in "So and so" and what he did. As far as the counselee is concerned, no one has ever had his particular problem. In every interview, the counselee must be the center of primary concern.

It is vital to be a good listener and to speak only when necessary to ask for clarification or to keep the counselee talking. Repeating back to the counselee the last few words he has said helps him to elaborate. For example, the counselee comes to the end of an incident, then adds, "And so we went to the beach for a weekend . . . ." He pauses, stops. Counselor: "You went to the beach for a weekend" (not a question—but a mere statement). The counselee will probably continue then to tell about the trip to the beach.

Sometimes the counselor might say, "I don't quite follow you —would you mind going over that again?" Or, "What do you mean?" This conveys to the counselee that the counselor is very much interested in understanding correctly the problem as seen by the counselee.

INTERVIEWING THE OTHER SPOUSE

Having completed the first interview with one spouse—usually the one who arranged for the marriage counseling —the counselor must see the other spouse. It is very difficult to do much in resolving a marital conflict unless one can see both partners. Of course even if this is not possible, interviews with either one can have therapeutic value for that one, and may lead to a better marital relationship.

If and when the other spouse comes, the first interview would proceed as suggested below.

A word of caution is necessary: one must be careful that nothing said by the other spouse is relayed to the second one. He or she may say, "Well I suppose my husband (or wife) has told you everything. Now you probably want to question me." Never do it!

The counselor might say, "Well I have heard something of the situation. But I would like for you to tell me about it as you see it." This brings relief to the present spouse who may have expected to be called on the carpet. Relieved by this, the counselee may then say, "Did he (or she) tell you about this?" The wise counselor will answer neither Yes or No, but say, "Suppose you tell me," or "Would you like to tell me?" He must feel sure that the counselor is neutral.

Sometimes the second spouse may say, "Well I guess you are on his (or her) side." The counselor then should explain that he is not there to take sides, but to help both think through their problems, work out their difficulties, and make their own decision as to a resolution of the situation.

After laying all the facts on the table one or the other spouse may appeal for a judgment, saying, "Now don't you think I am justified in asking for a divorce?" The counselor must not enter into a discourse on divorce, but refer the question back to the individual saying, "How do you feel about it? That is a decision you and your husband (or wife) must make. I cannot judge."

Both spouses should feel that the counselor is trying to understand and wants to help them toward a constructive solution, whether this be to continue the marriage or to dissolve it. This attitude sometimes helps a person who had decided on divorce to reconsider and in the end to reconstruct the marriage.

A wife came in for ten interviews before she could get her husband to come. He had told her he was through with the marriage. He had moved out of the house and was working in another city. She wrote him that she had consulted a minister-counselor of their own church and that the minister had indicated his willingness to talk with him. Although she received no reply, I received a wire asking for an appointment. When the man came in, the first thing he said was, "I am here only because my wife asked me to come and said you wanted to see me. I am through with her and her family. I am going to get a divorce. I am not going to live with her. I do not love her. We quarrel all the time. I don't want to waste your time talking about it. My mind is made up. I'm getting a divorce." This went on with much elaboration for an hour or more. But as he talked, he mentioned their courtship, their love, and the causes of the quarreling, which were mother-in-law trouble and finances. Before he left, he had decided to cancel his flight back to where he was living and to go to the city where his wife was working and talk with her. Interviews with both of them continued for about six months. The end was reconciliation and the marriage reconstructed on a firmer foundation.

VISITING THE HOME

The minister-counselor is often familiar with the family environment, particularly if the family is a member of his parish. As previously indicated, it is best not to counsel in the home. Counseling is done best in the minister's office or study.

However, after several interviews it may be helpful for the minister-counselor to visit the home to see how the family functions as a unit. The outsider sometimes notices needed improvements in the physical arrangements, of which the couple is unaware, which would facilitate harmonious relations.

The Smith home is an example. Here was a well-to-do family of six living in a large house but crowded into three bedrooms. Another room, available for a bedroom, was virtually unused. For very little expense it could be made into a room for the eldest girl, and this would lessen the friction in the family. Somehow the use of this room as a bedroom had not occurred to them.

In another instance the counselor had some difficulty, from the description of the couple, in understanding the arrangement of the house, which seemed to cause friction. It was not until he visited them and was shown over the house that he understood this problem. It turned out that it was not the arrangement of the house, which the wife reiterated time and again was threatening the marriage, but the childishness of both regarding the husband's hunting equipment which he kept in his room at one end of the house and the wife's extreme fastidiousness about her room at the other end. The husband finally agreed to move back into the wife's "feminine" room with its fancy canopied bed during the closed hunting season, and to his "masculine" room during the open hunting season. Conferring with the couple in the home saved considerable time in interviewing.

ARRANGING FOR THE NEXT INTERVIEW

People sometimes come to the minister for counseling, thinking that one interview may be sufficient.

During the initial interview the counselor should explain the counseling process and that marital difficulties do not happen overnight; therefore, they cannot be adjusted quickly. He should make it clear that he will need to interview both spouses, and that time and patience and their cooperation will be required.

Some counselors wish to set up in advance a series of several interviews with each spouse, a week apart. A few days or a week should elapse between interviews to give each one time to assimilate the material and to try out new patterns of behavior presented in each interview.

The husband and wife should not discuss between themselves any material taken up in the interviews. This is quite important because usually each one has criticized the other, and if they begin to discuss their interviews, they begin quarreling and set back the whole counseling process.

Furthermore, both spouses should avoid quarreling and arguing during the counseling period. They will generally agree to do this, and of course since each has aired his views and possibly discharged a great deal of emotional feeling in the interviews, it is not hard for them to be more objective and less quarrelsome.

In saying this, it is not meant to imply that they should pretend with each other that they have no interpersonal problems. There is such a thing, however, as creative quarreling. What I refer to above is the continual playing over and over of the same old "tape recording" of all their past and bitter conflicts. This they should stop, taking instead a new look and a new stance, and developing a new mental set. Most couples find that if they can do this, a better relationship develops, and as the counseling continues, the relationship improves steadily, though not always upward on a straight line. It is rather a going up and down, forward and backward, but the general trend is up. The counselor should not be surprised, after a couple reports improvement over two or three counseling sessions, for them to report that everything has blown up and the situation worse than ever. But the "blowing up" may have removed a considerable amount of accumulated debris of misunderstanding, subjectivity, and suspicion, and may have opened the way for real and permanent improvement.

The author also suggests that each one strive to do what he knows the other likes and refrain from doing anything he knows the other one dislikes. After discussing these likes and dislikes, the wife may say, "Well, I can cook his favorite dish for supper." Or the husband, "I can mend the fence which she has been after me about for three months." They will think of many little things they can do for each other, and things they can refrain from doing.

If the counselee wishes to continue with the counseling, the counselor should not end the initial interview without a definite appointment for the next one. In other words do not end it with, "Well, call me when you wish to come back," or "I'll see you in a week or so." It is important to be definite. This accomplishes three things for the counselee:

(1)   The minister really is interested and wants to be of help by arranging his schedule for another or several interviews.

(2)   It gives the counselee a definite date to work toward improving the marital relationship—to do his or her "homework."

(3)   It indicates to the counselee that he or she has a responsibility to the counselor to do that "homework," which is the implementation of insights and the various plans or decisions which the counselee himself may have made during each interview.

PLANNING THE NEXT INTERVIEW

It is helpful immediately or soon after an interview to go over it and plan for the next one by noting significant material presented, reactions of the counselee, suggestions offered, and the direction the next interview might take. An unplanned

interview may get nowhere, leaving both the counselor and counselee frustrated.

THE SECOND AND SUCCESSIVE INTERVIEWS

Each interview should begin where the inter-
viewee is. The above suggestion that the interviews be planned does
not mean that the counselor should start in with his notes and
decide what should be taken up next; he should have these in mind
to bring up where they fit in but should allow the counselee to start
wherever he wishes.

There are times when points noted to be considered after an
interview cannot be taken up for several interviews. The interviewee may come back each time filled with problems not mentioned
before. Each interview opens up new insights. Each one begins
where the counselee *is*.

This also prevents the counselor arriving at an early diagnosis.
It usually takes several interviews with both spouses before an
outsider can pinpoint the trouble. If he thinks he knows what
lies behind the couple's difficulty, he may anticipate them and
suggest some course of action which they are not ready to consider.
The interviewee should go at his own pace. This is definitely the
best way for the minister-counselor to proceed.

SUMMARY

The trained and experienced minister-counselor
is quick to sense the need for counseling as he meets with his parishioners in the daily course of events. But as the need arises, he does
not seek to meet it casually, though it may be revealed in casual
conversation while fishing or golfing. He seeks to transfer the conversation to a counseling session in his study or office.

Definite appointments should be made as opportunity arises
in conversation or over the telephone.

It is recommended that spouses be seen separately and then
together, depending on the progress made in the initial interviews
or later interviews. A two-hour appointment for a couple is recommended for the initial interview with each spouse being seen separately and then both together.

Ample time should be allowed for the first interview. The

counselor should not give the impression that he is rushed or impatient. For the time being the counselee should have his undivided attention.

The counseling procedure should be explained to the counselee. It should be pointed out that several interviews with each spouse may be required, as well as several with the couple together. Finally, a terminal interview will be set.

The interview begins when rapport has been established. The counselee should be allowed to begin where he is or wishes to begin. If he shows apprehension, the counselor should point out that the interview is private and that whatever is said will be kept in strict confidence. The test of good counseling lies in the amount of talking done by the counselee. The counselor's percentage of the time should be a minimum. He should be a good listener. Pertinent questions are asked to keep the counselee talking.

Whenever possible, both spouses should be counseled. Occasionally, a marriage can be helped through one spouse, but since marriage is an interpersonal relationship, the best results are obtained by counseling both spouses. The counselor's role is not to carry information from one spouse to the other, but as both reveal the same information to help them view it objectively. By all means the counselor should be neutral.

A visit to the home will often be of value in understanding its environmental effect upon the marriage. If the couple belong to the minister's church, he probably already knows the home environment. But a visit to the home in the light of the counseling may be very rewarding.

Definite arrangements should be made for each succeeding interview. Time appointments should be made. This adds interest to the "homework" or reality testing to be done between interviews.

SUGGESTED READING

Mudd, Emily H. *et al., Marriage Counseling: A Casebook.* New York: Association Press, 1958.

Stewart, Charles, *The Minister as Marriage Counselor.* Nashville: Abingdon Press, 1961.

Sullivan, Harry Stack, *The Psychiatric Interview.* New York: W. W. Norton & Company, Inc., 1954.

Terminating the Counseling

4 The terminal interview is nearly always a dramatic and exciting one. It takes place after several interviews have been held with the spouses, individually and as a couple—interviews in which personal problems have been dealt with. Some quite serious moral problems may have been faced and worked through both to a better understanding of the motivations behind them and to a better understanding of how to deal with such temptations if and when they arise again. Each has gained an understanding of the strengths and weaknesses in his personality and has learned how to make personal and social adjustments within and outside the family. The couple have also learned how to modify their environment so as to lessen tension and conflict. New skills in interpersonal relationships have been learned and reality tested in their daily life. Now the couple, feeling that they are ready to terminate the counseling, come together. This is an important experience for them and for the minister-counselor.

It should be pointed out that the counseling is terminated sometimes by the counselees without discussing the matter with the minister. This may happen either in the case of one counselee or when a couple is being counseled. They may feel that they do not need further counseling or that the counseling is not accomplishing for them what they had hoped for. When this kind of termination takes place, it is best for the minister-counselor not to bring the matter up again unless some initiative is taken by the counselee—which may occur some time later.

Mr. and Mrs. Wallace had been coming regularly for their personal interview for about a month when he failed to keep an appointment. Before her next appointment Mrs. Wallace phoned that she would be unable to keep hers and did not wish to make another. Both were at church the following Sunday. No reference whatever was made to the counseling. They were both quite cordial. Several months passed. They continued to attend church and were seen on other occasions. Finally, Mr. Wallace called and asked if he and his wife could come together for an appointment. They both apologized for stopping counseling as they did, but now had several problems they wanted to discuss together. This turned out to be their terminal interview.

But some who stop before the counseling has been terminated never show up again. Perhaps they become discouraged because of the time consumed and because they can see little or no progress. Some do come hoping for a quick solution to a problem they may have had for years.

DEPENDENCY

Then, also, there are those who wish to continue the counseling indefinitely. They become very dependent on the counselor. When the matter of terminating the interviews was mentioned to one woman, she said, "Oh, I don't want to stop coming. I would like this to go on forever." A man who found that the counselor gave him a lift each time he came did not want to stop "because," he said, "I always leave feeling that I can do anything."

It is not always easy to terminate counseling when a dependent relationship has developed. It is essential that such persons be turned toward their spouses and that their spouses both be awakened to the needs shown in this dependency and attempt to meet those needs. It may be flattering to the counselor to have people dependent on him, but unless he transfers that dependency to those to whom it rightfully belongs, he is doing the counselee great harm; in marriage counseling it may provoke jealousy on the part of the other spouse.

It should be emphasized again that the minister-counselor

must be very careful that he does not become emotionally involved with any counselee.

A woman who had lost faith in her hubsand and was becoming dependent on the counselor was greatly relieved when he said, "Your husband is a very fine man." She replied with considerable spirit, "Do you really think so? Everybody has run him down." Actually the man had been "run down" only by her friends to whom she pictured him as a "drunkard and a wife beater." He drank occasionally and had hit her when she provoked it. But she had been deriving from her friends' commiseration a martyr's compensation. The man had an excellent business reputation and standing in the community. As we discussed his good qualities, her confidence in him began to be restored; with his understanding of her needs a good marital relationship was reestablished, although the wife had filed for divorce when she first came for counseling. The man stopped drinking. Persons can be very lonely, discouraged, and full of self-pity in such situations as both these individuals found themselves. They reach out to grasp and depend on any understanding person who can help them to see themselves and their problems objectively. The wise counselor will be quick to recognize their dependence on him, and equally quick to seek ways to transfer it to where it properly belongs.

Some parishioners come to the minister with full confidence that he has both the knowledge and wisdom to direct their lives. "Here is the situation. Tell me what to do," is said countless times in every minister's study. The minister who is untrained in counseling may make evaluations, interpretations, criticisms, or give praise and reassurance without a clear understanding of the motivations and feelings which may be behind the situation, thus bringing about a dependent transference. Rogers makes two hypotheses:

> When the client is evaluated and comes to realize clearly in his own experience that this evaluation is more accurate than any he has made himself, then self-confidence crumbles, and a dependent relationship is built up. When the therapist is experienced as "knowing more about me than I know myself," then there appears to the client to be nothing to do but to hand over the reins of his life into these more competent hands. . . .[1]

---

[1] Carl R. Rogers, *Client-centered Therapy* (Boston: Houghton Mifflin Company, 1959), p. 215.

Transference attitudes are perhaps most likely to occur when the client is experiencing considerable threat to the organization of self in the material which he is bringing into awareness.

It is the author's experience, in agreement with Rogers, that dependence is less likely to occur with the client-centered therapist because "his respect for every client utterance as being, at that moment, a responsible expression of the self as it exists at the time, would undoubtedly convey an expectation of independence rather than dependence." [2]

THE EXPECTATIONS
OF THE COUPLE AND THE COUNSELOR

What are the expectations of the couple? What are the expectations of the counselor?

In all likelihood the couple sought out a minister-counselor in the first place either because they wanted help in saving their marriage, which may have begun in the Church, or because after marriage they became identified with a church, and found that they were falling far short of the Christian ideal of marriage. "As our marriage deteriorated, we began to lose interest in the Church," spoke one client. "Our quarreling led to one of us staying home on Sunday morning. Then we began to send the children. Somehow, we did not feel comfortable going to church after bitter words and in ugly moods. This is not right. So we felt that we should first consult a minister. We realized that we needed help with our marriage, and we want to have a Christian home." At the terminal interview such a couple come to be united once more—to make a new start. They come full of hope, looking to the minister to give them some suggestions for accomplishing this goal.

The minister-counselor also has expectations of this terminal interview. He has worked hard with the couple individually for many hours. He has remembered them in his prayers. Now they are people whom he has come to love and esteem. He wants more than anything else to see them happy and their marriage rebuilt on the solid rock of Christian faith and morals. To help them he must believe in them. He must reassure himself of the ability of

---

[2] Rogers, *Client-centered Therapy*, p. 215.

people to change when properly motivated and free of constricting bonds—such as guilt, self-depreciation, and hostility.

THE INTERVIEW

During this interview the counselor should arrange for the couple to sit near each other—either on a sofa or on chairs close together. Many couples hold hands, or the husband may put his arm around his wife.

Some of the problems previously discussed with them separately are then reviewed briefly.

Mrs. Kay had been very jealous of a daughter by her husband's first marriage. Although the daughter lived with her mother, Mrs. Kay would become very much upset whenever her husband sent money for the daughter's support. She thoroughly disliked the child. This had caused Mr. Kay to stop seeing the child and finally to stop payments for the child's support. (For some reason the child's mother made only feeble requests and soon stopped asking.) Mr. Kay began feeling very guilty about this neglect of his daughter, but any mention of it to his wife created a terrible scene. When they came for counseling, he had not mentioned the child for some time and had not seen her for several years. He had become sullen and withdrawn and had engaged in a mild flirtation with another woman. This caused him so much guilt and confused thinking that his efficiency in his job dropped, and at home he withdrew from his wife and children.

These problems were resolved satisfactorily in the counseling. He discussed his daughter and the need to make contact with her and resume payments for her support. Confessing his guilt helped him greatly. His wife was also able to discuss the daughter with the counselor, resulting in her recognition of the rightful love of her husband for his daughter, which relieved her jealousy.

The flirtation had been so brief and mild that after discussing it, Mr. Kay did not feel that he needed to tell his wife. The counselor accepted this.

The man's confused state of mind cleared almost immediately. In the interview next to the terminal one he told of organizing a Little League baseball team on which his two boys were playing. His job efficiency was back to what he considered his best.

In the terminal interview the counselor reviewed with them the father's attitude toward his daughter and his need to renew his relationship with her. Mrs. Kay agreed smilingly. They had already discussed it.

The case of Mr. and Mrs. Ronald was terminated successfully with the marriage continuing but only after many personal interviews with each of them. Mr. Ronald had a long history of promiscuity and extravagance. His business required him to take long trips of a week or more duration. He regularly traveled by plane. Through experience early in his career he had learned how easy it was to take some young woman with him. For years his wife knew nothing of this; however, about two years prior to their coming for counseling she became suspicious. By chance, she found that he had a bank account unknown to her. Later a check made out to a woman in another town appeared by mistake in their joint account. She confronted him with it. After repeated denials and after Mrs. Ronald's calling the woman long distance, he admitted this affair and others. This resulted in a separation.

However, the Ronalds loved each other and were not happy separated. Their three children were greatly upset over the separation and had been given no adequate explanation of it.

Such was the situation when they came for counseling. Eight personal interviews were held with each. After the second interview Mr. Ronald returned home. In his interviews he was very frank and cooperative. He showed genuine sorrow for what he had done. The question naturally arose as to whether he was fully aware morally of his infidelity, or whether he was full of regret because he had been found out. The counselor came to be convinced that the former was correct in his case; Mr. Ronald's conscience had been troubling him for many years. Mrs. Ronald loved her husband very deeply and showed a remarkable capacity for forgiveness and a readiness to do her part as a redemptive agent.

In this terminal interview it did not seem wise to discuss again his unfaithfulness, but rather to emphasize the positive and creative aspects of a durable partnership based on Christian love, forgiveness, and mutual esteem. Mr. Ronald expressed himself as having found the real meaning of marriage, and Mrs. Ronald felt that the crisis they had gone through had helped both to realize how dependent they were upon each other.

USING THE DECLARATION OF INTENTION [3]
FOR MARRIED COUPLES

I have found that the Declaration of Intention (see Appendix I), with one change, makes an excellent outline for the terminal interview. By striking out the first clause, "desiring to . . . ," the Declaration reads, "We . . . do solemnly declare that we hold marriage, etc." I have added to the Declaration two clauses which make it acceptable to members of churches other than the Episcopal. The amended Declaration appears on page 70.

Each minister who may use this Declaration of Intention will of course develop it in his own way and according to his church's teaching on marriage. It would be presumptuous on the author's part to attempt to do this for him.

The author has the Declaration mimeographed, and a copy is handed to each partner. It is then read together. After reading it over each item is taken up and related to whatever phase of the previous interviews is indicated.

For example, in the Ronalds' case, without mentioning specifically his infidelity, it was possible to discuss what is meant by the complete sharing of the body with one's spouse in terms of St. Paul's saying that one's body belongs to one's spouse and is to be shared in Christian love and with understanding of the other's sexual needs. "Even so husbands should love their wives as their own bodies. He who loves his wife loves himself. For no man ever hates his own flesh, but nourishes and cherishes it, as Christ does the church, because we are members of his body." [4]

In discussing the Declaration with Mr. and Mrs. Kay, it was appropriate to apply "the complete sharing of . . . spirit" and, further on, "mutual . . . understanding" to his need of sharing with Mrs. Kay his emotional problem about his daughter and her need to try to understand his love for his daughter and his guilt because of his neglect of her. Both learned a great deal about empathic

---

[3] For use in premarital counseling, see J. Kenneth Morris, *Premarital Counseling—A Manual for Ministers* (Englewood Cliffs, N.J.: Prentice-Hall, Inc., 1960), pp. 39–59.

[4] Ephesians 5:28–30.

In the Name of the Father, and of the Son, and of the Holy Ghost.

Amen.

DECLARATION OF INTENTION

We

_____

and

_____

do solemnly declare that we hold marriage to be a lifelong union
of husband and wife *(with the complete sharing of body, mind
and spirit in a cell of Christian love) as it is set forth in the
form of Solemnization of Holy Matrimony in the Book of Common
Prayer *(or in Holy Scripture).

We believe it is for the purpose of mutual fellowship, encouragement, and understanding, for the procreation (if it may be) of
children, and their physical and spiritual nurture, for the safeguarding and benefit of society.

And we do engage ourselves, so far as in us lies, to make our
utmost effort to establish this relationship and to seek God's
help thereto.

_____
Signature of husband

_____
Signature of wife

Dated _____ A.D.

*This portion in parenthesis is not a part of the official
Declaration of Intention.

70

understanding as the key to a closer and more realistic relationship.

In discussing the last paragraph of the Declaration of Intention, two points may be emphasized very strongly. These are "our utmost effort" and "to seek God's help thereto," for a marriage succeeds only to that degree for which the couple is willing to work and sacrifice. A happy and successful marriage must be the goal intended from the beginning and kept in mind through the years. Whatever disagreements and difficulties may arise must be overcome by the determination to let nothing interfere with the marriage achieving its goal. (See section entitled "Working at the Marriage" on page 105.)

Successful marriages reflect the maturity of the spouses, or at least of one of them, to plan for the future and to work for its realization. In some cases one spouse may be a sufficiently strong and mature personality to carry the marriage through happily to a bright and satisfying future. He can solicit the cooperation of the other spouse and children and, assuming the leadership, guide and motivate them to the goal, which he alone may fully comprehend. But of course it is far better when both spouses are mature enough to comprehend and plan for the future.

Neither the minister nor any other counselor possesses magic formulas that can guarantee any marriage. But many marriages that have ended in divorce might have been saved had the partners worked as hard to preserve them as they did to destroy them. A couple must work at their marriage twenty-four hours a day, every day. There are no rest periods and no vacations in this job, but it's the kind of job which brings such satisfying rewards that one never tires in doing it. In fact, it even may be said that those who are mature enough to express their love for each other in kindness, consideration, and respect are really unaware of the effort they make. This is characteristic of love at its best, love that does not will to love and cherish the loved one any more than one wills to breathe and stay alive. To love one's spouse and to sacrifice for the marriage becomes a way of life.

"To seek God's help thereto" is essential for the Christian couple. The whole concept of Christian marriage is rooted in the belief that since God Himself instituted marriage, His help and guidance must be sought in building a marriage. There are many ways in which this may be done: private devotions, family prayer, and church attendance. "The family that prays together stays together" does not always hold, however. In counseling I have known couples who prayed and read their Bible daily but who were at such odds that divorce seemed to them the only answer to their unhappiness. Nor is church attendance necessarily a stabilizing influence. Underneath these aids must be the motivating influence of mature love.

Given mature love, however, family prayer and church attendance can enrich family life and its "togetherness" as no other aids can. God is concerned with every marriage. He is distressed as deeply over the unhappy ones as He is pleased with the successful ones. All spouses are His children whom He loves equally, and not for what they do but for what they are. Therefore, a couple can pray to Him and worship Him knowing that in every sincere and honest endeavor they have His blessing and the guidance and help of His Spirit.

SIGNING THE DECLARATION OF INTENTION

Some couples, in fact most couples, wish to sign the Declaration of Intention as amended. This is done at the terminal interview, but never under pressure. It is a matter they must desire to do as a sign of a renewal of their marriage vows. The interview then closes with a prayer. The following prayer seems very appropriate:

O God, who hast so consecrated the state of Matrimony that in it is represented the spiritual marriage and unity betwixt Christ and his Church; Look mercifully upon these thy servants, that they may love, honour, and cherish each other, and so live together in faithfulness and patience, in wisdom and true godliness, that their home may be a haven of blessing and of peace; through the same Jesus Christ our Lord, who liveth and reigneth with thee and the Holy Spirit ever, one God, world without end. Amen.[5]

A blessing may follow the prayer.

---

[5] *The Book of Common Prayer*, p. 303.

A PRAYER FOR A MARRIED COUPLE

The following prayer is one which may be given to those couples who intend to build or reconstruct their marriage along Christian lines:

O God, for whom all fatherhood is named, who hast instituted marriage; Grant that we may be so bound together in mutual love and esteem that we may always show kindness and consideration toward each other. Enable us to forgive each other's trespasses and to believe the best about each other. Inspire us to be trustworthy. Strengthen us in all goodness. Help each of us to rise to the other's best as each strives to achieve his noblest ideals. Give us patience and wisdom as we grow and develop into mutual fellowship and understanding. Through Jesus Christ our Lord. Amen.

A FOLLOW-UP INTERVIEW

It is well to set a follow-up interview with couples a month or more after the terminal meeting, especially where there have been some very destructive elements of marital discord which time alone can repair. Those couples welcome a later interview. It signifies to them that there will be a time to evaluate once more their situation, and if the marriage should slip back, there will be a time to pull things together again.

I find this follow-up interview is a very welcome one for most couples, but all couples do not feel this way. Some say they will call if things do not work out. No pressure is exerted upon them. But they need to be reassured that the minister is always ready and willing to counsel with them whenever they feel they need him.

If a follow-up interview is desired, a definite appointment should be made, entered on the desk calendar or appointment book, and written down and given to the couple. Just to say, "Well, come back in three months," is not definite. The chances are they will not come back, even though they may need to. All appointments for counseling should be definite: date and hour. To say, "Come by the study sometime and we will talk about it," is to say, "Do not come." But to say, "Let us make an appointment now for a follow-up interview. When will it be convenient for you to come to my study?" will indicate to the couple the minister's real concern about their marriage as well as the minister's desire to be of further service.

After the terminal interview or the follow-up interview—as well as during the whole period of counseling—it is the author's feeling that the minister should never refer in any way to the counseling when he meets the counselee or is making a pastoral call. For instance, he should not ask, "How are things going now?" The counseling, and whatever may be said or done (e.g., confession), should never be referred to outside the pastor's study. If the parishioner makes reference to it, the pastor's reply should be such as not to invite a repetition of the counseling or a discussion of it at that time. If the parishioner introduces some new material, the minister should suggest that he or she come to the study or office for another interview.

THE CONTENT OF THE FOLLOW-UP INTERVIEW

The real purposes of this interview are to check on the reality testing in regard to the points of conflict which were disturbing the marriage at the time the couple first came for counseling, to reinforce improvements in the relationship, and to give encouragement in whatever areas are indicated. As Dollard and Miller [6] point out, the counselor should never content himself with mere knowledge or good intentions on the part of the counselee.

A couple who had felt they were ready to terminate the interviews came for their follow-up one. During the three month interval since their last visit, at which time they felt that all their problems had been solved, they had become careless in using the skills they had learned. They had begun to quarrel violently about differences in child training, the wife's laziness in housekeeping, and the husband's indifference toward the family. A good deal of mutual hostility was shown in the interview. Both agreed that they should renew the individual counseling. Appointments were set up and several sessions held with each over a period of several months.

---

[6] John Dollard and Neal E. Miller, *Personality and Psychotherapy* (New York: McGraw-Hill Book Company, 1950), pp. 349ff.

Then another terminal interview was set and after that another follow-up interview. This time the couple made it successfully. In this case the initial three month interval was too long—a month would have been better.

The follow-up interview may result also in a decision to dissolve the marriage. In this case the interview may be of great value to the couple in facing this crisis with the counselor so that it may come about as amicably as possible, especially where children are involved. Divorce is disturbing enough to children, but if parents can maintain a friendly relationship and share the children happily, the children may take it more easily. If each spouse realizes the need of the child to esteem his parents and to know that each loves him, the child will feel less insecure.

The author feels also that if couples must secure a divorce and have had marriage counseling with a minister, in later years they can tell their children that they used the best aid available in the Church in an attempt to save their marriage but that in the end it seemed best for all concerned to dissolve it. Then the children will have a better understanding and appreciation of their parents' marital problems.

All marriages cannot be saved, such as, for example, one which was formed under parental pressure because of premarital pregnancy. The couple probably would never have married because a mature love had not developed. There may even have been serious clashes before the marriage. Now, a few years later, they find that the marriage is not working out satisfactorily. Both are miserable, but they come for counseling. Some improvement in their relationship is made as long as they see the counselor weekly. Although they come for their terminal and follow-up interviews, the early conflict of personalities with its frequent blowups and recriminations continues. Plainly, they do not love one another. They cannot create a wholesome home atmosphere conducive to good child development. They come to the follow-up interview convinced that divorce is the only way out of their unhappy situation. This was the experience of Sam and Louise. They discussed it calmly and objectively with the counselor. Each accepted his share of the blame. Each felt that he understood himself and the other one better because of the counseling, and that an amicable relationship could be maintained "but only out of the marriage," said Sam. Because they belonged to the same church and would continue to live in the same town, Sam decided that he would transfer to another church while Louise and the children would continue in theirs. Sam moved out, and divorce proceedings were started by Louise. There were no ugly feelings, and financial arrangements were made which were acceptable to both.

Because there are more happy marriages than unhappy ones, and because marriage is still a popular institution, far more couples are helped in marriage counseling toward successful marriages than toward a dissolution. The follow-up interview, therefore, is usually a very satisfactory one: couples report continuing progress; matters which once were barriers to communication have been dealt with as they arose; immaturity has given way to growth; skills learned have been further developed; church involvement has increased. Some report an improvement in their finances, or promotions in their jobs. Naturally such news gives the counselor great pleasure. Many relate amusing incidents; they have learned to laugh at themselves, at each other, and together. One husband said, "She is the best dressed-for-bed-wife in the city." "How would you know that?" his wife replied, with a sparkle in her eye. One of his complaints had been that she wore "old flannel pajamas"! A wife who had had the habit of letting her husband get his own breakfast at six o'clock while she stayed in bed until nine said that the counselor had played havoc with her beauty sleep, because she was getting up to get his breakfast. Her husband's point had been not that he wanted her to get up just to prepare his breakfast but that because of his working hours there was little opportunity for them to talk together. They were now finding a new companionship at this early hour. "Of course, after he leaves, I go back to bed!" she remarked on the side.

"I'm coaching a Little League team and getting a real kick out of it. John is one of the players," said a father who was discovering his son for the first time. "We do more things now as a family," said another. "I don't worry any more about house cleaning. My husband and children are more important," said a wife. "We all go to Sunday School and I'm helping in the nursery." "I've taken a class of boys at church. They are great kids." "I've put too much emphasis on my practice to the neglect of my family," said a physi-

TABLE 1 Marriage Counseling Process

Precounseling	Counseling Process						Post-counseling
	First interview: individual	Husband-wife together	Between interviews	Subsequent interviews: individual	Subsequent interviews with couple	Terminal interview	
Decision by one or both spouses to seek counseling	Basic background material set forth verbally or by Schedule IA	General overview of problems presented	Reality testing	facing specific problems in interpersonal relationships and how to resolve them	Confidence gained in expressing hostility and/or love	Husband and wife find strength in union	Couple leave counseling and continue reconstruction of marriage in accord with purposes related to Christian faith
Couple in conflict threatening stability and permanence of the marriage	Facing reality of problem	Tensions relaxed	Rediscovering each other and mutual responsibilities			Purpose of Christian marriage	
		Hope and reassurance	Conflict decreasing	Freedom in expressing feelings of animosity, love, guilt, and forgiveness	Meaning of love forgiveness, restoration	Goals to achieve	
		Energy released for reconstruction of marriage	Understanding gained		The three purposes of sex		
				Guilt resolved			
				Reinforcement of creative psychic forces			

cian. "I've rearranged my schedule. My family comes first. I never realized that it could be done."

Can a minister spend his time in any more profitable way for his church and community than in helping his people grow in their marriages and be happy? The minister trained in counseling will be able to fulfill his pastoral responsibilities with joy and satisfaction as he achieves a ministry of reconciliation between the spouses of his congregation.

Table 1 outlines succinctly what has been discussed as marriage counseling in Chapters 3 and 4.

SUMMARY

The terminal interview should be anticipated by both husband and wife and counselor. It marks a conclusion of the interviews during which counselees have shared experiences with the counselor and solved many problems. It is an important occasion for all.

Sometimes, however, the counseling is broken off by the couple, without benefit of the terminal interview. Again, sometimes these couples may return later and seek further help. But some are never heard from again unless of course they are parishioners of the minister-counselor.

It is easy for individuals to become dependent on the counselor. This is more apt to occur with the untrained counselor because he may not recognize the psychological danger inherent in it or know how to transfer the dependency to the spouse, where it rightfully belongs. Dependency, which can get out of hand if the counselor becomes emotionally involved with the counselee, is less likely to occur in client-centered therapy.

The couple and minister-counselor bring many expectations to the terminal interview. The spouses may come to be reunited spiritually with each other and the church. They wish to make a new start. This is also the hope of the minister, for he has come to love and esteem the couple and has prayed many times for their happiness.

The arrangement of the interview should be such that the couple can sit together on a sofa, or in chairs near each other. Their oneness must be emphasized. Salient points in the counseling will be touched on according to their nature and resolution. The general atmosphere should be hopeful and reassuring.

The Declaration of Intention as revised for a married couple can be used with much effectiveness, and usually the couple will want to sign it. An appropriate prayer concludes the interview.

Usually it is advisable before closing the interview to plan with the couple for a follow-up interview to take place a month or several months in the future. If agreeable to the couple, a definite appointment should be made.

The purpose of the follow-up interview is to check on the reality testing in regard to the points of conflict which were disturbing the marriage when the couple first came for counseling, to reinforce the improvement in the relationship, and to give further encouragement and reassurance.

SUGGESTED READING

Alexander, Franz and Thomas M. French, *Psychoanalytic Therapy,* pp. 35–37. New York: The Ronald Press Company, 1946.

Brammer, Lawrence M. and Everette L. Shostrom, *Therapeutic Psychology,* pp. 200–208. Englewood Cliffs, N.J.: Prentice-Hall, Inc., 1960.

Johnson, Dean, *Marriage Counseling: Theory and Practice,* pp. 125–27. Englewood Cliffs, N.J.: Prentice-Hall, Inc., 1961.

Sullivan, Harry Stack, *The Psychiatric Interview,* Chap. 9, "The Termination of the Interview." New York: W. W. Norton & Company, Inc., 1954.

Thorne, Frederick C., *Principles of Personality Counseling.* Brandon, Vt.: Journal of Clinical Psychology, 1950.

Special Concerns
of the Minister-Counselor

5 The minister-counselor should never overlook his unique relationship to those who come to him with their personal and marital problems. He holds a position in the community as a man of God who has dedicated his life to the service of his fellowman through the Church described in the New Testament as the Body of Christ. It is, therefore, to such a person that men and women bring their problems. This should give him a deep sense of humility and cause him to reach out in love and concern to all who come to him.

SOME PERTINENT QUESTIONS FOR THE COUNSELOR

When the minister sits down to talk with a person whose marriage is breaking up, many questions will come to mind.

What caused this couple to marry each other? Were they in love? If so, what has happened since marriage to undermine that love?

All marriages are not for love. Marriages exist in which a spouse is seeking economic security. One woman frankly admitted that she had married not for love, but because she was tired of working and thought Jack would be a good provider. After six years, she realized that receiving economic security without giving love was worthless. He had loved her, however. After she had expressed her reason for marriage and her guilt for having married under false pretenses, she began to see her husband in a different light, soon found herself in love with him, and began to respond to his love. They had children whom both loved. The husband had reacted against her indifference with ridicule and sarcasm. When he understood this, he became more considerate.

It is not always possible, however, to have a marriage which began without love on the part of one or the other turn out so well. Where there was no love to begin the marriage and none developed, not much can be done to repair marital damage. There are those, of course, who will continue to live together because of children and because they do not believe in divorce. For the sake of the children involved, couples have been known to work out an amicable relationship but devoid of expressions of marital love.

Some ministers would raise the issue of duty versus love. They would say that a couple having married have a duty toward the sacrament of marriage and toward the children born of the marriage, a duty requiring them to continue in marriage and to find a reasonable basis—platonic, perhaps—on which to continue the marriage and be faithful to their marriage vows. In the framework of the indissolubility of marriage this has merit. Certainly, couples cannot escape their responsibility to provide a secure and happy home environment for their children. It might be argued also that since one spouse entered the marriage contract without reservations and because of love, he has a right to expect the other spouse to fulfill his duties and obligations in keeping the marriage. However, a marriage held together solely because of duty without love could be intolerable for some people.

The commands of duty are absolute, and true freedom lies in self-constraint of our personal interests and gratifications in accordance with the dictates of a higher universal law. Moral good transcends all natural impulses and particular emotions, just as personal relationships belong to a different plane from that on which questions of status and equity are determined.

Now it is the moral "ought" which today has lost its compelling power in the modern world. The imperative of duty is no longer binding on the universal conscience of mankind as in former times, and the impulse towards liberty has been replaced by the claims of equality and justice with scant regard for responsibility and obligation. The husband-wife relationships as a complementary partnership in a joint personality has been resolved into a dualism of male and female rights, status and freedoms, so that the fundamental nature and purpose of marriage have been lost in a struggle for equality and social justice in isolation from the biological and domestic context in which, in its natural setting, the institution of marriage occurs.[1]

Was this a forced marriage without love? If the woman had not become pregnant before marriage, would these two people have married each other?

Perhaps no marriage is more tragic than one of this sort. As the years go by, each spouse, because of his or her unhappiness, may build up great resentment against the other. And yet both may love their children very much and for their sakes wish to hold the marriage together. Sometimes this sort of marriage produces in one or the other a neurosis, or it may bring on a latent psychosis.

When a couple whose marriage was forced upon them without love come for counseling, the minister needs to be very understanding and nonjudgmental, and to show in every possible way that he identifies with them in their problem. Even though there may be no good solution to their problem, if the couple come to a minister, he may be sure that they believe he can be of help. The minister has much to offer such a couple. In the first place, he can help them toward forgiveness of themselves, for the chances are that each hates himself for having gotten into the marriage, and also holds resentment toward the other whom he or she may blame. And then, too, there is the unwanted first child, and now, perhaps, several children. Sometimes the couple resent the first child because the child symbolizes the forced marriage, or they feel guilt toward the child or children. To have the minister-counselor listen patiently and understandingly, entering empathically into their problem with them, means that they may be able to forgive themselves and each other. The veil of resentment begins to lift, and life takes on a happier mood.

Sometimes divorce may be the only answer. Their feelings may be so deep and the wounds of bitterness and resentment so unhealing that further attempts to rebuild the marriage are useless.

---

[1] Edwin O. James, *Marriage and Society* (New York: John de Graff, Inc., 1955), pp. 186–87.

This calls for counseling, then, for divorce—helping the couple to consider its many problems. Divorce may solve some problems, but it inevitably raises others. The couple will need much help in facing the future. They will need legal advice. The minister should know the legal resources of his community well enough to suggest to them how to go about selecting a lawyer if they do not know one. The minister himself should not attempt to give legal advice.

If and when the divorce or a legal separation is granted, the couple will still need counseling. It might be well for the minister to encourage each one to come back when the case is settled.

Some cases are quite complicated. A man who was happily married and had two children had an affair with a divorced woman. The man had a record of promiscuity. He and the woman went off for a weekend, and she became pregnant. The man told his wife who divorced him. He then married the woman so the child could be born legitimately. However, neither spouse loved the other and neither one was capable of loving and continuing faithfulness to one spouse. Each resented his marriage, the man particularly because he felt the woman had trapped him. There was nothing to build on in the marriage, and a divorce was obtained. However, the minister-counselor was able to help each spouse to a better understanding of himself, one of them to repentance and a more wholesome way of life, with self-acceptance and a rediscovery of God.

When did difficulties of a serious nature start? What was taking place in the environment at that time? Was there some crisis?

It is frequently possible for couples to pinpoint the beginning of their difficulties. However, although they may not at first see the environmental crisis in relationship to their difficulties, they may soon come to do so.

For example, John and Mary had been unhappy for several years. Each said in the interview that he could not see the difficulty in relation to any particular event. They had been having trouble for eight years. Up to that time, they had been quite happy. Naturally, the question was, "What happened eight years ago?" They could not recall anything unusual. But as they talked, it soon developed that eight years before, John had changed jobs. This had happened before, but this time the job involved a lot of traveling and consequently a change of routine. Gradually, the wife began to resent the job that took her husband away, sometimes a week at a time. When she married, she had always thought he would be at home. Moreover, her father had also traveled, and on one of his trips he had become involved with a woman, resulting in the breakup of the home. Consequently, this was what a traveling job symbolized to her. Her anxiety over her husband's traveling became so intense that prior to her husband's leaving on his trips, she would be nervous and tearful—and finally began questioning his love for her. She expressed to the counselor her worst fears that her husband probably had a woman as her father had had. It is easy to see how the environmental change was the cause of the beginning of their unhappiness. Reassurance, her husband's understanding, his taking her with him when possible, and his seeking a position with the firm that would allow him to spend more time at home soon restored a happy, trusting relationship.

In the case just cited, when the emotional disturbance was resolved or dissipated, it was possible for the wife to become objective and gain insight into the nature of her marital conflict. Once this was accomplished, reorientation followed, resulting in a new relationship with her husband. Together they then moved forward toward new objectives and perspectives related to the counselees' needs, abilities, and resources, both personal and environmental. The plans and decisions made in the counseling sessions could now be implemented.[2]

What is there of lasting value in this marriage on which it may be rebuilt?

The minister-counselor will naturally want to save a marriage if he feels that it can be done and that happiness can ensue for the family. The counselor will seek first to discover if there was love in the beginning of the marriage. It is my experience that if there was love in the beginning, it often can be renewed. Real love is strong and flexible; it can be bent, but is not easily broken. Once present, it seldom completely vanishes.

---

[2] Emily H. Mudd *et al.*, *Marriage Counseling: A Casebook* (New York: Association Press, 1958), p. 44.

Encouraging a couple to talk about their courtship and marriage often helps them to recall tokens of love each had forgotten and to see them against the background of several years of living together.

Discussing romance with them, and going over many of the things they used to do for each other, may cause them to try again.

It is so easy for a couple to forget that romance must be kept alive. A man was asked if he had ever been in the habit of giving his wife little surprises—a box of candy, for example. He said he did until they began quarreling. Since he was very anxious to repair the marital rift, it was suggested that he give her a box of candy and tell her that he still loved her. He did, with an unexpected response from his wife who had also been counseled. She accepted his gift and his love as only a sweetheart could. They had little trouble rebuilding after that. In the counseling, both learned a great deal about himself and the other, and how to cultivate each other's love and good will.

It is surprising how many people give up selling themselves to their spouses. Neither would have gotten the other in the first place had each not put his best foot forward and "sold" himself.

Skip was a very successful salesman who knew how to sell himself and his product. He had a very warm, friendly approach to others. He knew the psychology of salesmanship. Even though a prospect might not give him an order, he always left a friend behind because he felt that some day the man might give him an order. He was proud of his ability to make friends. But of Olga, his wife, he had made an enemy. He had failed completely to keep her as a good "customer" for personal wares: his personality, his ability to love and to satisfy her sexual needs, and his companionship. As he compared his ability outside the home with his failure in the home, he realized that after marriage he had done what no good salesman ever does—taken his "customer-wife" for granted. No one wants to be taken for granted. Each wants and needs a continual renewal of appreciation of his worth as an individual, his value to the other person, and his status in his own right. No one likes to be stereotyped. Many a marriage has failed at this point because one spouse stereotyped the other as a "typical mate," casting him in a preconceived role without regard to that mate's peculiar personality traits. Couples who have allowed courtship and romance to die have lost the glow of love essential to a happy marital relationship. Neither should a spouse ever cease showing his best self to the other; it makes marriage an exciting adventure in love so long as each shall live. Many a marriage has been saved by helping a couple reorient themselves toward love and romance. Skip and Olga were quick to see what had happened to their marriage and set about rebuilding it.

Where there was love at the beginning of the marriage, often it can be reactivated on a more mature level.

Mature love seeks to give—not to get. As infants we were only concerned with getting. As mature individuals, we should be concerned with giving. To give to one's spouse love, affection, appreciation, security, and understanding; to put one's family welfare first and give to one's family time, interest, and security—these are all evidences of mature love. Each one can measure his or her own degree of maturity by this scale.

How will separation or divorce affect the family involved? What about the children? How far reaching will a separation or divorce be? What effect will it have upon the in-laws?

These are perhaps the first questions to arise in the mind of the minister-counselor when a couple consult him about the possible breakup of the marriage.

Some spouses become so embittered toward each other that they seem to forget the children. Parents should be asked to consider the rights of children: right to both father and mother, and right to a home environment that will give them love and security. It is interesting to see a wife's or husband's reaction to the questions, "Did your children ask to be born?" "Who was responsible for bringing them into the world?"

I recall a wife who had but one thought: to get rid of her husband, until she was confronted with the question, "Will you send the children back where they came from?" This question triggered an emotional value concerning the children—her love for them and her husband's love for them; how they had wanted to make a happy home for their children; the rights of the children to a father and a mother. With her thoughts centered upon the children, it was not difficult for her to see some of the good points in her marriage and in her husband. Both were willing to enter counseling and try to save their marriage.

MARRIAGE DISSOLUTION

I do not wish to give the impression that all marriages can be saved. Far from it. A wife, the daughter of a college professor and married to a fairly well-to-do engineer, came to consult us about the unhappiness in the home and its effect upon the children. The husband also came. But no reconciliation was possible, even after months of counseling. Divorce followed. The wife felt the children would be better off in the atmosphere of her parents' home.

In another case, in which the husband and wife were forced into marriage, no way for a reconciliation could be found. The wife got a legal separation. The two children involved presented a tragic sight. For a long time they were emotionally disturbed and had night terrors and enuresis. The father, when visiting, added to their problems by periods of indifference, showing partiality to one child, and spasmodically showering them with gifts.

Divorce, however, is not always bad for the children. A wife with three small children was married to an alcoholic. Even through prolonged counseling and AA, the alcoholic pattern could not be broken. The husband also showed marked immaturity and was diagnosed as psychopathic. The home atmosphere, disturbed by prolonged drinking, abuse, cursing, and quarreling, was having a bad effect upon the wife and children. The wife finally decided on divorce. This was several years ago. She and the children are happy. She has been able to provide them with a stable home atmosphere, ample love, and affection.

The minister-counselor needs to be realistic and recognize that all marriages cannot be saved, labor as he will to that end.

When a legal separation or divorce seems inevitable, he should be able and ready, as already pointed out, to counsel both spouses for meeting the new situation.

The minister-counselor has a responsibility to the whole family. He should utilize his knowledge regarding interpersonal relationships, child training, and social factors, as well as physical ones, to try to help all concerned toward a reorientation of family living on the Christian level. The minister is in an unusual position to help families achieve the goal of Christian family life.

THE MINISTER-COUNSELOR AS A CATALYST

I have already indicated that the minister must not take sides. For example, a parishioner consulted his rector on a marriage problem. His wife sometimes drank heavily, and when not drinking took sedatives and sleeping pills. They had two small children, yet this had been the behavior pattern for several years. Sometimes his wife was better, sometimes worse. The husband came to the minister after his wife had been drinking considerably more than usual. The husband was frustrated, angry, and pretty much fed up with the whole business. When he had finished a lengthy tale of woe, he asked the minister, "What shall I do? I cannot go on this way." Without hesitation, the minister said, as he (the minister) told me about it: "I told him to get rid of that woman; that he would be justified in getting a divorce; that he had had more than his share of trouble, etc., etc." Of course, this did not help the man. He loved his wife. He did not want a divorce. Nor did he want a snap judgment. He asked the minister if he knew of a marriage counselor who would talk with him and his wife. It should be noted that he did not ask if he could bring his wife to talk with the minister. Nor did he ask for a further interview for himself. By taking sides and pronouncing judgment, the minister had spoiled his opportunity to be helpful to a couple in deep distress.

When the minister is neutral, he serves as a sort of catalyst—that is, by both parties separately talking out their problems with him, the problems become identified, labeled, and objective. Emotions are vented, and attitudes are clarified. In a permissive atmosphere, individuals can fully express their feelings, and this results in great relief. Thus, an immediate result of counseling can be the reduction of hostility. The counselor should provide for and listen to the fullest expressions of hostility.

Rogers states that

. . . the experiencing with the client the living of his attitudes, is not in terms of emotional identification on the counselor's part, but rather an empathic identification, where the counselor is perceiving the hates and hopes and fears of the client through immersion in an empathic process, but without himself, as counselor, experiencing those hates and hopes and fears.[3]

Therefore, like a catalyst, the counselor, after the counseling, remains unchanged. But this does not mean that he has not gained in wisdom and learned more about human nature—its defeats and triumphs. The counselor does not sit apart as though he has all the answers or that failure, guilt, and suffering have not been his lot, too. There is no place in the counseling process for a holier-than-thou attitude. All have sinned. Many have made a "mess" of their lives. Many, too, have wrested from defeat victories which make them towers of strength to others struggling desperately to find their way to peace and happiness.

WHY THE MINISTER-COUNSELOR?

Certain of the author's observations as to why people with marital problems do not consult the minister were mentioned earlier. Let us now consider why some others do come to a minister when the marriage is threatened.

(1)   If they are Episcopalians, they may come because the canons require it.

(2)   If they were married by a minister, they may come because they feel the Church is interested in their marriage and might be able to help them.

(3)   One spouse may come because he feels that he is morally right and wants the reinforcement of the minister.

(4)   They may come because they are religious-minded and feel that the minister can bring the teachings of religion to throw light upon their marriage to show them where they have failed.

(5)   They may come because they believe that religion can give them support in strengthening the strong points in their marriage.

(6)   They may come because the minister in his pastoral relation-

---

[3] Carl R. Rogers, *Client-centered Therapy* (Boston: Houghton Mifflin Company, 1959), p. 29.

ship and in his preaching may have conveyed to his people that any problem which concerns them concerns him and that he is always ready to serve them and to be helpful.

(7) They may come because those ministers who do a thorough job of premarital counseling will have opened up to couples the potentialities of marriage counseling when marital difficulties arise. Those couples will be inclined to seek the minister as a counselor.

THE MINISTER-COUNSELOR AS A RECONCILER

Although the main emphasis in this book is upon the minister as a marriage counselor, his role as a reconciler must not be overlooked. Some couples prefer to counsel with a minister simply because he is a man of God; they believe that he will handle their marriage and their problems in such a way that whatever the outcome may be, it will be in accordance with the will of God for them and their children (if there be any).

Sin and broken relationships

Sin in the marriage relationship or in the family constellation cannot be overlooked,[4] and those who seek out a minister-counselor do not want it overlooked. The counselor must not attempt to explain away the reality of sin in human life. Wrongdoing destroys the very essence of good relationships. To let guilt be overshadowed by psychological explanations of the dynamics of some sinful act is to play loosely with the moral order emanating from God and governing all human society. Therefore, for a minister-counselor to gloss over these elementary factors inherent in human conduct is to let down those who seek his help as a reconciler between themselves and God and their fellows, and to weaken the fabric of their moral integrity developed out of their moral convictions.

No one disputes the fact that neurotic or psychotic people are indeed sick, but the tendency is to attribute the illness only to one's early environment or to some failure to meet the demands of

---

[4] Lawrence M. Brammer and Everett L. Shostrom, *Therapeutic Psychology* (Englewood Cliffs, N.J.: Prentice-Hall, Inc., 1960), pp. 399–407.

life, instead of realizing that the person may instead have violated his moral standards, gone contrary to his self-concept, and sinned. In the stress of some situation he chose to do what he knew to be morally wrong, and unable to remove the guilt, was overcome by remorse, self-disgust, and shame.

Some psychologists, led by O. H. Mowrer, are beginning to recognize that the recovery or constructive change or redemption of the neurotic

. . . is most assuredly attained, not by helping a person reject and rise above his sins, but by helping him *accept them.* This is the paradox which we have not all understood and which is the very crux of the problem. Just so long as a person lives under the shadow of real, un-acknowledged, and unexpiated guilt, he *cannot* (if he has any character at all) "accept himself"; and all *our* efforts to reassure and accept him will avail nothing. He will continue to hate himself and to suffer the inevitable consequences of self-hatred. But the moment he (with or without "assistance") begins to accept his guilt and his sinfulness, the possi-bility of radical reformation opens up; and with this, the individual may legitimately, though not without pain and effort, pass from deep, per-vasive self-rejection and self-torture to a new freedom, of self-respect and peace.

. . . for the only way to resolve the paradox of self-hatred and self-punishment is to assume, not that it represents merely an "introjec-tion" of the attitudes of others, but that the self-hatred is realistically justified and will persist until the individual, by radically altered attitude *and action,* honestly and realistically comes to feel that he now deserves something better. As long as one remains, in old-fashioned religious phraseology, hard-of-heart and unrepentant, just so long will one's con-science hold him in the vise-like grip of "neurotic" rigidity and suffering. But if, at length, an individual confesses his past stupidities and errors and makes what poor attempts he can at restitution, then the superego (like the parents of an earlier day—and society in general) forgives and relaxes its stern hold; and the individual once again is free, "well." [5]

Fear and anxiety

People come to a minister for counseling because they are troubled about something they have done or failed to do which has made them fearful, anxious, and "sick." They fear the conse-

[5] O. Hobart Mowrer, "Sin, the Lesser of Two Evils," *American Psy-chologist,* XV, No. 5 (May 1960), 301–4.

quences of their acts which may affect personal safety or the family relationship. A man who was dangerously close to incest with his daughter was not fully aware of the direction in which his attentions to her were carrying him until confronted with the facts in counseling. He then became frightened. But understanding the dynamics of his behavior, he began at once to change, and a tragedy may have been prevented. Counselees must not be led to believe that their fears of punishment are unfounded where some real and not imaginary sin has been committed. Even God does not promise relief from punishment or the natural consequences of wrongdoing. The incestuous father will be punished if found out, or he may suffer a broken relationship with his child. The counselor cannot mitigate the results of wrongdoing, but he can help the counselee toward achieving a new orientation toward rightdoing and building a good relationship where a broken one exists.

In discussing fear as it is expressed in counseling by the patient or counselee, Dollard and Miller have this to say:

> Naturally the patient does not extinguish anxiety to every possible sentence which he can make. To take extreme cases, he is not allowed to be without fear when he is planning murder, incest, or criminal behavior. This discrimination must be made quite clearly by the therapist. The therapist can, so to say, promise nonpunishment for certain activities—those which were once punished but are now no longer forbidden—but the therapist cannot tamper with life's realities. He cannot let his patient, for instance, think that apprehension, trial, and conviction may not follow upon murderous thoughts which lead to murderous acts. The therapist must therefore correctly interpret the real world and its danger signs. He can diminish only those fears which are already out of date in the sense that they are no longer followed by punishment in the actual conditions under which the patient lives. Here again the immense importance of the sociological conditions of the patient's life is evident.[6]

Sin separates—it separates man from God and man from his fellows. The latter may be his spouse and/or children. Therefore, sin and its effect upon the marriage relationship must not be side-stepped. As a reconciler the minister must be able to help the couple understand the meaning of repentance, forgiveness, acceptance, and restoration.

---

[6] John Dollard and Neal E. Miller, *Personality and Psychotherapy* (New York: McGraw-Hill Book Company, 1950), p. 250.

Unfaithfulness and repentance

This is particularly true when unfaithfulness has precipitated the marital crisis—precipitated, because usually many factors have contributed toward causing the unfaithfulness. If it is the husband who has been unfaithful, part of the problem may go back to an unresponsive, unaffectionate wife, or one who has never accepted the sexual relationship as a wholesome part of a happy marriage. Some wives say, and husbands too, but more often wives, that they felt guilty and ashamed after intercourse with their husbands. Some have said, "I know I am the cause of my husband's unfaithfulness." A young wife who had been unfaithful said, "I don't know why I did it. I did not even know the man except for a brief date. I should have known better. But I think one reason was because my husband was so indifferent and unloving. He seemed to want sex only for himself. He seemed to just use me. This man I met even in the brief time I knew him, expressed feelings of love and affection. I guess I was just dumb and fell for it. I do love my husband."

For one spouse to repent may not help much unless the other one is willing to repent also and each forgive the other. But spouses can be very hard on each other. Some men will freely confess repeated acts of infidelity and excuse them in themselves as the man's privilege, but not forgive their wives for one misstep.

The Christian man or woman generally wants to do something about unfaithfulness. The minister can help him with his problem of guilt as no one else can. His confession to the minister in the counseling room has a great value as a catharsis. It also gives the minister an opportunity to share with the individual the meaning of love, redemption, the infinite love of God, and the great promises of God which give to every repentant sinner joy and hope. An explanation about making a formal confession in the church audibly, before the minister, prepares them to go one step further and put a finality upon their unfaithfulness. Absolution can bring great assurance and peace. With some individuals, however, it is better to do this in the office or study at the time the confession is made. There is no rule to follow in dealing with human beings in times of great stress; what may fit one person may not do at all for another. Sometimes a formal confession in the

Church is better delayed until the person expresses a need for it. Using the Church's discipline tests the minister's love and care for people and his empathic understanding of their needs.

But then comes the question, Should the person tell the spouse of the unfaithfulness, in cases where the spouse does not already know? There is no way to answer this categorically. The counselor should never advise it either way, but help the individual decide whether or not to do it. In some cases it should certainly not be done unless the spouse has been prepared for it. Let us consider the following case.

Ethel and Felix had been married several years. There were two children. The family was close to their church and pastor. The parents were active members, especially Ethel, who taught in the Sunday School and participated in the women's activities. Felix had a great desire to take a more active part in the church but felt inhibited by his previous drinking problem and notoriety as a "woman chaser."

When they came for counseling, both were terribly mixed up in just about every relationship including their relationship to their church.

Ethel arranged for the counseling and on her first visit was not sure that her husband would come. Several years ago she had stopped going to church but had begun attending again about six months previous to this visit. She complained of severe headaches, nervousness, and nightmares, and of being very unhappy. Her physician had put her on tranquilizers. When he was consulted, he said that there was nothing organically wrong but that she was nervous. He was glad that she had entered counseling.

Ethel vividly described a recurrent dream from which she always awakened frightened and with a severe headache. The dream took various forms, but in every case it ended with her being alone; also, sometimes in her dream she thought of death and if after death she would be alone. Sometimes she woke up crying and terrified, broken out in a cold sweat. She also said that God seemed very far from her, and in her dreams she felt that He had abandoned her; also, Felix was not with her, which troubled her considerably. As she told of her dreams and fears of death, she cried and would say, "If only I felt that God was with me. But He is not."

After several interviews, when nothing had been said by her to give a logical basis for her fears, I said to her, "Somewhere, you seem to have omitted something. Things don't add up. Is there not something quite significant that you are concerned about and have not brought up?" After a moment, she replied that there was, but that she had not been able to bring herself to the point of discussing it because she would be embarrassed. I answered simply, "In other words, it is a sex problem?" From there on, she related several acts of infidelity. In time, she made a formal confession, and her fears and dreams ceased.

But then one day she said, "I know I must tell my husband. But I am afraid it will upset him and start him drinking again." She felt very strongly that if she were to be free to develop her potentialities as a wife and mother it would be necessary for her to tell him, but we both felt that her husband should be prepared for it. She arranged for him to come for counseling. After talking with him, I realized that there was one thing he believed completely about his wife and that was her faithfulness. He readily admitted that he had been unfaithful. But she was his ideal of a wife and mother.

In discussing forgiveness he said, "I can forgive everything except unfaithfulness."

"Then," I replied, "you cannot truly forgive anything."

"What do you mean?"

"I mean that for one to truly forgive another, one must realize what God has forgiven him, including the lies, lustful thoughts, unfaithfulness, dishonesty, or what have you. One cannot say, I will forgive this but not that. Complete and sincere repentance manifested by genuine sorrow for what one has done demands complete forgiveness on the part of the one sinned against."

Felix wanted to discuss this more fully. It brought him down to bedrock thinking. He then related incidences of his own unfaithfulness, picturing himself as a first-rate liar. Tears came into his eyes as he confessed that time and again he had deceived his wife with lies. At the close of the interview he said, "I've got to have time to think this over."

After several interviews in which we had discussed more fully his own problems and the meaning of love and forgiveness as they related to him, and after he had expressed himself on his feelings about God's forgiveness and acceptance as an expression of God's love, I felt that he was ready to hear his wife's confession and so informed her in an interview, but again helped her to be sure that she really wanted and needed to tell him.

Reconciliation

She told him as planned. I saw both of them separately several times after that. It was a shock to him. But through the preparation he had been helped to make, he said that he was surprised at his reaction. He said, "I could only hold her tight, as we both cried. I don't believe I have ever loved her as much as I did then and still do."

The couple returned for further counseling several times over a period of about a year. It was rewarding to see them come to self-forgiveness and self-acceptance.

When they entered counseling, each one had brought with him a considerable amount of self-depreciation and loss of self-esteem. They hated themselves for what they had done in the past and for the cloud which they had caused to darken and threaten their marriage. But after being assured of God's forgiveness and their worth to God in terms of our Lord's redemptive act on the Cross, they began to see themselves in a new light and to realize that the next step in their renewed relationship to God was to forgive and accept themselves as forgiven, accepted, and restored children of God. Their self-esteem returned and along with it a surprisingly new and wholesome relationship with others and with their church.

Felix had felt that others in the church looked down upon him as he looked down on himself, but now, with the barrier of guilt removed, he found to his surprise that he could speak and associate with them without any feeling of inequality. And they accepted him. In fact, a few months later they elected him president of the men's organization and later a member of the church board. A whole new life in the church opened to him.

And Ethel found that she could teach her Sunday School class without "those awful feelings of being a hypocrite and unworthy." She became more active in the women's organizations.

At the time they came for counseling, both had been so

concerned about their own personal problems that they had neglected to give their children the time and attention needed by
them. Here, also, a better relationship developed. They felt free
to develop this relationship by planning family outings and games
and by working together in the yard. Relieved of their own guilt,
fears, and insecurity in their own love relationship, Felix and Ethel
were able to create a relationship within the whole family constellation which reflected love, understanding, and mutual respect.

The minister's role as a marriage counselor is but a part of
his priestly role as a reconciler of men to God and man to man.

AVOIDING A QUICK DIAGNOSIS

After the first interview wth a couple, the
counselor may feel that he already knows the trouble, but he can
be greatly mistaken. The complaint first mentioned may not be
the chief cause of trouble. All the facts will not come out in the
first interview. In fact, the real cause of the trouble may not come
out until several interviews are had, as just related in the case of
Ethel and Felix. A hasty diagnosis may lead the counselor to work
toward an impossible and unacceptable solution.

Rogers [7] feels that the counselor may become so occupied
with arriving at a correct diagnosis that he may side-step the real
purpose of the interview, which is to provide "deep understanding
and acceptance of the attitudes consciously held" by the counselee
as he moves closer into the dangerous areas which he may have
been repressing and was afraid to admit to consciousness.

One should avoid telling the couple what he thinks the cause
of the conflict is. He should let them discover the cause. They will
if allowed to, and if the counselor does not try to rush them or
to push his idea on them. If they discover the cause, they will
accept the solution suggested by it. It will then be their solution.

The counselor will arrive in time at some sort of diagnosis
of what he considers to be the basis of the marital difficulties:
immaturity, selfishness, neuroticism, or a paranoid trend. But he
must not relate to the counselees his diagnosis; rather, he should
let them become aware of the basis of the conflicts as a result of

---

[7] Carl R. Rogers, "Significant Aspects of Client-centered Therapy,"
American Psychologist, I, No. 10 (October 1946), 415–22.

the counseling. As said before, if the counselor feels that the counselee is in need of psychiatric treatment, he should make the proper referral.

MODIFYING THE ENVIRONMENT

In some marriage counseling cases, it is very obvious that little can be accomplished unless environmental changes are made at home, work, or in the community. One couple solved a family problem by moving to another town, another by changing neighborhoods. A change in a work routine helped another.

The change in the environment may be social and/or psychological. A better relationship developed in one family when the wife began organizing the home life more in keeping with her husband's wishes. In another case, a strained relationship between husband and wife had produced anxiety in the children. When the couple understood this and began to show affection toward each other in the presence of the children, their anxieties subsided.

Kirkpatrick [8] lists four fundamental factors which bear directly upon the family. These factors must be considered by the counselor. They can not always be changed, but often the effect upon the family can be understood and modified.

Any family is dependent for its existence on *natural environment*, such as soil, mineral resources, climate, and the plants and animals characteristic of a region. There is also *man-made environment*, such as houses, railroads, highways, and business districts. A wife brought up in the rural environment of the White Mountains may be very unhappy on a treeless Texas prairie, or in a large industrial district near Detroit.

There is not much the counselor can do about *heredity*. But insight into its results in particular cases may ameliorate a marital problem so that reasonably good adjustments can be made. To blame a spouse for what may be due to hereditary factors is to fight against impossible odds.

---

[8] Clifford Kirkpatrick, *The Family* (New York: The Ronald Press Company, 1955), pp. 19-20.

The *cultural factor* has already been mentioned. Culture is the ever-accumulating totality of uniform, socially acquired objects and impressions. Material culture includes such things as buildings, automobiles, and tools. Nonmaterial culture includes such things as customs, religious creeds, institutions, and scientific knowledge. The ways in which culture affects marriage is obvious, for the family is involved daily in meeting the demands of living within an established milieu. Changes and adjustments must be made constantly. The counselor can assist to this end by helping a couple understand the effect of cultural factors upon the marriage. The term *variable behavior*, according to Kirkpatrick, might be applied to unique and unstandardized interaction to distnguish it from uniform, ritualistic, standardized behavior which is a part of culture. Thus, rejection of a child because he resembles a hated relative is to react in terms of variable behavior. Marriage, modes of worship, and government are parts of culture. Conformity to standardized behavior and understanding one's variable behavior should follow effective marriage counseling.

The counselor should be on the lookout for changes or modifications in the environment as aids toward repairing broken family relationships.

HUSBANDS AND WIVES AS THERAPISTS

The home is the only institution with a built-in therapist. People are quite conscious today of the need for psychotherapy. Words like psychology, psychiatry, psychoanalysis, psychotherapy, and counseling are used freely—however, not always intelligently. Popular magazines carry numerous articles on different aspects of analysis. Many people go from one professional to another seeking relief from some form of maladjustment. I have been consulted by persons who have been to psychiatrists, ministers, marriage counselors, and, of course, the family doctor and friends, never finding the solution to their problems because the solutions they want have already been determined by them. Some of these people are in a serious state of mental disorder, but others are more in need of understanding, appreciation, affection, or a change of environment—all of which might be accomplished by a spouse who is willing to accept and learn the role of therapist. It does not require a degree in psychology. Here are a few things the minister-counselor may suggest to wives and husbands to help them build happier marriages.

Do not argue about spouse's personal emotional problems

Here is a husband who has had a hard day at the office. He has had a run-in with a good customer whom he could not afford to offend. He wanted very much to tell him where to go, but this would have been "poor business," and he could not risk it. He comes home seething with resentment and self-depreciation because, like a whipped dog, he has his tail between his legs. He hates himself for having taken it lying down. By the time he reaches home, he is in a foul mood.

His wife, however, has had a pleasant day. The maid came. The house was cleaned, and a nice dinner is ready. She looks pretty and fresh as she greets him at the door. He is not unmindful of this and brightens up. But, quickly, his ugly mood sweeps over him. She asks what the trouble is. Did things go badly at the office? With this, he lets loose with a volley of invectives against the so-and-so whom he could not offend. His wife tells him, "Get off your high horse and leave your work at the office. There is no need taking it out on me, I haven't done anything."

"No," he says, "you never want to hear what goes on at the office. You have everything so nice here at home. You don't realize the problems I have."

"And you don't realize mine either. Remember, I've been working all day, too."

By this time he has no desire to lay before her the problem that has so distressed him that he may digest his dinner poorly and not sleep well. He goes over and over in his mind what the customer said and what he could have said in reply. He tells him off, now, in his thinking, but he needs to do it verbally. He needs to express his feelings—but to whom? Because his wife has no patience or understanding, he represses his feelings and after dinner sits gloomily playing over again and again like a phonograph record the conversation with the customer and how he might have answered him.

Be understanding

The understanding wife would have handled the problem differently. She would have inquired about the trouble and then would have encouraged him to tell her about it. She would have let him express his feelings, to shout at her if necessary, to bang on the table and to say to her what he could not say to the customer. She would have listened very patiently and unemotionally, asking him questions that would help him in ventilating, until at last he could have said, "Well, anyway, that is the way it is in business. I feel better now. Let's eat." And no doubt he would have slept well—in the security of knowing that his wife loved him, respected him, and that he could tell her anything and she would listen, understand, and not argue.[9]

Be neutral

A good therapist does not take sides. In the above illustration the wife might have said to her husband, "Well, I think the man was right. You should have known better than to handle it that way." This would have increased his anxiety and resentment and made him feel that he had really failed.

Or, she might have sided with him, saying, "I think you were absolutely right. Why didn't you tell him off? I wouldn't stand for such treatment." This, also, would have increased his sense of failure, making him more angry over the affair and clouding his mind to objective thinking.

Here again spouses need to be neutral until all ventilation has been completed, and the person is able to be realistic and to make an objective evaluation of the situation. Then together they can be on the same side; or, in the above case, the husband might have concluded it by admitting he had been the cause of the misunderstanding and could rectify it the next day. Taking sides for or against a person under emotional stress accomplishes nothing so far as helping the person work through the problem.

What has been said about spouses is, of course, applicable

---

[9] George R. Bach, "The Path to Wedded Bliss: Get in There and Argue," *Life,* May 17, 1963, pp. 102–8.

to the counselor and is part of the technique of good counseling practice.

Be a good listener

Many anxieties [10] arise in everyday living. One may be anxious over conflicts of duty or responsibility. Many and varied are the demands made upon one's time and energy, probably more today than at any period in history. Decisions that may be distasteful and in conflict with ideals have to be made. Whatever the anxiety may be due to, it is a fortunate person who has an understanding spouse to whom he can relate his anxieties without fearing criticism, knowing that he will be understood.

Mowrer gives a good illustration of the cause of anxiety and his relief through a discussion wth his wife:

> While working on a monograph a few years ago, it became necessary to give the final examination in a large introductory course. The writer [Mowrer] personally proctored the examination, during the course of which he felt a mounting tension, verging on anxiety. This feeling continued on into the evening, at which point he discussed it with his wife. As a result of this conversation, it became apparent that the tension represented a previously unrecognized conflict between (a) the wish to push ahead with the monograph and (b) the obligation to get the examination papers marked quickly and the grades for the course to the proper authorities. As soon as this conflict was fully acknowledged and the decision made to read and mark the papers as quickly as possible, the tension lifted completely.[11]

Spouses as therapists are always available to each other and should encourage frank and open discussion about their problems, no matter how trivial or how great they may be.

TRIVIALITIES AS SYMPTOMS

Trivialities play a big part in our lives. A triviality may sometimes seem to be the crisis that causes a whole

---

[10] O. Hobart Mowrer, *Learning Theory and Personality Dynamics* (New York: The Ronald Press, 1950), pp. 550–61. Copyright 1950 by The Ronald Press Company.

[11] Mowrer, *Learning Theory and Personality Dynamics*, p. 551.

new chain of events to happen, and yet the triviality in itself may not be the real cause behind an explosive crisis but only the surface wave indicating a deep disturbance beneath. The movement of the ocean cannot be controlled by the ship tossed about on the surface. In the words of Edmund Bergler, "An inner conflict cannot be resolved simply by altering external circumstances." [12]

In marriage counseling the counselor should not be misled into dealing with trivialities and fail to detect the deeper motivations which lie behind the apparent upheaval.

The marriage of Joe and Evelyn seemed to be plagued with trivialities. Any little disagreement precipitated a crisis. After a few days of happiness one or the other would say or do something which would be so upsetting as to open a wide rift between them.

They came in one day barely speaking to each other. The difficulty was over a bank account. Now, a bank account of large proportions could well cause a crisis in some marriages; however, this bank account amounted to only a few dollars. It was a joint account which Evelyn wanted to move to a bank where a friend was working. Joe did not mind moving the account, except that he saw no particular reason for doing it. He had had it in the present bank from his college days and was known to the people there. Evelyn said that there would be no service charge in the bank where her friend worked, but the service charge was seldom over 50 cents a month in Joe's bank. Although Joe had agreed reluctantly to move the account about a week before, he felt that banking was a part of the husband's role in marriage and that he would decide when to change banks. Evelyn, without asking Joe, one day called her friend to drop the signature cards by the house on his way to lunch. Then she called Joe and told him that the account could be moved that day. Joe "blew his stack."

Why did Evelyn precipitate this crisis? Why did Joe get so upset? It could not have been the amount of money involved, for at the most it was only a small amount. It was not a question of one bank's being better than another. It was not a matter of convenience. When all phases of the crisis were analyzed, it proved to be symptomatic of competition in their roles of husband and wife and a failure to understand and accept those roles. Evelyn

---

[12] Edmund Bergler, *Unhappy Marriage and Divorce* (New York: International Universities Press, Inc., 1946), p. 13.

wanted Joe to "wear the pants," but she was very ambivalent about it and felt herself to be competing with him for the "top place" in the family structure. It was hard for her to understand and accept marriage as a partnership.

In the case of James and Laura the problem concerned James's eating, another triviality which frequently brought about a crisis. Table manners vary from family to family, culture to culture. Some people's table manners are unacceptable to others, but viewed objectively, we do not leave the table, walk out of the restaurant, or become nauseated because of the unpleasantness of the eating habits of friends and guests. Yet Laura could not endure James's table manners. Although he was brought up in just as refined a home as she, he had to eat as she wanted him to or else he reminded her of a relative whose manners were unacceptable to her family. She could accept the unpleasant table manners of others, but not James's. To show her disgust, she would leave the table and eat in the kitchen alone or with the children. The real problem? There were several.

Laura felt inferior to James, and at the table she unconsciously reduced him to the level of an atrocious relative who "ate like a hog." In like manner she criticized his other manners and was always correcting him because he embarrassed her. She knew that his family excelled hers in education and in his father's profession, but her mother had taught Laura to excel over others by following a rigid set of rules in table manners and in matters of courtesy. There was only one correct way to behave socially. If James happened to hold his fork the wrong way, it touched off this whole syndrome of inferiority feelings and created a crisis.

Matt had a lovely wife and three beautiful children. He and Ruth had been married about 10 years. Ruth became aware that Matt began asking her each day what she planned to do and where she was going. It soon became irritating to her. One day when he asked her, she refused to tell him. He became abusive and accused her of having an affair. He began to brood and pout. He had been coming in late two or three nights a week for some months saying that he had to work. This Ruth accepted without question. Why had he become so inquisitive about whether she went to one supermarket or to another, or whether she went at nine in the morning or three in the afternoon? Trivialities. What then lay behind his questioning? Matt himself was having an affair. He felt very guilty about it, for he loved his wife and children. Along with the affair his drinking increased. He came to understand, through counseling, that his own waywardness was being projected onto his wife. He broke off with the woman, the marriage returned to normalcy, and Matt's drinking decreased to a normal social drinking pattern—also his "night work" ceased!

In these three cases we see one partner unconsciously struggling against the other instead of engaging in the struggle to resolve his own inner conflicts, and we see that the surface trivialities were indicative of deeper and more complex psychological problems.

WORKING AT THE MARRIAGE

One evening while the author and his wife were entertaining a guest whose marriage was not a happy one, my wife went to the kitchen and soon returned with glasses of ice cream and ginger ale. Our friend seemed rather surprised. As my wife proffered me a glass, he remarked to her, "You really work at your marriage, don't you?" "Yes," my wife replied, "we both do—the only way to have a really happy marriage is for two people to work at it every day and work hard at it. What I mean is: each must be thinking and planning how to please the other, rather than what one can get from the other for onself."

"Give," said Jesus, "and it will be given to you; good measure, pressed down, shaken together, running over, will be put into your lap. For the measure you give will be the measure you get back." [13]

This simple and obvious axiom the author has given to many couples. For example, Sam and Mary had been married long enough to have three well-spaced and beautiful children. Sam traveled. Consequently, he was away several days a week and sometimes on weekends. His wife worked hard looking after the house and children. They were very much in love with each other, but when they came for counseling, their marriage had begun to weaken. In fact, Mary said in her first interview that she could not go on giving, giving, giving, and getting little in return. When

---

[13] Luke 6:38.

the counselor asked what she meant, she said that Sam had become thoughtless and indifferent. Formerly, he had always shared with her his work and told her about his problems, where he had been, about this customer and that. He had helped with the children and usually had some plan for their weekends. But now, "He just comes home." With tears in her eyes she said, "He doesn't even want to share himself with me. Our sex life is awful."

When Sam came for his interview, he too was disturbed. He could not explain what had happened. Somehow their marriage was changing from a happy one to one held together more by determination and duty than by love. But Sam was far from understanding the part he had to play in bringing the marriage around again to what it had been. He was not a mature individual. In fact, he gave the impression of being a "bouncing baby boy." He loved Mary, but now that she was the center of the home surrounded by three children, the home had become a symbolic anchor of security. He wanted to come home from his travels because he found safety, relaxation, food, and a place to sleep—just as it had been when he was a boy and came home from school or play. That he had some responsibility toward the home and contributions to make toward the family's enhancement had not occurred to him seriously. He seemed to realize that he was failing somewhere, but could not label it.

They discussed Mary's contribution to the home. He mentioned her artistic ability in attractively decorating the home, her care of the children, and her ability to cook and serve attractive meals. He felt that she was a good sex partner—when he occasionally wanted her. "Occasionally?" the counselor asked. As the home, together with Mary, came more and more to symbolize security and became identified with his childhood home, the less frequently he desired her as a sex partner. This had disturbed him for a while, but now he thought it was due to his increasing age. He was all of thirty! Nor was he seeking sexual satisfaction outside the home; of this the counselor was convinced.

There were many interviews with both of them for they sincerely wanted to make their marriage a happy one. Mary came to understand Sam's attitude toward her and the home, to realize that they both had to recapture romantic love, and to know that she would have to help Sam grow into emotional maturity so that he would assume his responsibilities as husband and father. It was to require a lot of patience and hard work on her part.

Sam finally came to realize that he was taking all he could get from Mary and giving nothing in return except his pay check. He recalled their happy courtship and early marriage days when they were sweethearts; how in those days his mind was filled with thoughts of her and later of the children and what he could do for them. He now began to plan again along those lines. As he thought of ways by which he could satisfy her needs for love and emotional security, he also began to see her again as his sweetheart and himself as her protector and the protector of their children. He began to work at his marriage and to give of himself in time and interest when at home. Soon it was evident that a new and more mature relationship was developing as both tried to outdo the other in giving. They found that each could give to the other "good measure, pressed down, shaken together, running over."

Once they reestablished this sort of happy, generous working relationship, their sex life, with a few suggestions from the counselor, took care of itself. Their working and sharing together toward the common goal of a happy marriage resulted in a satisfactory sexual relationship based upon mutual love and a strong desire to complete each other.

Those who get married and stop there cannot hope to achieve a successful marriage. The minister has no magic power to guarantee such a marriage. His premarital counseling will come to naught unless the couple work hard to make their marriage what they want it to be. To settle down, as some couples do after a year or so, taking each other for granted, dooms a marriage to unhappiness. Spouses must continue to seek ways of pleasing each other just as they did during the courtship period. No one wants to be taken for granted. Marriage is what we make it. But we—husband and wife—have to make it and that calls for hard work day in and day out. It calls for sincere appreciation of each other, for never failing courtesy, and for self-sacrificing labors involving time and interest. But those couples who are willing to pay the price and give generously of themselves can expect great rewards in a satisfying love life, security, self-esteem, and the realization of their ideals of home.

WAITING TO GROW UP

Every minister today is faced at some time with the unhappiness in a marriage between two people who married quite young, unprepared to assume marriage responsibilities. These marriages may or may not have taken place had the young people waited. But in some cases the girl became pregnant, or one or both parties felt guilty because of their sexual relations and believed marriage was their only alternative in righting a wrong.

Tad and Jane were both sixteen years of age when they discovered that Jane was pregnant and decided to run away and get married. They had been having sex relations for about six months. In fact Jane was fifteen when they first engaged in intercourse. Both of them felt guilty and ashamed, but once having experienced it and with no one to instruct or guide them, they continued their heavy petting and intercourse once or twice weekly. They were going steady and believed that they were really in love. Because they had never discussed the future, planned their marriage, or communicated their goals to each other, they realized, in retrospect, that there had been only the sexual attraction between them. Their relationship had been purely physical.

They had been married about a year and a half when they came for counseling. They were very confused and uncertain as to their marriage, the child, their families, and their future. Tad felt that Jane did not love him, which she also substantiated, whereas he did love her, which she also believed. Their families were helping him to get his education, but there was a great cultural barrier between their families. He was from "the other side of the tracks." Her people were professional people, highly educated, and prominent socially, whereas his people were daily wage earners with little education. Soon after marriage Jane rejected his people completely, refusing even to visit them. She could not tolerate "their uncouth ways and illiterate speech."

Jane's family was relieved that she had married and saved them from "disgrace." His family was pleased over the marriage because they felt that religiously it was right. He was accepted by her family only because they needed him to give a legitimate birth to the child. However, since they did not approve of divorce, they decided to do what they could financially and otherwise to make the marriage last.

In high school Tad had been outstanding as an athlete and leader among the students. He and Jane were married in May. When he returned to school in September, he found that all his prestige had been completely swept away. "Everyone knew what had happened. Jane could not attend school. I was not allowed to play football or take part in school activities. My friends turned away. One would have thought I had leprosy. This was my senior year. Because of my marriage I had lost everything I had prized. I began to resent my marriage. There were times when I was so lonely I cried. In previous years I had made good marks, now I made very poor grades. My teachers were unsympathetic and unhelpful." However, Tad did graduate, and on the insistence of both families entered college.

Jane had not known his family until after the marriage. Her first visit was a terrible shock. What she saw in them was transferred now to Tad. She felt humiliated to be married to him. She began to blame him for her pregnancy and marriage, but when asked if he had forced himself on her, she said, "No. But I just did not realize what could happen. No, I really can't blame Tad. We were both to blame."

Sexual relations for her had become unpleasant and disgusting. She no longer reached a climax. She manufactured every kind of excuse for not having coitus. Sometimes they would go a month without intercourse, causing Tad anxiety, frustration, and lack of concentration on his studies and work (he also had some night and weekend employment). He was becoming depressed and could see nothing hopeful in the future. His grades were falling fast, and he was afraid that he might fail and be dismissed.

Their first concern, which seemed to be one of guilt, was the point at which we began counseling. They were seen separately. Both expressed considerable relief after they had talked out their premarital sex experiences. The catharsis was very beneficial. This took place during several interviews, because each time they found need to face up to their behavior again. Finally, however, the guilt seemed to be resolved. After both were willing to accept the blame, resentment toward the other lessened. Their confession was related to God's forgiveness and redemption, and how they could each forgive and be a redemptive agent for the other. Placing their experiences in the framework of Christian teaching seemed to bring considerable relief and an orientation in which they could rediscover each other. They had stopped going to church—because, they said, that only emphasized their guilt and shame. Now they began to attend church again and expressed their happiness in the renewed fellowship.

The problem of their family backgrounds was very difficult to resolve because of the obvious facts about which we could do nothing. The two families were what they were and would always be. Tad, for his part, showed no divided loyalty. He liked her family, appreciated the help they were giving them to enable him to go to college, and got along well with them. They apparently liked him now and had forgiven him and Jane for their early marriage. They loved the grandchild. Tad realized that his family was below hers culturally and accepted it. This is not always the case with an individual from the culturally lower class: The acceptance of the other spouse's family seems disloyal to his own family, and instead of accepting the other he may reject and ridicule his spouse and her family. Tad liked his father-in-law especially and found in him a good pattern to follow. He was also able to recognize his own father's limitations and the effect of his environment upon him. In a mature manner he was evaluating himself and the two families, drawing some good conclusions.

Jane, unfortunately, lacked the maturity to do this. She seemed to understand the cultural factors, but she could neither comprehend them nor make any adjustment to them.

Her next problem was to reverse the process of transferring to Tad her unfavorable attitude toward his family. She had to come to see him as a person in his own right. She was stereotyping him as an uncouth, illiterate, uncultured person, whereas he was quite the opposite. He was headed for a professional career as a lawyer. He had ambition, dressed nicely, and was beginning to be well read. It is true that his family traits showed up at times in table manners and social customs, but this he realized and was trying to correct. He welcomed her suggestions and was trying hard to be like her people. Gradually, Jane began to differentiate between him and his family and to think of him in terms of what he was becoming. She found that by praise and appreciation she could do much to encourage him and boost his morale.

The counselor, also, was able to do much in this direction by helping Tad evaluate himself and his potentialities. It was commendable that in addition to a full college load, he was willing to work in his spare time so that Jane's family would not have to bear the entire share of their support. His mental ability was average; when relieved of his anxieties and with his self-esteem restored, he began at once to improve his grades. This was most gratifying and reassuring to Jane.

The sex problem was complicated, of course, by all of their conflicts and frustrations. But as these were resolved, they became more affectionate with each other, and the frequency of intercourse became weekly, then two or three times a week. This brought them much satisfaction and a sense of belonging and of being needed by each other. They required some factual instruction on sex anatomy. They completed the Sex Knowledge Inventory, Form X, expressed surprise at their ignorance, and also were pleased with what they learned as the counselor went over it using the manual. Soon Jane reported that she had achieved orgasm. This had a very good effect upon Tad for he had blamed himself for her failure to reach a climax, thinking that he was failing her and was not completely virile.

When last seen, they were quite happy and very appreciative of the counseling.

One thing that seemed to help both of them was the explanation that they had married before either one was mature and ready for marriage. They were not, at that age, prepared emotionally to accept the responsibilities of marriage and parenthood; however, they were growing into maturity. If they remained married, they would probably find the mature love on which every true marriage must rest. They were encouraged to be patient with each other as they grew up and to help each other toward maturity. During the counseling, which extended over nine months, they matured considerably. A follow-up interview was set for them.

It would have been helpful for the counselor to see the two families, but this was not feasible because of distance.

In the follow-up interview several months later, progress in the marital relationships was continuing nicely. Owing to a change in the counselor's position, this couple was not seen again for over two years. On this occasion he was invited to visit the home. They were rejoicing in the birth of another child. They had matured considerably in every way since last seen and were quite well adjusted in all their relationships including those with both sets of in-laws. They seemed grown up.

SUMMARY

The minister-counselor stands in a unique position in relation to those who consult him because he is in their eyes primarily a man of God who has dedicated his life to the service of his fellowman.

Therefore, when couples consult him, he must ask himself many questions regarding the basis on which the marriage was formed to see what prospects there may be to rebuild it, or to help the couples toward an acceptable and amicable dissolution.

The minister, like other counselors, serves as a catalyst to precipitate the real problems so that they become identified, labeled, and objectified.

The role of the minister as a reconciler must not be overlooked, for this gives him a special concern for those who come to him with marital problems. Sin separates and cannot be set aside in the marriage relationship. Some psychologists recognize that the redemption of the neurotic is best attained by helping him accept his sins so that he may find forgiveness and freedom. People come to the minister for counseling because they are fearful, anxious, or "sick" morally. They fear the consequences of their acts. Unfaithfulness separates and leaves deep hurts requiring the healing of a skilled counselor, and the way back to marriage unity may be long, tedious, and painful. The minister's role as a marriage counselor is but a part of his priestly role as a reconciler of men to God and man to man.

One can seldom make a sure diagnosis after one interview. All the facts may not come out until several counseling sessions. A hasty diagnosis may lead the counselor to work toward an unacceptable solution.

Environmental changes are often required before a satisfactory resolution of marital conflict can be arrived at. This change may be social and/or psychological.

Husbands and wives should learn to become good therapists. A counselor, if his work is to last with a couple, should be sure that they know how to help each other—some of the simple principles of psychotherapy might be given them.

It should be impressed upon couples that successful marriages do not just happen but are planned and worked for patiently through the years. Those who marry and stop there cannot hope to achieve a happy marriage, but those couples who are willing to pay the price and give generously of themselves can expect a satisfying love life, security, self-esteem, and the realization of their ideals of home.

A young marriage is of special concern to the minister. Many of these young people are unable to assume the responsibilities of marriage. Many are disillusioned and fearful of the future. Some of them can be encouraged to hold to each other until they grow up. During this period the minister can be a great source of strength.

SUGGESTED READING

Bennett, Edward, *The Search for Emotional Security*. New York: The Ronald Press Company, 1959.

Carrier, Blanche, *Free to Grow*. New York: Harper & Row, Publishers, 1951.

Carrington, William L., *The Healing of Marriage*. Englewood Cliffs, N.J.: Prentice-Hall, Inc., 1961.

Genné, Elizabeth Steel and William Henry Genné, eds., *Foundations for Christian Family Policy*, Proceedings of the North American Conference on Church and Family, April 30–May 5, 1961. New York: Department of Family Life, National Council of the Churches of Christ in the U.S.A.

Johnson, Paul E., *Psychology of Religion*. Nashville: Abingdon Press, 1959.

Landis, Judson T. and Mary G. Landis, eds., *Readings in Marriage and the Family*. Englewood Cliffs, N.J.: Prentice-Hall, Inc., 1952.

Mudd, Emily H. *et al., Marriage Counseling: A Casebook*. New York: Association Press, 1958.

The Family Constellation

6 Psychology speaks of a constellation among people. Any group of people held together by some force, such as mutual interest, business, politics, or family, may be called a constellation. This is a particularly appropriate designation for a primary group such as the family, for members of every family are held together by tensions—love, loyalty, duty, authority—which produce between the members strains and stresses due to the constant interaction of their personalities as each seeks to achieve his goal.

In some families the tension between its members may become so weak that one or more members may drift beyond the influence of the constellation and actually lose all contact with the other members. Also, the strain of the pull of one member may reach the breaking point and the member literally fly away, severing all connection with the other members. A mother, who was domineering and sought to control her divorced daughter, Mrs. Rand, and Mrs. Rand's family, produced so much stress and strain that the daughter solved the problem for herself and her children by severing all relations with her mother, refusing even to receive her letters and phone calls. Having thus made the break, the daughter felt that her immediate family constellation returned to a balanced state.

THE PULLS OF STRESS AND STRAIN

Let us show a family constellation diagrammatically (Fig. 6.1).

When a man and woman marry, a family constellation takes shape immediately. There is primarily the husband (H) and wife (W) relationship. The arrows in Fig. 6.1 indicate the direction of tension—solid line primary, broken line secondary. The interplay of their personalities produces a certain amount of stress and strain

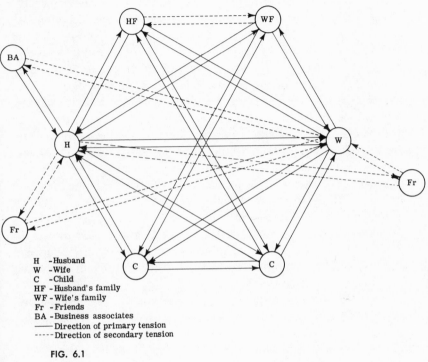

H – Husband
W – Wife
C – Child
HF – Husband's family
WF – Wife's family
Fr – Friends
BA – Business associates
——— Direction of primary tension
----- Direction of secondary tension

FIG. 6.1

A Family Constellation

in both directions. While the basic force holding them together is love, loyalty, duty, or authority, the family is subject to the stresses and strains that undulate upon it as the years pass. If their personalities are in constant conflict and crises are continually precipitated, the unifying force of their love may become too weak to hold them, and the constellation may fall apart in divorce.

If the marriage relationship is in general satisfying, mature couples will make adjustments to their conflicts in order not to allow the tension between them to reach the breaking point. For instance, they will consciously try to avoid getting angry at the same time. In anger one is very apt to return to a juvenile level of behavior; therefore, if husband and wife both become angry at the same time, they may act like two children fighting, and this may possibly have disastrous results. In angry episodes one spouse should always try to remain calm and objective.

Any association of persons produces relationships that in turn produce tensions and problems. These are normal in every family constellation. As each individual strives to find the meaning of life for himself in relationships with God and his fellows, and as he seeks to solve the problems produced by his attempt to satisfy his needs, he will find himself time and again caught in a bind caused by this emotional complex. It is his attempt or struggle, however, which develops his potentials and his capabilities to grow into full maturity. The child who has everything and is spoiled and pampered is very apt to remain immature and self-centered in adulthood, lacking self-discipline and the ability to deal successfully with the normal tensions of an adult society. The tensions and stresses of the family constellation serve two functions: (a) To hold the family together so that it creates an orderly and stable environment in which each individual has status, and (b) to require each individual to exercise his emotional, moral, and spiritual forces against these tensions and stresses of interpersonal relationships so that his capabilities to wrestle with the problems of socialized living will be strengthened.

Now in the case of the newly married couple the constellation also includes the families on both sides (HF) and (WF). These in-laws also produce tension upon the husband and wife and sometimes between themselves. The interaction of their personalities again produces stresses and strains in both directions. As long as the in-laws recognize the independence and right of self-determination of the young couple and lend emotional support on a basis of equality, the constellation will be well balanced. There are many such families, just as there are more happily than unhappily married couples.

But in-laws can and do produce strains and stresses which spoil many a good marriage. Undue interference on the part of either of the in-laws can bring to the breaking point the tension between those in-laws and the young husband or wife or both. In order to avoid this situation a conference with the in-laws before the marriage of the young couple is often indicated. The author has held such conferences with very good results. It is a rare parent who does not want his son or daughter happily married. Parents are usually glad to have any help the minister-counselor can give them.[1]

When children (C) come to the new couple, new lines of tension are set up with accompanying stresses and strains. These involve not only the parents but the grandparents. The serious situation of Mrs. Rand mentioned above was due largely to the grandmother's objection to her granddaughter's dating.

The number of interpersonal relationships within a family constellation increases with each addition to the group.[2] For example, where there is only husband and wife, there are two relationships. When a child comes, this increases to six; two children, twelve; three children, eighteen, etc. When we add other members of the constellation such as in-laws, friends, and business associates, the number of relationships becomes astronomical. To keep all the tensions well balanced requires mature, adjustive, and objective individuals. Integrative people can and do revise and restructure their behavior in the light of experience and reality testing.

This family (F) constellation may also involve relationships with various secondary groups shown in Fig. 6.2. Here we have the school (S) or PTA; the church (C); the commuuity (Co) including activities such as scouting and activities at community centers; the lodge (L); the club (Cl); social groups or bridge clubs, and political meetings (P). All of these activities produce tension between their claims and the family needs. The mother and children may quarrel with the husband because he will not attend the PTA. The meeting nights of the lodge and the bridge club may conflict. The husband may complain that the wife spends too much time in church activities to the neglect of home duties. The wife may accuse the husband of caring more for his hunting lodge or fraternal lodge than he does for his home. All of these interests are good in themselves, but produce tensions within the family, which may throw the constellation out of balance. Husband and wife must be aware of

---

[1] For a fuller discussion the reader is referred to J. Kenneth Morris, *Premarital Counseling—A Manual for Ministers* (Englewood Cliffs, N.J.: Prentice-Hall, Inc., 1960).

[2] Compare Harry J. Baker, *The Art of Understanding* (Boston: The Christopher Publishing House, 1940), pp. 185–86.

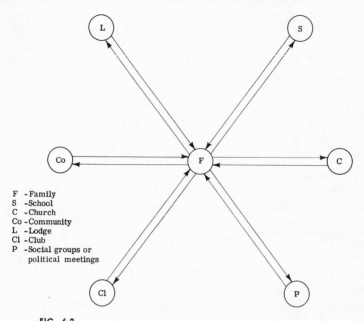

FIG. 6.2

The Family Constellation in Relationship with Secondary Groups

these factors of adjustment and keep them in line. Although the family must take precedence, it also must realize that it has a role to play in the community and that the community has a rightful claim upon its members for assistance with its many programs. One family cannot engage in every activity; it must choose those its members feel they can best serve. The activities they engage in may also depend on the ages of their children. The mature, well-adjusted family will welcome opportunities to serve and thereby make its contribution to the community life.

The resolution of these conflicts lies in an understanding of the cultural background of the individuals and of the role concept held by them. A wife who comes from a society-conscious family that places a culture value on membership in the country club and the DAR may have serious conflicts with a husband whose family looks down on such things as "high brow" and out of his class. In seeking to locate the strain in the interaction of personalities between members of the family constellation, it is necessary that husband and wife know the culture values in each other's families, evaluate them objectively, and agree to incorporate into the new family the best out of each, rejecting those culture values that are detrimental to the new family's well-being. Many couples do this unconsciously and keep the family constellation in good balance; others are unable to do this without the help of a counselor. A minister who knows his families and community intimately should be of great service to families having conflicts in the area of culture values.

AN UNHAPPY FAMILY CONSTELLATION

In the average family that we may describe as "happy," the lines of tension which hold the constellation together may be designated by positive ($+$) signs. This does not mean that there are never negative ($-$) forces. In all families there are negative or dissonant forces from time to time caused by quarreling, disobedience of children, misunderstandings, or even by more serious matters such as infidelity and character disorders. But healthy family constellations, even though temporarily thrown out of balance, sometimes to the point of disintegration, are able to readjust and pull the members back into strong relationships with each other.

Such was the case in the Smith family. The husband left the family for another woman, and temporarily, the family constellation fell apart. Yet, one would have said that this family constellation was a very strong and stable one; the wife even said that she had no idea that her husband was interested in another woman. Although all the forces described by her to the counselor were positive, her husband suddenly left and joined the woman in another city where he was working temporarily. The wife was distraught. The children felt rejected by the father. Having been close to him, they became insecure, fearful and unable to eat or sleep.

When the husband came later for counseling, it was clear that his affair with the woman had been going on secretly for several months, so that actually there were negative forces before he left which were weakening the constellation. Since the positive forces were also apparent, we have both positive and negative forces ($\pm$) (Fig. 6.3) from the husband toward the wife and children, but strong positive forces between the husband and his paramour (P).

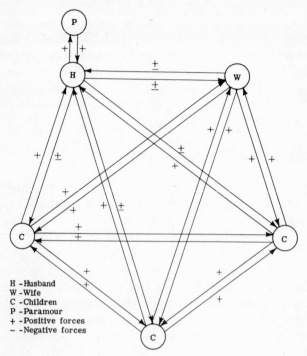

FIG. 6.3

An Unhappy Family Constellation

The family constellation when the husband left is represented in Fig. 6.4.

Notice that many negative forces were now weakening the family constellation. The husband was being pulled out of his orbit by the strong alien force of his paramour.

The wife felt very bitter (—) toward her husband, but still loved him (+). The children turned against him, but the oldest one blamed the mother (—).

The wife, however, refused to give way to the other woman. She maintained that because of her love for her husband, she had as much right to keep him in the family for herself and the children as he felt he had to leave them. She went to the city where he was working and confronted him and the woman, demanding that he return to the family—which he did. He was a very confused person when he came for counseling, and also very much ashamed

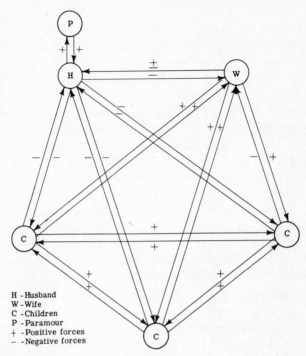

FIG. 6.4

The Family Constellation When the Husband Left

of his behavior, but he was happy to be back with his wife and children. Readjustments were made, and the family constellation gradually returned to normal (Fig. 6.1).

After several years the reunited family has continued, with a few ups-and-downs, to remain well balanced.

DIVIDED LOYALTY

It is only natural that a person have a sense of loyalty toward his parents. When one grows up, marries, and establishes his own family constellation, this does not mean that he necessarily moves out of the strong influence of his parents and the constellation in which he was reared. Both spouses move toward and away from their parental constellations. This does not mean that one renounces one's parents; one includes them in a new perspective.

If one of the young couple is an only child, the parental pull may create a tension strong enough literally to draw this spouse away from the other and disrupt the marriage. If both young spouses are in the only-child category, and if their parents exert pressure upon them to draw them apart or to control their marriage, again the tension between the young spouses may reach the breaking point. This situation is even more complicated in the only-child and often in the youngest-child situation where the relationship between the parents has been weak and where one or the other parent has sought to find in the child the love and affection he neither received from nor gave to his spouse. A dependency thus develops between parent and child, detrimental to the latter in developing a good marital relationship with his own spouse.[3]

Situations such as these create in the married son or daughter the problem of divided loyalty. One is pulled in two directions, toward the parental constellation and toward the new family constellation. The influences producing divided loyalty may be over-affection, overdependence, cultural emphasis, or all of these expressed toward the parents to a stronger degree than toward the spouse.

Willard's parents worked in a mill. In fact, so did his grandparents and most of his close relatives. They lived in a mill town, belonged to the local church, and were among the more successful families in the village. His father finished elementary school and his mother the fourth grade. Willard was the only one in the family constellations, including those of near relatives, who had a college education and a professional degree. His whole family was very proud of him, but reminded him frequently that he must not think of himself as "too good for them."

While in college, he fell in love with a girl whose family was well established in the same town. Her father was a professional man, and most of her near relatives had college degrees. They moved in an elite social circle and were well-to-do. They did not approve of Mildred's going with Willard, and when she accepted an engagement ring from him, they were very demonstrative in their opposition. However, when they realized that the two young people were determined to marry, they accepted it.

---

[3] See Morris, *Premarital Counseling*, p. 150, for illustration of a mother who moved her daughter and grandchild back to the parental home.

Then, instead of waiting a few months and allowing time for Mildred to visit and get to know Willard's parents who lived some distance away, the couple decided to run off and be married. Both families were shocked by this but accepted it.

Willard was hesitant about taking Mildred to visit his family, not knowing how they would receive her or she them. The visit did not turn out well. Everyone felt uncomfortable. In fact, innuendos were expressed by his family, which hurt Mildred. She went to the bedroom and cried. Willard was sorry and apologized for his family but indicated to her a strong loyalty toward them.

As time went on, Willard began to resent Mildred's family. He felt out of place with them and felt that they had not accepted him. He became very self-conscious around them. The style of life in which they lived and which Mildred was creating for them was, he felt, separating him from his own family. He made fun of Mildred's friends. Soon he was visiting his family without her.

Willard felt that if he accepted Mildred and her family, he had to reject his own. This he could not do. In the counseling she said that she realized the cultural differences in their families, but that she admired and loved Willard for what he was. She believed that he had a fine future and together they could surmount this problem which had produced so much unhappiness as to threaten seriously the stability of the marriage itself.

Willard was reluctant to enter counseling. He came only once or twice. He was unable to gain insight into this problem of divided loyalty or to cooperate in reevaluating his marriage. Although his family gave him no support in stabilizing his marriage, they were opposed to divorce on religious grounds and felt that Mildred should "come off her high horse" and be one of them. They resented her speech, manners, and dress. His parents felt out of place when they visited the couple on two occasions and met her parents.

The tension between Willard and Mildred became so intense that they began to quarrel, and he had struck her on two occasions. Her family then showed their resentment toward him and the marriage. They separated for short periods, and after three years Mildred obtained a divorce.

Willard's divided loyalty caused the breakup of his marriage. He was unable to separate himself from his family culture to the point where he could accept himself as an independent person in his own right and respect himself for his own accomplishments. He could not understand that to be loyal to Mildred and their marriage did not mean disloyalty to his parents or any lack of love and esteem for them. He had not chosen them in the first place! They were fine people but limited in their outlook by lack of education and by having at least two generations rooted in a small mill town. Nor was Mildred responsible for her family and their cultural advantages. Her training, however, made it easier to accept his family than vice versa. She had no problem of divided loyalty. She believed that they could build on their own inner resources of love and mutual esteem a strong marriage with good prospects for Willard's success in his profession. If Willard had continued in counseling, he too might have reached this conclusion, but he resented the counseling, identifying the counselor with Mildred and her family, and feeling that even discussing his family realistically was being disloyal to them or to that constellation.

FORSAKING ALL OTHERS

This problem of family loyalty may be shown graphically by using the sketch in Fig. 6.5.

FIG. 6.5
Loyalty to Parents Before Marriage

Before marriage each one is sailing on the ship of his parental family and must be loyal to that flag. Each can be very proud of his family flag. Each ship carries a valuable cargo: family customs and traditions, education, knowledge and experience in forming relationships of various kinds, religious convictions and ethical standards, duties and responsibilities as members of the community. These are all family treasures varying in degree in each family.

Next, the young man and woman come together in marriage, board their own ship, and raise their own flag (Fig. 6.6), This now

FIG. 6.6
Loyalty to Spouse After Marriage

is the flag under which they are to sail and to which they both must be loyal. In the marriage service, with the words "forsaking all others keep thee only unto her (him) so long as ye both shall live," [4] each forswears allegiance to his parental family flag. Yet each brings over into the new ship treasures from the parental ship —but not without critical evaluation. Some family customs may not be agreeable to both spouses. Each one must be objective and realistic about the family treasures and bring over only those which fit in and support the kind of marriage and home the couple wish to build. Willard could not do this; he felt it was being disloyal to his parents to make a realistic evaluation of their family ways. Mildred was willing to evaluate her family—but Willard felt their treasures to be of more value than those of his family, which made him feel inferior.

In another family the wife complained because her husband

---

[4] *The Book of Common Prayer*, p. 301.

never took her out to dinner or the movies and never wanted to go to parties. In counseling it was found that the husband's family had lived austerely on a small income. "Going out" was frowned upon as a waste of money. As the husband said, "There just never was any money for such things." From an early age he had to work hard, but now he was successful, and although he could afford a moderate social life, he found his own family culture values would not allow him to enjoy it. But as he came to evaluate these culture values, he found that wholesome recreation was necessary for him and his wife and that he could accept and enjoy it. He began taking his wife out, and thus an area of conflict was eliminated and the balance in the family constellation restored.

The ability to evaluate objectively one's family, rejecting their outmoded, unlovely, unprofitable, and superficial ways, and yet holding to their good and profitable ones, enables a couple to fashion a strong and beautiful marital fabric that can withstand the strain and stress of all the forces which will exert tension upon the new constellation. When seen in the right perspective, in-laws can be a source of strength and encouragement to a young couple as all sail together as a united fleet.

COURTESY ESSENTIAL

Inconsiderateness is mentioned so frequently by couples who come for counseling that it may be said to be characteristic of unhappy marriages. Is inconsiderateness related to immaturity and selfishness, or is it another way of showing independence in a family setting? Why does an intelligent, successful professional man disregard his wife's convenience? Why does a woman who expresses love for her husband do things she knows he dislikes? Why do spouses neglect the small courtesies between them which they observed before marriage? How easily couples fall into the familiar stereotype of husband and wife as though they were destined to continual warfare!

The counselor's ability to help spouses recreate consideration for each other in the ordinary daily routine leads to great relief of tensions between them and a strengthening of their mutual dependence on each other. This results in the concomitant feeling of each being necessary to the other's happiness.

Mrs. Longman complained that her husband never picked up his clothes. She also worked, and as she expressed it, "I have two full-time jobs—my household work and my secretarial job. I must get up early, get the children up, and my husband—the most difficult one to get out of bed. I have to straighten the house and get their breakfast. All must leave the house for school and work by eight o'clock. I get home about 5:30 in the afternoon and must prepare dinner. The children help with the dishes. But by nine o'clock I'm completely worn out. My husband refuses to help because, he says, 'I've been working all day. I'm tired!' He sits up late watching television and gets mad because I go to bed early."

We might say that the husband in this case has reverted to childhood and comes home to be cared for as he did when a child. But when in counseling, the home situation was discussed and he heard someone else (the counselor) enumerating these points of friction between him and his wife, he began to realize that he was being very inconsiderate; in verbalizing his feelings, he was able to plan how he could be more considerate of his wife and more appreciative of the fact that she was holding two jobs to his one. He began getting up in time to help with the children and do some straightening up of the house. He also found that he could be orderly about his dressing and other personal habits in order not to impose on his wife chores that he could do. He also took over with the children some of the evening jobs around the house. His wife showed appreciation, not only verbally but by being more considerate of his comfort. They also became more courteous toward each other.

A machine runs smoothly when properly oiled. Courtesy pays off in big dividends when practiced in the family, just as it does in other relationships. Consideration, kindness, understanding, and courtesy can change strained relations in any marriage and pave the way for resolving many difficulties.

ROLES

Roles also play a great part in the interaction of personalities in the family constellation. Roles in families today are varied and mixed, but in marital conflicts involving social roles the problem lies in a misunderstanding of the role concept—husband, wife, father, mother, sibling, and grandparent. Also, there are those who avoid assuming their roles.

A husband complained because he regularly had to get up early, cook breakfast, and dress the children for school while his wife stayed in bed. He insisted it was not that he minded doing it so much as that it was not his role. It had started several years before when the wife was ill. She had deliberately allowed him to continue—sometimes feigning a headache. When she realized that she was shirking her duty and came to a better understanding of her role as wife and mother, she began to take over the early morning jobs, and this source of stress was removed.

Because we internalize social values in our culture, we assume roles from an inner disposition to conform outwardly or overtly to those values, thereby making them real within our environment. For example, social values are attached to the roles of husband and wife, father and mother, brother and sister, and on through the whole family constellation. We have a fairly good idea of how these roles should be manifested, but sometimes the pattern from which we gained our first knowledge of these roles, as for instance in early childhood, may not have been a good one. Consequently, these internalized social values, when exhibited overtly, may not be those which would produce the best relationship in marriage. Then, too, because social values acquired outside the family are internalized also, these sometimes produce conflicts within the individual so that his behavior may be erratic and frustrating to others. He knows the socially acceptable role which he should assume, but it is contrary to the role his inner disposition favors. Consequently, when he is outside the home, he may feel compelled to conform to those behavior patterns if he is to maintain his status in the social group, but when he returns to the home, he may revert to the behavior pattern toward which he has been predisposed owing to the early internalization of social values acceptable within his childhood family, even though they were not good norms.

In marriage counseling it is very important that the husband and wife understand this process of internalizing social values so that they may discriminate between what is good and bad behavior and consistently manifest good patterns of behavior both in and out of the home.

Mrs. Ward was proud of her husband's sociability and politeness whenever they went out to some social affair where he was always the perfect gentleman. But at home he was crude and thoughtless. He would sit in the living room in his shorts, eat carelessly, and show her no consideration. This was the way his father acted—a man who had had very little education and who had come from a lower cultural level than his daughter-in-law. Now following this example was his son, a college graduate and a success in his profession. Through counseling both Mr. and Mrs. Ward came to an understanding of their conflict. Mr. Ward was quick to see what caused these two types of behavior. He realized that his father's home was not up to the social standards of the kind of home his wife and associates held, and which he really wanted, too. He began to reevaluate social values as they related to his home and to carry over into the home the behavior patterns he had learned so well in college. But it was important that he not become a "snob" in viewing his parents' home, that he accept it as good for them. Mrs. Ward had to realize that the behavior she saw in her husband's home was proper and acceptable on its own social level so that when she visited her in-laws, she could try to be one of them, in a natural way without condescending. In this way she was able to appreciate her in-laws for the basic social values of kindness, goodness, love, and courtesy that they had internalized and which they exhibited in a behavior acceptable in their group.

Merton [5] and Coser [6] point out that ritual conformity takes place only under conditions of observability but behavioral conformity is better achieved if its observability is restricted. Mr. Ward was very careful that he did the proper things in the proper way in public or at social functions: ritual conformity. There he was being observed. But at home he was insulated, and his real internalized social values came out in his behavior. The system of relationships within the social structure must be maintained by certain signs of deference and demeanor. The same holds for the relation-

---

[5] Robert K. Merton, "Conformity, Deviation and Opportunity Structures," *American Sociological Review*, XXIV, No. 2 (April 1959), 177–89. Also see in the same issue articles by Dubin, Cloward, Meier and Bell, Nettler, Kitsuse and Dietrick, and Scott.

[6] Rose Laub Coser, "Insulation from Observability and Types of Social Conformity," *American Sociological Review*, XXVI, No. 1 (February 1961), 28–39.

ship between husband and wife. If both come from the same cultural level, their behavior will probably be acceptable to both, but if from different levels, then there may be conflict, as in the case above. The standard of home behavior acceptable to husband and wife must be agreed upon if peace and harmony are to prevail. What we do when unobserved reveals our real internalized social and moral values. The home is not to be a place of restriction, but neither is it to be a place of unrestricted license. There is a structure to be maintained. It can be maintained only as the couple have some agreement on the kind of home they want.

In fact, we may go further and say that in the ideal family, there is nearly always observability, though restricted at times, as the members act out their roles in the presence of each other. Where there is mutual respect between parents and between parents and children, the behavior pattern will be influenced by it, and each will strive to present his best self or his best internalized social values at all times. Each one will endeavor to organize these values as well as his various roles into a consistent, stable way of life, but one which allows flexibility without disrupting the basic integration of the self.

INTERCHANGING ROLES

Hostility may develop when roles are interchanged, when, for example, the wife dominates the family or makes more money than the husband. (See p. 153.) The husband may reach the point where he is continually hostile toward his wife. In fact, the two may find it impossible to work together, and the home may disintegrate.

Thad was several years younger than Mable. She had a better job than he. She was the more mature and aggressive. Things went fairly well for a while; then he began to show hostility. He stayed out late. Instead of using his money for the family, he began to "throw it away." His wife used more and more of her income until she soon was practically carrying the whole load. The situation for him became intolerable until finally he asked for a divorce. In this case that his wife was much superior to him was revealed to him only after the marriage relationship began. Whereas he had understood his role to be "the head of the family," he found that actually he was not. He could not tolerate a woman as the head, or as directing him. He even found himself having to ask her for money. More and more he resented her as being in his place. The marriage became impossible.

It would be reasonable to expect any wide difference of opinion by husband and wife on the correct roles of the spouses in marriage to cause friction, and if so, divorced couples should be expected to exhibit a greater degree of disparity in their attitudes toward the roles of husband and wife than do married couples. Jacobson [7] tested this hypothesis by scoring 100 married couples and 100 divorced couples on a pretested attitude scale. The divorced couples were found to be *four times as far apart* in their views of correct roles for self and spouse as were the married couples. Also, the married women tended to be closer to the "submissive" end of the scale than were the divorced women. This is in line with Terman's finding that his happily married women seldom objected to playing subordinate roles, but his unhappily married women were inclined to be aggressive and dictatorial. Further, his happily married men tended to be equalitarian toward women, but the unhappily married men tended to play commanding roles. [8]

ROLE STRAIN

Assuming too many roles often results in excessive role strain, [9] which produces anxiety—anxiety that in turn may cause tension between husband and wife. Let us take, for example, the minister who, like the average wage earner, has two roles: his family role and his pastoral role. If his pastoral role is well planned, he should be able to be a good husband and father and at the same time a good pastor. But if he assumes other roles, such as membership on several community boards, or leadership in politics he may find that these roles, one by one, crowd out the time and

[7] Alver H. Jacobson, "Conflict in Attitudes Toward the Marital Roles of Husband and Wife," *Research Studies of the State College of Washington*, XIX, (June 1951), 103–6.

[8] Ray E. Baber, *Marriage and the Family* (New York: McGraw-Hill Book Company, 1953), pp. 210–11.

[9] William J. Goode, "A Theory of Role Strain," *American Sociological Review*, XXV, No. 4 (August 1960), 483.

consume the energy needed for his pastoral role or his family role. Soon he is neglecting one or the other of his two major roles and begins to show the strain of trying to keep his time, interests, and energy in balance. He may become impatient with his wife and children, show indifference toward his parishioners, and feel guilty. To compensate he may try even harder to act out all his roles, wearing himself out physically and mentally.

What has been said about the minister can be said also about the business and professional man or woman. Sometimes roles are multiplied, and the individual is so busy being busy that no time is left for the family role—some do it to escape this role, saying the wife nags, the children fuss, "I'm met with problems, problems, problems, as soon as I open the front door." But a multiplicity of roles and busyness does not solve the major, underlying problem. It only increases role strain with its stress and anxiety.

We all have responsibilities in several directions: family, job, church, community, and friends. These all compete for our time and interest. They pull one this way and that. The strain they produce in a normal community is a cohesive force. These many activities bargain for the individual to assume this or that role or many roles. Kept in proper balance, excessive role strain of that individual should not appear. In many ways our various roles complement each other and produce much ego satisfaction as well as increase self-confidence, all of which can result in family esteem and happiness.

A CLASSIFICATION OF FAMILIES

In the discussion of the family constellation it was seen how there is always a certain amount of wholesome and necessary tension within a family, or any group for that matter, if it is to be held together as a homogeneous unit. Those tensions created by love and affection, obedience and disobedience, dependence and independence, and security and insecurity are all natural to normal family living. But these tensions are held in proper balance and resume their normal function better in some families than in others. In some, disobedience combined with insecurity or lack of love may be devastating, causing a member to go beyond the point of resilience by snapping his relationship to the family group. This is one cause of delinquency among young people. A misunderstanding of the adolescent's striving for independence and too strict discipline may cause such resentment that the strain cannot be handled in the family and the unity of the home is destroyed.

Some families seem prone to produce maladjusted and unhappy individuals, while others turn out into society mature and happy persons. Wherein lies the difference in these families?

We may classify families under three headings commonly done in sociology: authoritarian, laissez-faire and democratic.

Authoritarian

In the authoritarian type of group or family organization one of the parents, generally the father, is dictatorial and overbearing as a disciplinarian. He lays down his unquestionable rules. If he thinks young people should come home at 10:30 P.M., they come in at that time—or else! The "woodshed" is always handy. If he believes the wife's place is in the home—she stays in the home! Sometimes this type of authority is exercised by both parents. All rules are made at the top, and unquestioned obedience is demanded.

In his commentary on Ephesians, John A. Mackay says:

The authoritarian principle expresses itself when one member of the family, the father or the mother, or per chance, a sister or a brother, presumes to exercise absolute control in the family circle and to rule by pure force of one kind or another. The result is a doll house or a mad house. We have sepulchral quiet and orderliness imposed by fear; or we have chaotic disorder inspired by exasperation. In the one instance there is no spontaneity of behavior, no initiative in action. In the other instance, there is nothing but frustration and neurosis. In either case the idea of the home and the reality of family life are destroyed.[10]

Laissez-faire

Another type of family is just the opposite. This is the laissez-faire type. In this family there is no consistent discipline. No one cares what anyone does. Parents and children come and go as they

---

[10] John A. Mackay, *Gods Order* (New York: The Macmillan Company, 1953, p. 189.

please and where they please. Studying, school, and church attendance are fairly arbitrary becoming matters of convenience and disposition. Severe punishment may be given for minor infractions of rules, and serious problems may be overlooked or even laughed at. There is no consistency. There is no authority to provide stability to the world of the growing child. His attitude toward other institutions reflects the attitude he develops toward his family. From such homes come many delinquents.

Democratic

The third type is the democratic family. In this family there is well-recognized authority resting in the parents who consistently present a united front to the children in disciplinary matters. But the authority does not flaunt itself; it is not boastful and domineering. It is deeply rooted in love and maintains an understanding attitude. Where small children are involved, it seeks to get into the child's world and view the adult's world as the child sees it. This authority defines rules in terms of what is best for the family as a whole and for the society of which it is a part. It is never willfully arbitrary, but seeks to be consistent in disciplinary measures. When a child disobeys, the parent realizes that he takes the combined role of judge, prosecuting attorney, defense attorney, and court of final appeal. Therefore, he is particularly careful not to punish in anger and to see that the punishment fits the "crime"— neither too harsh nor too lenient. In this way the child learns to respect authority, to value it, and to realize that it is exercised for the personal welfare of the child, the family, and the social order.

In the democratic family every person is appreciated as an individual who has personal rights. In matters of punishment the older child and adolescent may be asked the extent to which he should be punished, and to help fix the penalty—deprivation of privileges, reduction of allowances, making restitution, etc. Here the parent must be careful that the child not inflict on himself too severe punishment.

The democratic family plans together, each member striving to work for the good of the whole. As the children become older, their opinions, likes, and dislikes are fully considered.

In family worship every member participates according to his age, and moral principles are discussed—matters of honesty, lying, and disobedience. Family worship is an excellent time for passing on to the next generation our Christian heritage. As the child realizes that his parents are sincerely trying to live the Christian way even though they fail at times, he will come to accept the Christian way as the one which makes for fullness of life. He will not expect his parents to be perfect—but to be honest and to strive for right living. We can always recognize and accept wrongdoing in others if we can believe that they are sincerely sorry and are conscientiously striving to do that which is right. Even their failure, as well as their determination to rise above it, can be a great inspiration. All fail at times in the moral struggle, but not all care. The child or the adolescent who learns in the family circle to hold fast to his moral integrity will not be easily overthrown when he moves out into the world torn by competition, deceit, and status seeking.

Freedom to develop one's capabilities is a primary need. Frustration can be devastating to a personality if it occurs time and time again. Everyone has his breaking point. And everyone has something he yearns to accomplish. The little child building a house of blocks is expressing his creativity. His potential lies there. Or it may be finger painting. Or it may be reading. Whatever it is, it is important to him, and it must be recognized. In the democratic home his rights are respected. His work is appreciated. He feels free to express himself in any way that does not interfere with the rights and freedom of others. He knows that he is loved for himself, and in that love he feels secure. Someone has given this formula for child raising: Love him and leave him alone. Good advice. Most children brought up in a democratic family will not abuse their freedom. And they will respect the rights and privileges of others.

If, then, the family constellation is to be wholesome and tensions between the members are to be exerted evenly and congenially, every member should find within it peace, happiness, and freedom. But these flourish neither in the authoritarian family nor in the laissez-faire family, but in the democratic family.

In marriage counseling it is very important to know what type of family one is dealing with, and in what type of family the husband and wife grew up. This may throw considerable light on their present marital problems.

A MARRIAGE THAT FAILED

Not every marriage can be saved. One might say, also, that every marriage should not be saved. The marriage I wish to discuss had little to commend it in the first place and almost everything against it in the second place. Even the love Tom and Jane had expressed for each other before marriage carried a question mark. But there had been no deterring them in their romanticism and in the girl's determination to make at least one decision in her life without her mother's dictation.

Both of these young people were active in their churches. They came from religious families, each with long traditions of Christian devotion. But here their agreements ended. As we shall see, they were unable to construct a constellation strong enough to resist the stress exerted upon it by their respective families.

The premarital counseling

They came together to arrange for the premarital counseling. A schedule of appointments was set up for them together and separately.[11] They seemed very eager in their desire to make a happy and successful marriage and faced squarely the various factors discussed below which presented serious obstacles. There were cultural differences in their family backgrounds, particularly in Jane's maternal family. Their paternal families were much alike. Jane's overdependence on her mother and the overpossessiveness of her mother were discussed, as well as Jane's identification with her mother. Jane was very hostile toward her mother at times because of her overdependence; she recognized this and tried to break it during the premarital counseling period. In fact, she came to feel that a much more mature relationship with her mother had started.

Jane both loved and pitied her father, who was completely dominated by his wife. He seldom expressed an opinion contrary to hers and was subject to long periods of silence. There was no communication between husband and wife. Jane found it hard to talk with him, but he was kind to her, and she afforded him

---

[11] This followed generally the plan for premarital counseling as outlined in *Premarital Counseling—A Manual for Ministers* by the author.

an outlet for his affections, which his wife denied him. But he was not a forceful individual, and Jane sometimes felt ashamed of and resentful toward him. Because he provided no satisfactory male or father image for her, she was always seeking something from him which she never quite received and did not understand.

Jane was attractive, but not pretty, and had had very few boy friends. Indeed, Tom was the only one she had dated steadily. She expressed some apprehension in the premarital counseling that she might lose him. She was very insecure in her love life. Whereas Tom was very ardent and his love for her seemed mature, but her love for him seemed rather shallow and "starry-eyed."

Although they both faced the obstacles to their forming a lasting marriage and even discussed the possibility of breaking off the engagement, they never reached that decision. Since they were determined to marry each other, the counselor tried to reinforce whatever he could find of enduring value: the nature of love and how it can be enhanced; their religious devotion and the part religion can play in making a marriage successful; Tom's job and future which appeared good; Jane's cultural advantages which could be a real asset to the home; the sound health of both; the similarity of their educational backgrounds; their high yet realistic ideals for the kind of home they wanted; their both wanting children and wanting to be good parents. By the time they had completed the premarital counseling, the prospects for a successful marriage seemed to be good.

Background material

Jane's parents never came for counseling, but her mother did call once or twice to discuss the marriage.

Jane's mother had married a rather mediocre man much beneath her family's cultural level. As a small merchant he was a hard worker, but was never able to give his wife and daughter anything more than the smallest comforts. In order that the girl might have educational and social advantages such as her mother had had, it was necessary for the mother to work—"Something no lady in my family ever did!" she remarked one day. Fortunately, she lived hundreds of miles away from her parents and therefore in her mind did not offend them. Once a year she took Jane to visit her parents and relatives. Most of the mother's earnings were used to provide Jane with this "taste of culture I was reared in." There were horses to ride and, when Jane was old enough, fox hunting to enjoy, as well as a whirl of parties and dances. The visits usually lasted a month. Then they returned home to its rather monotonous life and the mother to her job.

Jane's father, from what the mother and daughter said, was not too bright and came from an unknown family who lived in a small rural community. "Just nobodies," was his wife's comment. But she had met him when he was in military service. "I don't know now what I saw in him—except his uniform. I fell madly in love, and we were married. It was not until I visited his family that I realized my mistake. But I was then pregnant. It was too late to do anything but accept the marriage. There had never been a divorce in our family. I don't think that ever occurred to me as a possible way out. I determined to be a dutiful wife. I had made my bed; I would lie in it."

The mother set everything by her daughter. She would live her life in her daughter. She would give her all that she had had and more if possible. Her family helped her some financially, which, together with her income as a clerk in a store, made it possible for her to create for her daughter something like the cultural climate in which she herself had been reared. She dreamed of the day when her daughter would marry a wealthy, charming man, highly educated and socially prominent—perhaps a banker, or a diplomat. Always she would tell Jane that never must she make the mistake she had made and marry beneath her; she must hold her love only for some outstanding person like her uncle, a wealthy socialite. Her mother would describe the man as tall, dark-haired, broad-shouldered, athletic. "Truly a knight in shining armor."

But her mother had failed to reckon with Jane's love for her father. He was a weak man dominated by his wife who merely suffered him to be around. He had to wait on her until he had an injury which put him to bed for several months. This finally re-resulted in more or less permanent disability—however, Jane had married before this came about. As a child Jane never argued with her mother, but many times she felt sorry for the way her mother treated her father and resented the things she said about him and his family, whom she was never allowed to know intimately.

During her early adolescence Jane felt very close to her father—it was then that he had had his accident. She waited on him and helped him about the shop, often going there from school just to be with him.

When in college, she met Tom. He was a very quiet, sincere person, several years older than Jane. He had a good job with a large concern which offered a fine future. But he was not handsome; indeed, he was small in stature and wore glasses. He drove an old model car. When he came to her home to take her out one evening and met Jane's parents for the first time, there was the barest of polite greeting on their part.

Soon Tom was Jane's escort to various social affairs, but no one knew Tom. All invitations were because of Jane and her mother. As he frequented the home more and more, two factors came into play: the mother's rejection of him as a suitor, and the father's jealousy of him as a rival for Jane's affections. The mother was at times very haughty and actually rude to him. She begged Jane to stop dating him. She would sulk and not speak to Jane for days. She would tell her how she was letting her family (the mother's) down. "What do you see in such a nincompoop?" she would ask.

Jane's father used a belittling nickname for Tom. He would call him "Insect," a play on his name, calling him this to his face while laughing loudly. Tom would become embarrassed and confused, which would make Jane furious with her father. She and Tom would try to console each other—Jane, because of her mother's domination, Tom, because he did not know how to cope with her father's ridicule. All of this drew Tom and Jane closer together.

Finally, he gave her a ring, a far more expensive ring than he could afford, but he felt he had to impress her parents, especially her mother. The ring created an episode that nearly proved tragic. The mother went into a tirade, expressing her disappointment in Jane for becoming engaged to a person such as Tom. The father all but ordered him out of the house. Jane went to bed crying, and Tom returned to his room depressed and with a considerable loss of self-esteem.

However, they finally married. Jane's family made much of the wedding. Everything had to be perfect. No expense was spared. Her uncle helped pay the bill.

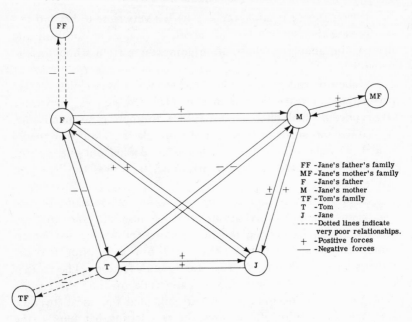

FIG. 6.7
The Family Constellation at the Time of Marriage

Figure 6.7 shows the direction of the positive (+) and negative (—) forces of stress existing in the family constellation at the time of marriage.

After the wedding

The house they occupied was small and the furniture cheap —two facts Jane's mother never failed to point out. She avoided Tom as much as possible. Emotionally, she felt all the disappointment in this marriage that she had felt in her own marriage. She saw her daughter's life as being as drab, hard, and uninteresting as her own. Unable to accept the marriage, she began planning on breaking it up—probably not consciously—by pointing out Tom's inadequacies.

Jane's father went far in accepting the marriage; indeed, he and Tom became fairly good friends. But the father still used his nickname for Tom and often irritated him by his ridicule, with the result that Tom began to see himself as a weak, unpromising young man, lacking in self-esteem and full of self-depreciation.

Soon this began to show up in the marital relationship. Tom found himself being very critical of Jane and her housekeeping, as well as of her friends.

When the baby came, things were better for a time, but soon Tom was criticizing her for the way she cared for the baby. He fussed about Jane's appearance when he came home at night. He complained about her housekeeping and cooking. Nothing she did seemed to please him. He then began to make fun of her, her friends, and her family and their aristocratic manners.

Jane retaliated by using the nickname her father had given him and by ridiculing his family—about whom she knew little.

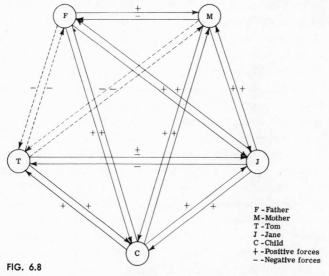

FIG. 6.8

The Family Constellation After One Year of Marriage

F - Father
M - Mother
T - Tom
J - Jane
C - Child
+ - Positive forces
− - Negative forces

Figure 6.8 shows the direction of the positive (+) and negative (−) forces of stress existing in the family constellation at the end of the first year of marriage and at the time Tom and Jane came for marriage counseling.

The marriage counseling

This rift between them had been widening for about a year when they came for marriage counseling. When it first began, Jane had asked Tom to see a counselor and agreed to go with him, but his answer was that they could work things out if her family would leave them alone. Her mother was a constant visitor and never failed to criticize Tom and his "failure" to provide better for his family. Her attitude, confirmed by both Jane and Tom, was such that she always left trouble behind. Each felt less and less secure in the marriage.

By the time they came for counseling, the situation had just about reached the breaking point. Jane was convinced the marriage was over, claiming that she no longer loved Tom and repeating some of the things her mother had said about him before the wedding. Asked why she came for counseling, she replied, "For the sake of the baby, I thought I should see if things could be patched up." But her cooperation with the counselor was nil. Her parents wanted her to leave Tom. Her mother still believed a "knight in shining armor" would ride in from some direction and carry Jane to his castle. Why should she throw herself away on Tom?

"Why did you marry Tom?" Jane was asked.

"Frankly, I think I felt sorry for him."

"Just as you often felt sorry for your father?"

"Yes, I suppose so. In many ways they seemed alike. Both, quiet and reserved. But I hated Dad when he would ridicule Tom. Then after the marriage I felt our marriage was also a duplicate of Mother and Dad's."

The parallelism was quite striking. But there was this difference. Tom rebelled when Jane tried to dominate him as her mother dominated her father. Another difference that made it easier for the parent's marriage to hold together was the separation in distance from the wife's family. Her mother apparently rarely visited them—only an uncle came once in a great while—whereas Tom and Jane lived in the same town where her family lived and where Jane grew up. This meant that their friends were first Jane's friends. Tom's family lived in another state, and his friends were there. The environment was all Jane's, and Tom felt like an outsider.

Jane came only once for counseling.

Tom was very cooperative in the counseling and professed his love for Jane and the baby. He began to gain insight into his own problems in the marital relationships and the dynamics underlying his motivations in seeking to belittle Jane. Tom continued in counseling for some time.

It is a very common psychological expedient to boost oneself by degrading another person.[13] (See section on Symbiosis, page 232.) Tom could do nothing about the fact that Jane's family excelled his in education, refinement, and prominence. This he readily admitted and before the marriage felt that he had accepted it. But the intimacy of marriage, the daily contacts, and her desire for luxuries he could not provide made him more and more aware of the disparity between their families. Further, Jane felt she should teach him proper table manners and other amenities of the social graces —all of which he interpreted as reflections on his family. So, out of loyalty to his own family, he began to pick flaws in Jane and her housekeeping activities.

Then, too, Jane got a job—just as her mother had done. Now she would work to see that her child had all the advantages to which a girl with her heritage was entitled. This impressed upon Tom his inability to provide the things Jane seemed to count as essential.

When Tom came for his second interview, he reported that when he came home the night before, Jane and the baby were gone, and all of Jane's things had been moved. Where was she? Her

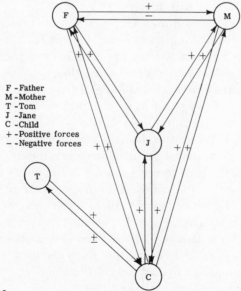

F – Father
M – Mother
T – Tom
J – Jane
C – Child
+ – Positive forces
– – Negative forces

FIG. 6.9

The Family Constellation at the Time of Divorce

mother refused to tell him. He had spent the night trying to find her. She had given up her job.

Tom felt he was obligated to support the child at least and left money with Jane's mother. It was about two months before Tom located Jane. She was still in the city but had moved several times for fear he would find her. She refused to see him or correspond with him. She had secured the services of a lawyer and divorce proceedings had started.

Figure 6.9 shows the family constellation at the time of divorce.

Dissolution

This marriage ended in divorce. Contact was lost with Tom, who moved to another city. After a year or so an announcement appeared in the papers that Jane had married again, but from the announcement it was clear that she had not improved in her choice of a husband. She had, however, moved a little further away from her parents. Later inquiry revealed that her present husband is much like her father. Jane dominates him, and she has to supplement their income with a job.

The mother's dream of a knight in shining armor riding his white charger and dashing up to sweep Jane in his arms and carry her to his castle never came true. But Jane is wiser and has moved away from the pull of her family constellation.

Jane's marriage to Tom should never have taken place. There were too many factors against its success, perhaps the greatest being the differences on the cultural level, which caused the mother to reject Tom consistently. Also, being a very dominating individual, the mother tried to control her daughter's selection of a mate, but the daughter had begun to rebel against her mother's domination and was determined that in this instance she would make her own decision. This blinded her to the salient factors necessary to a successful marriage, such as the social, economic, and psychological factors. Although these factors were discussed in the premarital counseling sessions and an understanding of them obtained, neither Jane nor Tom was properly oriented toward them nor had the maturity to cope with the problems they presented.

If they had come for counseling when the rift first opened, perhaps some drastic changes could have been made that would have saved the marriage. For example, Tom might have found work in another city. That would have thrown the couple upon their own resources, and Jane's mother could not have visited so often and exerted so great an influence. They would have become more dependent upon each other. Also, they would have made friends together, and Tom would have felt more comfortable in such friendships.

There was no apparent conflict in religion. Soon after marriage Tom joined Jane's church, and from what both said he proved a loyal member; together they engaged in church activities. Although it was never brought out in the counseling, Tom may have felt that in joining her church he was proving somewhat disloyal to his own family, and this may have increased his dissatisfaction with Jane.

Although Tom and Jane expressed no concern over their sexual adjustment, their sexual relations became less frequent as the rift widened, finally ceasing altogether, along with other demonstrations of affection.

SUMMARY

Families form constellations in which the members are held together by the normal stress and strain of love, loyalty, duty, and authority produced by the constant interaction of their personalities. In some families the tension between the members may be so weak that they leave the constellation and drift away from all contact, or there may be strain great enough literally to drive away members. Family ties must be strengthened and conflicts resolved in order to create a strong and stable constellation; the converse of this is illustrated in the example of the unhappy family constellation.

The stress and strain may reach the breaking point through unfaithfulness, divided loyalty, lack of consideration, role confusion, or the types of family in which the spouses were reared, e.g., authoritarian, laissez-faire, or democratic. The case of a marriage that failed illustrates these points.

SUGGESTED READING

Bowman, Henry A., *Marriage for Moderns* (4th ed.), Chap. 4. New York: McGraw-Hill Book Company, 1960.

Burgess, Ernest W. and Harvey J. Locke, *The Family* (2nd ed.). New York: American Book Company, 1945.

Kirkpatrick, Clifford, *The Family*. New York: The Ronald Press Company, 1955.

Landis, Judson T. and Mary G. Landis, eds., *Readings in Marriage and The Family*. Englewood Cliffs, N.J.: Prentice-Hall, Inc., 1952. Part XIII: Reading 1, Mirra Komarovsky, "Cultural Contradictions in Sex Roles"; Reading 2, Paul Wallin, "Cultural Contradictions in Sex Roles: A Repeat Study"; Reading 3, Clifford Kirkpatrick, "Inconsistency in Marriage Roles"; Reading 4, Della Cyrus, "Problems of the Modern Homemaker—Mother."

Emotional Needs

7   There is no such thing as a self-sufficient person. Even one who may consider himself self-sufficient is dependent upon others as companions. On the purely physical level how can he be self-sufficient? For one to be self-sufficient, he would have to live the life of a recluse, raise and process his own food and clothing, and manufacture the lumber or quarry the stone for his dwelling. There would be no community for such a person, and because of his separation from others, he would soon become odd.

Self-sufficiency also means that one's emotional needs must be met within the limits of one's own inner resources. A Simon Stylates alone on his tower of stone might feel that he had achieved emotional self-sufficiency, but the chances are that he would be dependent emotionally upon the admiration of those below who could look upward and exclaim among themselves, "What a holy man!" or upon his own feeling that he had praise from God above.

Our actions are relevant to those around us. There is no escape from some kind of dependence upon others—either positive or negative. We are always members of some community, and within that milieu we grow and develop or we withdraw and deteriorate or stagnate. To develop we must give to and receive from those about us. And it is not the material things we give or receive that count but those which derive from our emotions, such as love, fear, anger, joy, hate, and praise. No amount of material things can make up for our unfulfilled emotional needs.

Henry Guntrip [1] rightly states that the fundamental human

---

[1] Henry Guntrip, *Psychotherapy and Religion* (New York: Harper & Row, Publishers, 1957), p. 20.

problems do not lie in the region of the intellect, but lie in the area of our personal needs and emotional relationships, and concern our basic satisfactions, fulfillments, and frustrations. Dallas Pratt lists nine basic emotional needs:

(1) To be the object of affection in terms of what one is rather than what one does
(2) To protect oneself and those with whom identified from harm
(3) To assert self as an independent individual, in thought and action; to be allowed to reach one's own decisions and participate in plans where one is the object
(4) To love others and have others dependent on one
(5) To identify with and be like others, to be part of a group
(6) To match self against the environment, physically and mentally, and to master and comprehend it
(7) To love within defined limits, to see order and structure in life
(8) To clothe reality in illusion; to create symbols, abstractions, art forms, and romance
(9) To be understood as one whose behavior is the result of many complex environmental forces, and not to be stereotyped [2]

THE NEED TO BE LOVED FOR WHAT ONE IS, NOT FOR WHAT ONE DOES

How many wives have said that their husbands bought them washing machines, automobiles, television sets, vacuum cleaners, and what not, thinking they would be happy with all these things, but that what the wife really wanted was for her husband to take her in his arms and say, "I love you." Things can never satisfy the yearning of the heart or take the place of companionship. Some individuals, of course, prize the receiving of things above their needing to share emotionally with their spouses or children, and then complain because they receive things only. Someone has said, "The immature person loves things and uses people; the mature person loves people and uses things." Those who heap up for themselves riches seeking to find happiness may become possessed by their possessions and never find what they are really seeking: emotional

---

[2] Dallas Pratt, "Making Environment Respond to Basic Emotional Needs," *Psychiatry*, XV (1952), 179–188.

security in the love of others; that is, to be loved for one's own sake, not because one seemingly merits it by gifts or otherwise, but only because of what one is.

One day a mother was overheard saying to her little girl of about four years of age, "If you do not behave and act nice, I won't love you." Again, some mothers may say to their little children, "You are a bad boy. Mother doesn't love bad boys." These probably are not true statements. Most likely those mothers do love their children whether they be good or bad, and if anything had happened to them after such statements, the mothers would have been overcome with grief and guilt for having said such things. Furthermore, there is the question of what these mothers mean by "nice" and "bad." Certainly they are not speaking in ethical terms. A child of four does not measure his acts according to a moral code. He is experimenting, testing, showing his desire for independence. The actions of the child must be understood from within the child's world, not from that of the adult's world. If the child has done something of serious consequence accidentally, such as breaking a valuable object, and is frightened and crying, he needs assurance that his mother or father does love him. It may be that what he has broken is so dear to his mother that she is crying. At such a time he needs all the more to know that in spite of what he did, she loves him.

Now, let us carry this over from the child's world to the adult's, for the adult's world view in time of emotional crises is not far removed from that of the child.

Jim and Betty were getting into a bad habit of finding fault with each other. Nothing either one did seemed to please the other. Jim seemed to be particularly harsh in his faultfinding, often causing Betty to cry. She was quite tearful in her first interview, and while Jim did not cry, he too was emotional in his first interview. Both said much the same things about each other: no interest in my work; faultfinding with care of the children, housekeeping, personal appearance, table manners, etc., etc. Each acknowledged his grievances as petty—and each asked, "If he (she) loves me, why does he (she) do (or not do) these things?"

The counselor asked Jim, "Suppose Betty were sick and could not do any of these things, would you love her?"

"Yes," he replied, "of course I would."

"How would you show her your love?"

"I would tell her, and do whatever I could to make her happy."

"Would you even do the things she wants you to do, but which you do not do now?" the counselor asked.

"Yes, I would, of course!"

"Of course—what do you mean?"

"Well, I know she wants me to do a lot of things—she says I don't play with the children enough. I know I don't. But as soon as I get home, she wants me to spend all my time with them. I'm tired. I want to rest a while, read the paper."

"And what is she usually doing?"

"She is getting supper."

"Who is looking after the children?" I asked.

"Well, I . . . she is."

"Do you have a maid?"

"No," he answered.

"What, then, is the family picture as you see it?"

After some hesitation he replied, "She does the housework, cooks, and takes care of the children. And when I come home, she tells me to help by playing with the children, that she's had them all day. I resent her asking me. I'm tired too."

"So you sulk and hide behind the paper. Do you love her?"

"Yes, of course I love her. If she would just stop nagging me when I get home."

"How do you interpret her nagging?" I asked.

"She just wants to be mean, I guess."

"You aren't sure?"

"I give her all I can. I think she loves me. There are times when we get along fine."

"Do you think what you call nagging might be a way of getting you to give her and the children some attention? To get from you some evidence of love that does not come through the things you give her?"

After a period of discussion of this idea, Jim seemed to realize that the motivation behind the nagging might be due to some unsatisfied need in Betty.

"I know I love Betty. I am sure she loves me, but we both hold back from each other. We used to be more demonstrative in our love. It was more spontaneous. Now there are times when I deliberately do not show her affection, waiting to see if she is going to show me affection first. I guess I should do as I used to—kiss and hug her tight when I come home, and play with the children. She must be tired with all the work she has to do."

The next time Betty came for counseling she said, "Well, I don't know what you did to Jim, but he has been a different person. He helps me and plays with the children. And he is much more affectionate. This past week has been the happiest in a long time."

Much the same line of questions and answers took place with Betty as with Jim. She began to realize his need for love, and that no matter how fine a meal she cooked, it could not satisfy his need for affection. Each of them had been selling his love to the other, the price being: "You be nice to me, do what I want you to do, and I will love you." When they discovered that love cannot be bought, sold, or bargained for, but must spring spontaneously from the heart because of what the other one is, they were willing and glad to outdo each other in the kind of behavior each had tried to force from the other.

It is an exhilarating experience to think and plan ways to bring pleasure to a loved one. In fact, this is how courtship starts, and one reason why the period of courtship is such a happy and rewarding one—it marks the discovery that one is loved for oneself. And as each one seeks to satisfy the love needs of the other, the courtship leads to marriage. But, unfortunately, many couples neglect to continue their courtship practices. The love needs become greater as the years go by and children come because there is no one else to love one for what one is except husband or wife. If the attention they give to each other begins to lessen and the demonstration of affection ceases, then fear of loneliness, rejection, and not being needed emotionally can be very depressing. As these things close in on one, nagging, fighting, and estrangement ensue. Some believe divorce may be a way out, but the chance of a happy remarriage becomes less as the years go by, particularly if there are children. The unsatisfied need for love can strike out in many cruel and harsh ways. It can produce anxiety and even result in a nervous breakdown.

Jim and Betty rediscovered their own need to be loved and their need to love, not because they could get material or physical comfort from each other but because they were a husband and wife needing to give and receive love for the completeness of their own personalities.

Betty's love need being satisfied, she found there was no need to nag in order to get his attention, thereby prodding him into loving her. Jim found new pleasure in giving her affection and playing with the children.

THE RIGHTFUL DEMANDS OF LOVE

So much misunderstanding about the meaning and nature of love in marriage exists that its normal demands and expectations are often wrongly understood. (This is apparent in many cases presented in this book.) These are the rights of love (agape) in marriage, which cannot be overlooked if happiness is to characterize the union:

(1)   To be accepted as a partner on the basis of shared interests—jobs, child training, in-law concerns, and pleasures
(2)   To be accepted for what one is along with one's failures
(3)   To be forgiven and restored when sorrow and repentance are shown, and not to have past sins and failures brought up again
(4)   To share in the successes, failures, and disappointments of the other spouse
(5)   To be free to develop one's own potentialities along creative lines
(6)   To show love to those who have a rightful claim upon one
(7)   To a satisfying sexual relationship which respects one's feelings and desires
(8)   To be alone at times
(9)   To live and grow in a peaceful and harmonious home environment
(10) To be respected, appreciated, and trusted when deserved

These rights in a Christian marriage are inalienable.

THE NEED FOR INTERDEPENDENCY

Interdependency is the need to be dependent upon someone and to have someone dependent upon one. As already pointed out, there is no such thing as a completely self-sufficient person; we are all dependent upon other people. It is a part of communal living and of socialization. We begin life by being completely dependent individuals, but we very soon begin to strive for independence. As the self-image develops, one wants to feel capable of making his own decisions and of planning his own life, but this must be consistent with his emotional dependence upon others in his immediate family constellation, and their dependence upon him. This is true for the adult as well. A mature, well-adjusted father would not deliberately abandon his family. He would appreciate their dependence on him and their feeling of rejection if he left them. But he would also feel his dependence upon them for love and emotional security.

In counseling, one deals with many maladjusted persons, some of them alcoholics, others discouraged and defeated in life. One cause for a husband's maladjustment may be a very capable wife whose earnings and position in the community excel her husband's, thereby leaving unsatisfied his need to have her dependent on him. Some have expressed considerable resentment and feelings of inadequacy in such a situation.

Mr. and Mrs. Y were facing a crisis in their marriage owing to his drinking and low income. For a number of years Mrs. Y had held an excellent position with an income of some $400 a month. Mr. Y had never made more than about $60 to $70 a week. His wife was charming, intellectual, and self-confident. It seemed that she had all the fine qualities he lacked, and he was very much aware of it. Yet they loved each other deeply. There were two children. Out of her income she supported the family: bought the groceries, paid the utility bills, and sometimes paid the rent. Mr. Y spent about a week's salary a month on liquor and gambling. In his interviews he would say, "But she doesn't need me. She's smart. She makes twice as much as I do. She buys the groceries. What does she need me for?"

In our culture a man is expected to support his family to the best of his ability. He needs to feel their dependence on him, and that he is providing the necessities of life for them: food, clothing, and shelter. If he is not allowed to do this by his wife, who may be quite able to do it for him, he feels inadequate and something less than the ideal husband and father. The husband image we build up in our boys is for them to see themselves someday able to have and support a wife and children. When these ideas were explained to Mrs. Y, she realized that in trying to prove her love for her husband she had actually deprived him of satisfying one of his basic needs and of realizing his self-image.

A plan was worked out with the complete understanding of Mr. Y that they would set up a budget and that he would give her every week, when he was paid, money for groceries, rent, and clothes. What remained he would use for recreation for the family, insurance, and taxes. They had bought a car and were paying on several items for the house. As these things could be classed not as necessities in the strict sense but as luxuries, it was decided that Mrs. Y would pay for them. The change in Mr. Y was immediate. He felt at last that he was supporting his family. He was not a failure. He also found under further counseling that he had some fine capabilities which he had never recognized and could develop. His drinking problem lessened because he now realized that his family was dependent on him and he had no right to waste his money. Mrs. Y was now able to save some of her salary with the hope that someday she could make the down payment on a house. She also came to feel that she could depend on him and that he could support his family.

THE NEED FOR SELF-REALIZATION

Creative activity is a great stimulus. (See p. 267.) Man has always sought to express himself in some form of creative art. Recently, a picture in *Life* magazine showed the crude art work of an American Indian dated some 30,000 years ago. Some man had carved the pictures of an antelope, a bison, and a mammoth. With what pride may he have looked upon his own reproduction of what he saw—he had captured for himself, in his own way, these animals to be his talisman.

Even the child will build great houses with his blocks and point with pride to his achievement. And to show that he is free to build or tear down, he may knock it all down. "See what I can do!" Children can be encouraged to develop their creativity by praise and understanding.

Adults carry with them this same desire to create. Those who have been stimulated in childhood by appreciative parents will seek to achieve great things.

Husbands and wives can also encourage each other to be creative in developing their potentialities. Each one brings to the marriage his own peculiar capabilities and bents, his goals, both near and far off, and his ideals and notions of how to achieve them. The family milieu can promote his capabilities or weaken them. His creative impulses can be stifled by destructive criticism and lack of appreciation.

John had an untrained but beautiful baritone voice, which he used in the choir and would have liked to have had trained, but ridicule from his wife discouraged him. He finally gave up the choir and singing altogether. A wife who loved her piano playing gave it up because of an unsympathetic husband. Everyone needs some kind of creative work for which he has a natural bent in order to release his emotional tensions and express himself in his own special way. Spouses should be aware of this need, and lovers early in courtship should try to discover the potentialities of the loved one. Their creative activities may change through the years, but, whatever these may be, they should be understood and appreciated.

Many husbands today have workshops and there find great relief from the tension in the business world. Some show remarkable talent for cabinet making, wood carving, and other crafts. There are others who find outlets for their talents in Boy Scout work or coaching a Pony League team. Some men find their daily work monotonous and tiring—not necessarily physically, but mentally and emotionally. Some are confined to jobs which are purely routine, such as assembly line jobs allowing them no initiative or originality. They need some afterwork activity which will allow them to express freely their creativity. A wise wife recognizing this need will make provision for it in the daily program. She will do all that she can to enable her husband to carry on the activities which allow for self-expression.

But the husband must likewise recognize his wife's needs for creative work. Most wives find this in homemaking and caring for the children. However, with many couples living in small apartments, there are wives who cannot fill their time with housekeeping chores. As one wife said, "I can do all my housework in one hour. What am I supposed to do the rest of the day?" She wanted to get a secretarial job, but her husband objected. She had studied to be a secretary, liked the work, and was apparently a very efficient one. Before her marriage she had held a fine position. Her husband had been brought up in the country where the women stayed at home. He had never thought that his wife would work. He especially disliked her being "some man's secretary." He could not understand why she seemed depressed in the evening. They were both disturbed by a lack of harmony and companionship. They had been married about two years, but there were no children although both wanted a child. This had been a disappointment to them and contributed to their frustration.

In counseling, the wife said that she knew she would be happier if she could work. "I am sure I would be a better wife and companion. I just don't like housework, and there is not enough anyway to keep me busy." She was so bored that by evening she was actually tired from doing nothing. She resented her husband's busy, active, interesting life in the business world—a world with which she was acquainted—friendly contacts, coffee breaks, lunch hours, interesting items of news and gossip, and especially her pride in her own efficiency and the praise of her boss. One study reveals that there are about 2½ million working mothers in the United States with children under six years of age.

It took some time for her husband to recognize the contrast between their positions, to accept the idea that a woman's place in an urban environment might differ from that in a rural environment, and to realize that there are women who dislike housework and have the need to work outside the home. It meant the reversal of his whole concept of wifehood, but it meant for her a break into freedom. She had no difficulty in getting a job, and her husband found once more the vivacious, intellectually stimulating, happy woman he had married.

Another case did not end so happily, because the husband could not accept the idea of his wife's working. They had two children. She felt that she would "go crazy" if she did not get out and find a job. (See p. 130.) So, disregarding her husband's wishes, she got a job in a public institution and employed a maid to look after the children. At first her husband seemed to acquiesce in it, but when she tried to discuss her work with him, he would sulk and make disparaging remarks about it and also about the men with whom she worked. The situation went from bad to worse. He discontinued counseling. She would not give up her work, but became more and more nervous and anxious. Their home life deteriorated. Finally, they separated and later obtained a divorce.

Much can be said about the wife and mother staying home, but also much can be said about her need for creative activity outside the home.[3] Some women find this in club work, church work, Girl Scout work, and other outlets. But there are some women whose personalities seem to demand a regular paying job outside the home and who, when this need is met, make better wives and mothers.

Some husbands object to their wives having outside activities of any kind or permit them only very limited activities. One husband was quite angry with his wife because she belonged to several organizations: the Red Cross, Women of the Church, a woman's Bible class, a civic club, and a bridge club. They could afford a servant, and she had her own car. There were several children. He said she was "never at home and always gadding about." She denied that her activities interefered with her home responsibilities and claimed that she was usually at home in the mornings and practically always in the evenings. She accused him of being noncommunicative when they were both at home and of going out frequently at night and leaving her alone. There were many problems disturbing this marriage, however. Their outside activities were only one of them, and these were becoming means of escape from more important matters essential to the happiness of their marriage. They were also using these activities to strike back at each other. They were very busy being busy, but both wanted to do something about it and came for counseling.

The result of the counseling was a recognition on the part of both of the needs of each for a reasonable amount of activity outside

[3] Ray E. Baber, *Marriage and the Family* (New York: McGraw-Hill Book Company, 1953), pp. 378ff.

the home. They had much to contribute to their church and community, but in order to make their maximum contribution and not to let it interfere with their marriage, it was necessary for them to select only the one or two organizations that seemed to fit their needs for creative endeavor and to give their best efforts to these. Their renewed recognition of each other's needs helped them to reorient themselves toward the goal of a happy and successful marriage, possible of achievement only through mutual cooperation.

People find their development toward self-realization in various ways: some through their profession—lawyer, doctor, housewife, nurse, teacher, and businessman; others through activities they find creative. These extra-curricular activities may be more important to one's happiness and self-realization than those by which a living is made. Everyone has the need to feel that he is moving progressively toward the goal of some form of creative work; whatever this may be, spouses will be wise if they encourage each other in it.

In the interpersonal relationships of marriage each spouse must have freedom to enhance his personality according to its capabilities without trespassing upon the same freedom allowed his mate. David E. Roberts observes that

. . . the causes of failure in marriage are identical with the causes of failure in human relationships generally. This seemingly trite statement is worth stressing because so many young people look forward to marriage as a means of solving all the problems that they have been unable to solve otherwise. Yet the ability to let a mate have his or her own personality is dependent upon a general ability to let others lead their own lives. If a person has not reached self-possession apart from marriage, he is not likely to reach it by means of marriage; on the contrary, he is likely to "read into" the mate's personality qualities which would fit his own neurotic needs, and if these qualities are not forthcoming an endless tussle begins. One seeks to make the other overly dependent, or, conversely, to make the other carry the whole load. If the mate cannot or will not take on the desired role, then one feels that marriage has cheated him. Instead of being a relationship in which two emotionally mature persons facilitate each other's development, the marriage becomes a rigid, frustrating deadlock.[4]

---

[4] David E. Roberts, *Psychotherapy and a Christian View of Man* (New York: Charles Scribner's Sons, 1951), pp. 22–23.

THE NEED FOR ROMANCE

Life can become very humdrum and monotonous. Day after day may actually be just one day following another. The routine of the husband's job or the wife's work at home can become almost unbearable unless lightened by exhilarating romantic experiences with one's spouse and anticipation of idealistic possibilities in the future. We are dreamers by nature. Make-believe continues from childhood except that with mature adults it is conditioned by reality. Studies of the problems of aging indicate that those individuals live longer who look forward and not backward as they grow older. A keen mind with healthy attitudes is romantic and idealistic, giving its owner a zest for living. Such a person looks forward to adventure and new experiences. Young lovers dream of the future; old lovers should also dream of the future. "What is past is prologue." One never overtakes the future; therefore, one can always dream of it, plan for it, and press forward toward it. But many married couples stifle the romantic in each other so that the mind becomes dull, pioneering in new experiences is fearful, and one settles down to an uneventful tiresome experience.

One of the author's saddest pastoral experiences was in calling on a woman, the mother of several children, who had once been a beautiful, happy girl but who was now a tired, plodding housewife of forty-five. Her face was expressionless as she went about her duties. Her daily routine was cooking, washing, and cleaning. Her husband left early and came home late. There was no greeting or communication between them. She had lost the art of conversation and rarely smiled. Her social life had become nil. The husband was a likeable person, pleasant enough to meet, but when he came home, his wife seemed afraid of him. He was gruff, profane, and drank rather heavily. Nothing could be done for this couple because the wife had given up and withdrawn into a world of her own and the husband had no conception of what had taken place and cared less. He had made his world outside the home among his drinking and card companions, alcohol, and women. When he had no place else to go, home was a place to come to, with food, bed, and another sex outlet—not a partner.

Another defeated wife, who came for counseling, was terrified at what she saw happening in her marriage. She was becoming bored with her housework, not because she disliked it, but because it had become devoid of any love relationship. There were children, but they were growing older (in their teens); she realized that they would soon be gone and her life then would be completely empty of daily interest. Her husband had his work, which, while remunerative, offered little opportunity for creativity. He was not at all an imaginative person. He went to work daily and came home regularly. He gave one the impression of having given up as far as any future advancement or growth was concerned and of withdrawing more and more from social contacts in church and community. One day she said pathetically and wistfully, "If only he would take me to a movie." She felt that she was fighting a losing battle. The husband said that he realized something was lacking in his marriage but that he was always so tired at night that he wanted only to stay home and rest. It was difficult for him to appreciate his wife's needs. Although he said that he would try to make life more interesting for both of them, this was never accomplished. Perhaps he lacked romantic comprehension or had withdrawn so far from social contacts that now he could follow only a compulsive daily routine.

Another couple, approaching this same situation, were able to comprehend what was happening and could happen in their marriage to destroy romance and determined it would not be so with them. They began to make plans for going out together, calling on their friends, and having them over for an evening of bridge. They had family picnics and engaged in family games. They planned evenings out with dancing. The husband would call his wife to have lunch with him. They also began to dream together of the future: planning a house which they might some day build, starting a scrapbook of house designs which they liked, planning for the children's college and investigating education insurance policies, and discussing the possibilities of advancement in his work. They said, "It is lots of fun dreaming and planning together."

Two couples went to the beach for a week's vacation; both couples were in their early thirties and had two children. We shall designate them couple F and couple G.

The husband in couple F spent much of his time in bed, rising about 10:00 A.M. or later. Putting on swim trunks, he drove off alone in his car toward the amusement center. Later, he slept a good part of the afternoon. On two or three afternoons, late, he would go to the beach with his wife and children. After supper he had a few drinks and went to bed. Little communication occurred between them. His wife cooked, washed, cleaned, and took care of the children just as she did at home. The children were not allowed to make any noise while their father was home. When he spoke to them, it was usually to tell them to be quiet.

Couple G also went to the beach. They had a wonderful time. The wife cooked, and her husband washed the dishes; they both cleaned the house and looked after the children. There was much play and laughter. In mid-morning and afternoon the whole family went on the beach where they built houses, caught crabs, and played in the surf. In the evening there was family talk, and after the children were in bed the low, pleasant tones of father and mother engaging in conversation.

Any comment on the contrast between these two couples would be superfluous—couple F was devoid of romance; couple G was keeping it alive and rejoicing in its stimulating influence.

THE NEED FOR PERSONAL ACCEPTANCE

"I'm not his wife," said Mrs. X, "I'm just his cook and somebody to satisfy him sexually. He does not love me for what I am. I'm a convenience."

Her remark was similar to that of Mr. C who said, "My wife cares nothing for me for myself. All she cares about is the money I'm able to give her." These two people were being stereotyped by their spouses. The former saw his wife as a convenient woman to have in the house, as one would have an electric razor. The latter saw her husband as a source of revenue, like a trust fund. When counseling began with the couples, considerable time was spent with each spouse in ventilating his grievances. In each case there was much criticism on both sides. Some of it was real; some of it was projected, but the main problem was something none was able to label: stereotyping.

Being able to label the counselee's motivations and emotional reactions is very important in counseling. In these two cases it was not no much that the stereotyping spouses did not care for their opposites as that they did not realize what they were doing to their spouses by typing them.

When Mr. X came to understand this, he was able to recognize his error and correct it. He was particularly sorry and gained good insight into the problem. He was really following a pattern observed in his own family in which his parents had apparently stereotyped each other. His father's attitude toward women was that they were to serve men. A married woman was to be at the beck and call of her husband. He had never learned to consider wives as having emotional needs such as we are discussing in this chapter. The wife was made to fit into a mold. Perhaps *housewife* is the word which gives them this stereotype—a title which many wives today rightfully resent. Mr. X was relieved to understand the problem and began evaluating his wife in terms of the qualities he had found in her when he fell in love with her but which had become latent. She stepped out of the stereotype of his family pattern to stand before him as "the girl of his dreams" in all her individual loveliness.

It was quite difficult for Mrs. C to grasp the idea of stereotyping. Labeling helped to some degree, but she was a domineering and scheming person who had learned how to hold her husband sexually as a means of gaining considerable money and luxuries. He would become angry and violent at times when she would criticize him during their intimate love-play. Then, on other occasions when she got what she wanted, she would be loving and cooperative. He would threaten to leave her, and she in turn would threaten to leave him. But she never was able to see him as anything other than her stereotype of a husband to be used and to keep her in ample funds. She probably would have been happy with any man—for she plainly did not love her husband for himself.

Every normal person wants to be accepted for himself on the basis of his personal qualifications. Perhaps we might take a lesson from the Church. The Church always deals with people as individuals. In the majority of churches, soon after birth the child is baptized and given a name by which he is recognized as a special individual. Baptism is always an individual matter. The Church, represented by the minister, takes the infant in its arms and baptizes that individual. The same is true in confirmation.

The bishop, pastor, or session lays hands separately upon each individual, praying for that particular person. Holy Communion is administered to each individual recipient. Thus the Church never stereotypes its members. Each one is accepted as a person in his own right.

The form of Solemnization of Holy Matrimony [5] used in the Protestant Episcopal Church and those forms used in other churches imply in the marriage vows that husband and wife take each other as particular persons—to be loved and cherished "for better for worse, for richer for poorer, in sickness and in health . . . according to God's holy ordinance." The names received in baptism are used, and the model of God's dealing with men is implied in "God's holy ordinance."

God always deals with us as individuals. He never stereotypes. He knows each one's peculiarities, motivations, and reactions to stress and frustration and seeks to meet our needs on an individual basis—needs of forgiveness, acceptance, redemption, and restoration. We humans need to deal with each other as God deals with us, for each one of us is an individual different from all other individuals, reacting in his own way to his environment as he seeks to develop behavior techniques adequate to his needs, frustrations, and conflicts. We refuse to be stereotyped; we detest the common mold. Each personality cries out to be accepted for itself. We hold firmly to our self-image—whether it be good or bad. It is *I* against the world, and no one else can be this *I*.

Spouses must find the individual in each other and love and cherish that *I*.

SUMMARY

No person is self-sufficient because no one is able to meet his own emotional needs. Our fundamental human problems lie in the region of personal needs and emotional relationships.

A primary need is to be loved for what one is and not for what one does. Things cannot replace a person's love. When one has sinned or failed, he needs to know that he is still loved for

---

5 *The Book of Common Prayer*, p. 300.

what he is—spouse, child, or parent. It is an exhilarating experience to think and plan ways to bring pleasure to a loved one. The unsatisfied need of love can strike out in many cruel ways, producing much anxiety. Love has its rightful demands which cannot be overlooked if happiness is to be characteristic of marriage.

There is also the need for interdependency. It is a part of communal living. The normal person has a need to be dependent on others and to have others dependent on him. Spouses who allow their need for independence—which also is a basic need—to rule out interdependence unwittingly undermine their marriage.

Everyone seeks, but not all find, self-realization. Some become so discouraged by the depreciating attitude of others in the family that they give up striving to be creative in the development of their capabilities. Men and women need opportunities to exploit their creativity: a job, housework, care of children, a workshop or collecting, community and church work, etc. Marriage should facilitate the development of every member of the family.

Life can become very monotonous unless relieved by romantic experiences with one's spouse and anticipation of an idealistic future. We are dreamers by nature. Make-believe persists long beyond childhood, but with mature adults it is based on reality.

The need for personal acceptance as a unique individual in one's own right is another need which couples must recognize and meet. No one likes to be stereotyped. Every normal person wants to be accepted on the basis of his personal qualifications. Here the Church sets an example, for it always deals with persons as individuals.

SUGGESTED READING

Baber, Ray E., *Marriage and the Family* (2nd ed.), Chap. 6. New York: McGraw-Hill Book Company, 1953.

Cameron, Norman, *The Psychology of Behavior Disorders*, pp. 103–86. Boston: Houghton Mifflin Company, 1957.

Coleman, James C., *Abnormal Psychology and Modern Life*, Chap. 3. Chicago: Scott, Foresman & Company, 1950, 1956.

Johnson, Paul E., *Psychology of Pastoral Care*. Nashville: Abingdon Press, 1958.

Maslow, A. H., *Motivation and Personality*, Chap. 5. New York: Harper & Row, Publishers, 1954.

Morris, J. Kenneth, *Premarital Counseling—A Manual for Ministers,* Chap 7. Englewood Cliffs, N.J.: Prentice-Hall, Inc., 1960.

Peterson, James A., *Toward a Successful Marriage,* Chaps. 4, 5. New York: Charles Scribner's Sons, 1960.

Sullivan, Harry Stack, *The Interpersonal Theory of Psychiatry.* New York: W. W. Norton & Company, Inc., 1953.

Witenburg, Earl G., Janet MacKenzie Rioch, and Milton Mayer, "The Interpersonal and Cultural Approaches," *American Handbook of Psychiatry,* Vol. II, Chap. 70. New York: Basic Books, Inc., 1959.

The Right Use of Sex

8 The modern age prides itself on its sophistication. We know about so many things—automation, nuclear fission, space travel, disease, the atom—that we think we know everything. But with all our knowledge we have not learned the art of good human relations and the way to peace, not even within families, much less nations. The elementary psychology of human relations should be taught along with reading, writing, and arithmetic and continued through college. By the time social studies and psychology are taken up in our present school curriculum, the child may have already acquired an inner set toward antisocial behavior. And along with elementary education the foundation should be laid for instruction in the right use of sex.

Inadequate, improper, and antiquated knowledge about sex causes more unhappiness in marriage than any other one factor.[1] Howard Whitman has called the age we now live in "the sex age." [2] In a recent book by that title he sketches the centrality of sex in our culture. With the motto, "Get some sex into it," advertising, television programs, and movies emphasize sex to the point where it becomes the motivating force for buying, spectator entertainment, recreation, and sales increase. Therefore, it does work! The American mind is set toward sex but without understanding its right use.

---

[1] Judson T. Landis and Mary G. Landis, *Building a Successful Marriage* (4th ed.; Englewood Cliffs, N.J.: Prentice-Hall, Inc., 1963), pp. 307ff.

[2] Howard Whitman, *The Sex Age* (Garden City, N.Y.: Doubleday & Company, Inc., 1962).

YOUNG MARRIAGES AND THEIR CAUSES

As a consequence of our not understanding the right use of sex, we have increasing teen-age sexual promiscuity.

Since we have failed our teen-agers in not giving them adequate sex knowledge, we have an increasing number of teen-age

TABLE 2

Marital Status by Sex and Age 15–19 *
(Percentage of total male and female white population of U.S.)

Year	Male Married	Female Married
1960	3.8	15.7
1950	3.1	16.7
1940	1.7	11.6
1930	1.7	12.6
1920	2.1	12.5
1910	1.1	11.3
1900	1.0	10.9

* Bureau of Census, U.S. Census of Population, 1960, U.S. Summary
Final Report PC(1)-1D, Table 177, pp. 1-436, 7, 8.

marriages. These young marriages shown in Table 2 are brought about by three main causes:

Infatuation

This is mistaken for mature love. Popularly referred to as "young" love, it used to be called "puppy" love. It is based on physical attraction and the awakening sex drive of two normal young people toward each other. It is a thrilling, starry-eyed experience. If one or more couples in a group run off and get married, others may do the same. Every year fifteen-year-old girls and sixteen- or seventeen-year old boys marry on this basis. Being too young to assume the responsibilities of marriage, there is little chance that they will make a success of it.

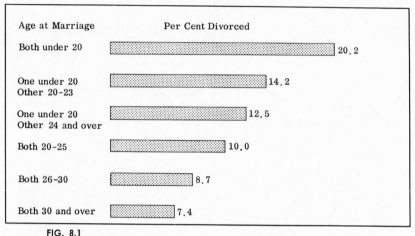

FIG. 8.1

Age at Marriage and Divorce Rate in 3,000 Marriages

Studies also show that the twenty-year old girl would not love or even be interested in the boy she may have been in love with at sixteen.[3] Our young people should understand their awakening sex drive and that for them infatuation and falling in and out of love are normal.

In the Bureau of Census report for 1960, statistics from 28 states reporting show the median age at first marriage for males was 22.7 and for females, 20.3.[4] The median duration of marriage in 28 states reporting for 1959 was 7.0 years.[5]

Landis and Landis report on a study of the divorce rate in 3,000 marriages.

All the couples were parents of college students, and therefore would not represent a cross section of the population. The divorce rate decreased in these families as the age of marriage increased. If one spouse was under twenty and the other was over twenty at marriage, the divorce rate was higher than if both were twenty years old at marriage.

All of these findings emphasize the fact that chronological age is related to the other kinds of maturity necessary to make a success of marriage. Certainly age cannot be isolated as the sole factor responsible

[3] Landis and Landis, *Building a Successful Marriage*, p. 127.

[4] U.S. Bureau of the Census, *Statistical Abstract of the United States, 1963* (84th ed.; Washington, D.C., 1963), p. 70.

[5] U.S. Bureau of the Census, *Statistical Abstract of the United States, 1963*, p. 72.

for the higher proportion of failures among youthful marriages. One hypothesis is that more of those who marry early do so to escape unhappy home surroundings or to defy parental dominance than is true of those who marry later. To choose marriage as a hoped-for means of escape from pressures may represent immature judgment and lack of the experience in problem-solving needed to make a success of marriage. Some who marry as an escape might not have the judgment to make a wiser choice even if they were much older, but many of them, if given time, would achieve a level of maturity not present when they marry at a very early age.[6]

Sexual activities

Dating no longer takes place at home or under a chaperon's supervision. The automobile has taken the place of the parlor and the porch swing. In five minutes a couple can drive to a secluded place, park, and pet. Since nature is amoral and biologically concerned only with reproduction, isolation, close proximity, and intimate kissing and embracing lead either to orgasm without penetration or to intercourse. But all teen-agers are not conditioned to accept this behavior without feelings of shame and guilt. While home, church, and school may not have specifically taught them anything about overt sexual activity, the impression is gotten over to them that this activity is immoral. The result is that some young couples feel that since they have engaged in activities which should be reserved for marriage, they should now marry in order to make right what they have done. And so they marry not because they may love each other but because of their guilt. After marriage they may find that the premarital sexual relation with its shame and guilt becomes a block to a satisfactory sexual adjustment, and that they have no love for each other.

A couple who had married early and were finding it difficult to be compatible came for counseling. The wife in telling about their premarital sex relations said, "I had always told myself that my body would belong to only one man: my husband. So after we had had sex relations, I knew I must marry him although I knew that I did not love him. Now I neither love him nor hate him. I just don't care about him. I can't stand for him to touch me. I just wish he would go and I'd never see him again."

---

[6] Landis and Landis, *Building a Successful Marriage*, p. 129.

Home, church, or school never spell out just what is meant by fornication, adultery, virginity, chastity, or the sanctity of marriage.

A young girl was brought by her parents to the author because she had admitted having sexual relations with a boy slightly older. She had recently joined her church after a period of special instruction. When asked if she had received any information at home, church, or school about sex, she answered, "No." When asked if the minister in his instruction had explained to the class the meaning of chastity, fornication, or adultery; explained the Seventh Commandment; or discussed boy-girl relationships, she again answered "No." Nor did she know the meaning of those words. She had no understanding of the right use of sex.

Another young girl who had become quite promiscuous and had borne an illegitimate child said her only instruction at home had been, "Don't mess around with boys." No one spelled out what was meant by "mess around." Another young girl had been afraid of boys because her mother had said, "Leave boys alone or they will hurt you." Not knowing what she meant and being a normal and attractive girl, she soon found boys delightful and had sexual relations with several until she became pregnant.

With all the sexual activity among teen-agers that we know is taking place, we still do not face up to our responsibility to teach them the right use of sex.

Pregnancy and contraception

Pregnancy, naturally, is a cause of teen-age or young marriages. Here again we have failed to give children adequate factual sex knowledge and an attitude toward the right use of sex which should help them deal wisely in controlling sexual desire. Many high school boys believe that "it is hard to get a girl pregnant." Consequently even those who know the use of contraceptives may not use them. Some girls, thinking boys are more sophisticated in sex matters, trust the boy to take precautions against conception without ascertaining what precautions, if any, he may be taking. So we have many young couples forced into marriage because of pregnancy.

Some parents demand that the marriage take place so that the child will be legitimate, intending to secure a divorce for the couple after the child is born. Some demand that the couple separate as soon as the marriage ceremony takes place and not see each other again. Other parents do not permit a marriage but seek abortion or send the girl to a home for unwed mothers and put the baby up for adoption. Others try to accept the marriage and help the young couple build a happy and successful one. Even so, the divorce rate is high.

In 1961 there were 240,200 illegitimate births in the United States.[7] It is estimated that there are about one million criminal abortions each year in the United States.

Misunderstood infatuations, early premarital sexual relations, forced marriages, illegitimate births, and abortions are filling our population with guilt-ridden, maladjusted persons and broken homes; yet we still surround sex with outworn and harmful taboos, allowing our children to continue to grow up in ignorance regarding the right use of sex.

Should our young people be taught the use of contraceptives? Or should we continue to allow our children to grow up in "innocency" (I shudder!) and continue in sexual promiscuity? Home, church, and school have already given their answers: "No" to the former question and "Yes" to the latter!

There is no logical reason why our children should be denied instruction in the right use of sex, any more than that they should be denied knowledge about the functions of the digestive organs. The reason parents do not teach their children is (a) their own ignorance, and (b) their own emotional reactions to sex, which is weighted for them with shame and guilt. The reason the Church does nothing is that (c) to be sex-minded is carnal and sinful and "the church is not the place to talk about such things." The reason the schools do nothing—though some are now making an attempt to teach the right use of sex—is that (d) sex instruction has been labeled "taboo" by the community. It is too threatening a subject to many adults and carries too much of an emotional charge to be permitted free discussion. The Bible and The Book

---

[7] U.S. Bureau of the Census, *Statistical Abstract of the United States, 1963*, p. 56.

of Common Prayer speak plainly, but Christian parents, teachers, and ministers "beat around the bush"!

My plea to all three of these institutions—family, church, and school—is to begin informing children and young people about the right use of sex—why we are sexual beings, God's purpose in creating us as such, and how sex in marriage can be a deep expression of love and trust and a protection against loneliness.

Of course, factual sex knowledge is not enough. The Christian attitude toward sex must also be conveyed to our children. This is something which is not so much "taught" as "caught." It is acquired as children see affection and trust set forth before them in the relationships between their parents. Children will come to associate correct sex knowledge with happy well-adjusted parents who express mature love toward each other in their daily contacts.

A WHOLESOME ATTITUDE TOWARD SEX

The minister will encounter various sexual problems among the couples who come to him for marriage counseling. It is therefore necessary that he have a well-founded and Christian attitude toward sex if he is to counsel on this intimate side of married life.

To have a wholesome attitude toward sex in Christian culture means first of all the recognition of sex as being of Divine origin and therefore good and beautiful. We are created sexual beings. In this we share with the animal world. Life, to continue, must reproduce. The biological function of sex is essential to the ongoing of the race. Since God through nature has ordained it this way, sex must be viewed along with other bodily functions such as elimination, digestion, and breathing as a normal, natural, and wholesome function in the art of living, which involves one's entire nature—physical, mental, and psychic. Indeed, man's whole nature is caught up in the sex act more completely perhaps than in any other of his activities. If the minister is to deal effectively with sex in marriage, he must view sex problems from this position: sex is a wholesome, God-given, natural expression of a basic physiological need of man.

REPRODUCTION OR PROCREATION?

There are two kinds of reproduction. Man, along with all members of the animal kingdom, reproduces physically. There is no mystery or magic about this. The male sperm fertilizes the female ovum, and an offspring is conceived. For humans, this kind of reproduction takes place in and out of marriage. Witness the large number of illegitimate children the soldiers of all nationalities leave in countries of conquest and occupation, and the large number of illegitimate children of mixed blood found in every nation. All of these fatherless children are the result of physical reproduction.

But God never intended that humans should reproduce on this level. For humans God had in mind spiritual reproduction. That is, children are to be conceived and brought into this world through procreation. Men and women are to marry on the basis of mature, self-giving love (agape) and to pro-create, that is, create for God, and in cooperation with Him, children made in His spiritual and moral image to be reared in a God-centered home which will enable them to grow up to be well-adjusted, happy, and creative persons.

God made us sexual beings. God instituted marriage in order that within that mystical relationship two persons may become one and create with Him another person in His spiritual image. This is procreation at its highest level.

SOME PROBLEMS IN DEVELOPING
A CHRISTIAN ATTITUDE TOWARD SEX

Church leaders are alarmed over the changing sex code in our Western culture. Christian standards as set forth in the New Testament and Church teaching are being set aside by great numbers of Christian people, especially young people. No doubt many of the old inhibitions are unwholesome and should go. Some of these are not found among other peoples.

In some cultures such as the Japanese, pregnancy is understood by children as a natural process, whereas in our culture, while the taboo on discussing pregnancy with children is changing, reticence and embarrassment hinder some parents and children from talking about it. Students of the field of marriage and family living feel that the whole matter of sex should be dealt with more realistically and that many taboos should be removed.

Some taboos are conducive to guilt feelings where there should be none. For example, it is taboo to look at a woman in the nude, yet there can be no ethics involved in either the nude female body or the act of looking. The female body is from God and is beautiful; so also is the male body. In Japan, where male and female are exposed in the public bath, there is nothing sensuous or immoral in this custom. However, an Occidental in such a situation may feel sensual, sexually stimulated, and ashamed, resulting in guilt feelings.

The author is not advocating the sudden discarding of all sex customs that have developed out of our Hebrew-Christian traditions, but he does call for a critical analysis of them in order to distinguish between what may be ethical and what may be matters of discretion.

In developing a Christian attitude toward sex we cannot go back to Old Testament standards for the answer. The Old Testament teachings definitely reflect ancient Semitic taboos and attitudes. We do not, for example, consider a woman unclean during her menstrual period, or after childbirth. The sin of Onan [8] was not that he had intercourse with one he thought to be a harlot, but that he withdrew and "spilled the semen on the ground," thus interfering with the biological laws of reproduction —in a population that was constantly being reduced by wars. Ham's great sin was that he saw the nakedness of his father, which was taboo.[9] But today many fathers and sons bathe together. Bathing together is one way by which a boy identifies with his father and a girl with her mother.

Nor can we follow blindly New Testament ideas regarding sex, for these are influenced by the Old Testament. Jesus said that a man should not look at a woman to lust after her.[10] But a man

---

[8] Genesis 38:8–10.

[9] Genesis 9:20–27.

[10] Matthew 5:28.

is not forbidden to look upon a woman. One is not to commit adultery, but is to be faithful to his or her spouse in sexual matters. In modern thought we stress the worth of the individual and say that fornication and adultery are wrong because they both disregard the effect upon the personality of those directly participating, and disregard the consequences to others who may be indirectly affected: children born out of wedlock, venereal disease, offended spouses and/or children, broken homes, or mental depression because of guilt and social condemnation.

The Church and legitimacy

The Church's strong position on legitimacy, although it is in the best interest of society, helps make illegitimacy a disgrace and the illegitimate child an outcast even among church members. How well the author remembers as a boy hearing the story of an illegitimate child with whom "nice" children did not play!

A boy of fifteen was brought by a teacher for testing and counseling. The boy was maladjusted in his school work and with his classmates and teachers. He was very antisocial and had run away several times from two institutions for incorrigibles.

Background material showed that the boy's father was the illegitimate child of the daughter of a prominent and wealthy church family who adopted but never accepted him and he grew up bitter and resentful. He had heard rumors of his birth so when he came of age, he went to the Bureau of Vital Statistics in his state and found confirmation of the rumor. He confronted his foster parents, began to drink and gamble, and was finally convicted of a crime and sent to the penitentiary. In the meantime, however, he had married a woman the family considered "bad." She bore a son—the boy whom the author saw. The mother deserted her husband and child and was later divorced.

The foster family refused to accept any responsibility for the child. He was not allowed in the home or to play with his cousins. Finally, he went to live with an elderly step-relative. Although innocent of his father's illegitimate birth, unfortunate marriage, and criminal record, the family and community had turned against the boy and made him practically an outcast.

The Church and sex

Finally, the Church needs new orientation in the area of sex. Continence before marriage is taught by the Church (although in some European cultures with Christian background, premarital coitus is acceptable among engaged couples), but its overemphasis and the subsequent denial and repression of natural sexual desires may result not only in a collapse of standards in the individual but in sexual promiscuity and preoccupation with sex as well. Nature will not be denied the biological function of the sex drive; however, it can be sublimated and sensibly controlled.

The minister should be familiar with the new directions in which the churches are beginning to move. An historic meeting was held at Green Lakes, Wisconsin, April 30 to May 5, 1961—The North American Conference on Church and Family—which gives considerable insight into the churches' concern about sex in modern society.[11]

The Lambeth Conference. The Conference of the Anglican Communion of 1958 set forth a theology of sexuality which should do much in the future to promote a sound, scientific, Christian attitude toward sex:

First of all, the family is rooted in the elemental processes of life itself. Human reproduction—human parenthood—is vastly more complicated than the reproduction of plants or the simpler animals. Mankind has rightly come to see depths and possibilities in the process, and in the relationships which it establishes, which are, at best, only faintly suggested (if indeed they exist at all) in the lower orders of life. Still the human family, even in its richest and noblest complexity, is at one with all of nature in its function as the means by which new life is begun.

The commandment in Genesis to "be fruitful and multiply" reflects this biological function. More significantly, it raises it to the level of God's creative purpose. Underlying the insistent drive of all life to reproduce itself is the creative activity of God himself, who ordered nature in this way and established the process and the urgent impulse, and reveals to mankind something of his purpose in so doing. Indeed, the

---

[11] Elizabeth Steel Genné and William Henry Genné, eds., *Foundations for Christian Family Policy,* Proceedings of the North American Conference on Church and Family (New York: Department of Family Life, National Council of the Churches of Christ in the U.S.A., 1961).

revelation expressed in Genesis implies that in this fruitfulness, to some degree, man shares in God's creative work, that he is admitted to a quasi-partnership with God in the establishment of new life. Therefore the process of human reproduction, from the earliest levels of Biblical revelation, has been seen as invested with a special and responsible dignity.

The Biblical revelation, however, does not limit the function of sexuality and the family to the reproductive purpose. Equally deep-rooted in Genesis is the reflection of a second factor—the need of man and woman for each other, to complement and fulfil each other and to establish a durable partnership against the loneliness and rigour of life. It was not good for man to be alone, and God made a helpmeet for him. This relationship of man and woman—of husband and wife—is rooted in God's creative purpose equally with the procreative function of sexuality. "For this reason shall a man leave his father and mother and be joined to his wife." [12]

Thus, in the heart of the Biblical teaching about creation, two great insights into the nature and purpose of sexuality and the family are lodged. They are not subordinated one to the other; they are not directly related to one another; their relationship, in the developing experience of Israel, is to be found in yet a third area—that of the place of the family in giving responsible security to the children born of the love of husband and wife.

To summarize, three purposes—three functions—are interwoven in human sexuality. Each of them is profoundly rooted in human experience and in God's revelation. The procreation of children, the fulfilment and completion of husband and wife in each other, and the establishment of a stable environment within which the deepest truths about human relationships can be expressed and communicated and children can grow up seeing and learning what mature life is really like—these are the great purposes which, in God's loving will, marriage and the family are created to serve. [13]

Three purposes of sex are emphasized:

(1)   The biological—procreation.
(2)   Sexual gratification as a pleasurable experience not to be denied. We must recognize our sexual needs, which rank along with the basic physiological needs of hunger and thirst. Just as

---

12 Genesis 2:18-25; Matthew 19:4ff.

13 *The Lambeth Conference, 1958, 1959* (London: The Trustees of the Society for Promoting Christian Knowledge, 1958; New York, N.Y.: The Seabury Press, Inc., 1958), pp. 2.142ff. © 1958 by The Seabury Press.

these needs are best met in the proper manner, under controlled conditions and with nourishing food and drink, so our sexual needs are best met under proper and controlled conditions. Christian morality demands that these conditions be satisfied only in the marriage state. The holy estate of matrimony was instituted of God, and within that estate the sexual needs of men and woman can be amply met. Christian morality does not admit of promiscuity in one's sex life.

(3)   The stabilizing and enrichment of family life.

Masturbation

This is a sexual outlet on which Christian ethics is divided. However, we have learned through our research in sex knowledge, both on the infrahuman and human levels, that masturbation is too universally practiced to be considered a moral problem per se; rather, it is an attempt to satisfy sexual needs, just as eating or exercise are expressions of other physical needs. We know that masturbation, which is a deliberate external manipulation or frictional stimulation of the sex organs, is enjoyed by infants and small children before they are able to appreciate the right or wrong of it as experienced emotionally by adults. May not masturbation be one way by which nature calls attention to and emphasizes the importance of sex? Medical studies show no physical ill effects from masturbation. However, it does sometimes accompany feelings of self-pity and association with unwholesome fantasies that are mentally unsatisfactory. Also, since masturbation in marriage deprives oneself and one's spouse of the expression of sex through the mutual experience of coitus, it therefore becomes a selfish act.

As the Lambeth Conference report says, sex is to be enjoyed as one expression of the consummation of married love. To the Christian couple it should be considered in its sacramental nature as "an outward and visible sign of an inward and spiritual grace." The love- or sex-play, which should always precede intercourse, should come from a very deep love that expresses itself in kindness, consideration, and courtesy. Nothing should be done which is offensive or displeasing to one's partner. Whatever is done should be on the high level of purity and holiness, each remembering that the other's personality is made in the spiritual and moral image of God and, therefore, is to be treated with loving tenderness and understanding.

SEXUAL PROBLEMS IN MARRIAGE

Let us consider some of the sexual problems causing maladjustment and unhappiness which arise in marriage.

Frigidity

"My wife is frigid" is a rather common complaint of many husbands. Frigidity means that the wife does not respond cooperatively and with warm emotional feelings in the sex act, either before, during, or after. Frigidity is a symptom of some emotional block which prevents the wife from cooperating.

The usual cause of frigidity lies in an unwholesome or warped attitude toward sex, sometimes accompanied by shame and guilt. For example, a married woman said she could never engage in intercourse in her parents' home because she felt her mother would not approve. Another wife said she was "petrified" whenever she and her husband had intercourse because the bed squeaked, and she felt sure the other people in the house knew what was going on. Both of these women felt that there was something about sex that was not good and were ashamed to think of themselves engaging in an act they had been taught was "nasty." Others have expressed the idea that sex is the man's privilege and must be tolerated. The thought of enjoying sex as a God-given right, privilege, and pleasure and sacred to the marriage relationship had been far from their minds, so convincing had been their training as children to regard sex as evil and dirty. To hear the minister say that it is good and to know that the Church believes it to be good brings them much relief.

Fear of pregnancy also causes frigidity. Fear causes tenseness and can produce such tightness of the genital muscles as to make intercourse painful. The use of reliable contraceptives can do much to relieve such women of this fear. Proof of this is that following the menopause when childbearing has ceased, many women begin to enjoy sex for the first time in their married life. Now they feel that they can relax and cohabit without fear of pregnancy.

Ignorance of sex anatomy and of what actually takes place in coitus may also produce frigidity. Some women have so little factual sex knowledge that they do not understand how intercourse is performed or its techniques. One frequently runs across this problem in premarital counseling. Women who have had no premarital sex instruction may be quite perplexed when they must cohabit in marriage. The author has counseled with mothers of several children who did not know the female sex anatomy well enough to explain techniques of intercourse and the woman's part in it. The minister-counselor should know and be able to explain with charts the male and female genital regions.

Failure of the wife to reach orgasm

This is also a common complaint. In practically all cases the husband reaches his climax, but the wife often does not. Many wives married for years state that they have experienced an orgasm only once or twice, and some never. One wife with three children learned from reading that she should have been having a climax. She had never enjoyed the sex act. She felt that sex was only for the man, the wife only to have babies. Her husband did not realize that anything was wrong until his wife began to show resentment because she was not experiencing a climax which she had learned she was entitled to. Considerable friction developed between them before they came for counseling. After several periods of counseling in which factual sex knowledge was given to both of them, but separately, and their attitudes toward sex and the roles of each as man and woman were gone over, both were able to experiment together to achieve a satisfactory sexual adjustment. The husband spent more time in love-making and learned to delay his own orgasm until his wife achieved hers. Her first climax was a very thrilling experience for both of them.

Conflicts

Some individuals enjoy sex more after arguing and fighting. But these are the exception who seem to use intercourse as a hostile act toward their partner. Most couples enjoy sex when they have planned for intercourse through the day or evening, indicating in subtle ways the desires of each for it. Love-making does not need to be confined to the bed. It should be spontaneous throughout the day so that intercourse in the evening becomes a uniting of two personalities in "one flesh."

A couple who were at odds complained each about the other that he or she would anticipate intercourse in the evening, only to have the other precipitate an argument which would spoil everything, causing one to go to sleep resentful and bitter. A husband complained that just as he was ready to penetrate, his wife would bring up a controversial subject which took away all his desire.

In both of these cases there was no lack of love. Each couple had been married several years. But there was a great lack of understanding and empathy. They were not entering into the feelings of each other in such a way as to sense the reactions of the other spouse toward the sex situation in which they were placed.

One man, whose wife complained about his arguing and then having intercourse, said that he did not see how that could have any effect since intercourse was merely a matter of friction of one organ against the other!

Menopause

The menopause, or climacteric, or change of life in the wife, is the cause of much friction, sometimes continuing to the end of the marriage. The beginning of cessation of the menses occurs generally between the ages of forty-five and forty-eight and may continue for several years. It signalizes the end of the childbearing period. It may take place prematurely as a result of pathologic physiology, surgical removal of the ovaries, irradiation, or other causes.

According to Kelly [14] the majority of women, about 80 per cent, pass through this period without any ill effects and, as far as their health is concerned, without even being aware of it. In most of the other 20 per cent the symptoms are mild, and in the few who really do have untoward effects medical science offers assurance of easy alleviation.

---

[14] G. Lombard Kelly, *The Doctor Talks on the Menopause* (Chicago: The Budlong Press, 1959).

Among the symptoms of the menopause may be mentioned hot flushes; nervousness; irritability; anxiety; fatigue or a sense of listlessness—even exhaustion; sleeplessness; general aches and pains, often transient; and headaches. The physician can do much to remove or alleviate these symptoms.

Even with all that is written about it in news columns and periodicals, the menopause is misunderstood by many husbands and wives. It seems to me that the family physician could render his patients, male and female, a great service by having them come in groups after office hours for him to explain the menopause and discuss the emotional problems which are generally related to it.

Time and again the author has counseled with women who believed that menopause meant the end of sex life for them and that their husbands, finding them no longer attractive sexually, would begin "running around" and being promiscuous. Great has been the relief of these wives to know that they would be just as attractive to their husbands as always, and that they themselves would enjoy sexual relations more now that their childbearing time had ended. There would now be no fear of pregnancy to cause them to be less cooperative in the sex act.

It is equally important that the husband understand the increased nervous tension that menopause causes at times in the wife and be patient and more attentive. The wife, because of her fear of her being less attractive physically after menopause, needs the reassurance of the husband's love and affection. If there are times when she would prefer not to have coitus, he should accept this, not as a refusal because of lack of love or concern for his sexual needs, but because of her emotional condition during the menopausal phase or cycle. No husband needs to seek release from sexual tension by seeking out some other sex partner. Nature, through the nocturnal emission, will take care of this. Continence in or out of marriage works no injury to a man but may do much to strengthen his self-discipline; when practiced in marriage out of deference to his wife's physical and mental condition, it can become an expression of mature love. Through sublimation of the sex drive into channels of devotion and service to her and the family, it can be a means of strengthening the marriage relationship.

Impotence

Impotence is the cause of much unhappiness in marriage and is greatly misunderstood. It may occur at any age owing to conditions inhibitory to erection such as grief, fear, quarreling, insults, sudden diversion of attention, worry, and guilt. But it is not always possible to be specific as to the cause. Fear of failure, detection, unwanted pregnancy, or any other kind of fear may prevent a satisfactory erection. Usually, it is deflating to the male ego; indeed, it may be so much so that he will not attempt coitus for a long time afterwards. Then he may be so fearful of failure again that with this uppermost in his mind, it does happen again. Since there are many reasons for impotency, when it first occurs, no particular attention should be paid to it. A wife who loves her husband should not ridicule him for his impotency but tell him that she understands and loves him just the same. It may never occur again. In normal, healthy men only very strong inhibitory emotions can prevent erection and a satisfactory sexual relation.[15]

When impotency occurs at night, particularly with older men, intercourse may be had in the morning. The early morning erection is common to men owing to the pressure of a full bladder. But after the bladder has been emptied, the erection can occur again and a satisfactory coitus obtained.

There are two types of erection: (a) cerebral erection, which is the normal and usual type caused by erotic thoughts, close proximity of the opposite sex, sexually exciting pictures and conversation; and (b) reflex erection, which is brought about by massage of the penis by the wife or oneself, with or without the use of a lubricant. Kelly comments,

> Although many men, unaware of the existence of the reflex type of erection, conclude that they are impotent, many others learn in one way or another of the reflex erection and realize that they are not impotent, but merely slow in getting started. . .[16]

Three types of impotence have been noted by Kelly:

---

[15] G. Lombard Kelly, "Impotence," in *The Encyclopedia of Sexual Behavior,* ed. Albert Ellis and Albert Abarbanel (New York: Hawthorn Books, Inc., 1961), I, 517. Copyright © 1961 by Hawthorn Books, Inc.

[16] Kelly, "Impotence," *The Encyclopedia of Sexual Behavior,* p. 518.

(1) Organic impotence is due to some anatomical defect in the reproductive organ, or in the brain or spinal cord. . . . (2) Functional impotence is caused by some disturbance of the various functions of the generative organs. It may be a nervous disturbance, affecting centers in the brain or spinal cord or interfering with nerve tracts or nerve endings; it may be a circulatory or inflammatory condition, resulting in congestion or erosions in the sex glands or in the urethra; or it may be due to subnormal activity of the male hormone glands. . . .

One of the principal causes of functional impotence is exhaustion. This may affect the central and peripheral nervous systems as well as the organs of reproduction. The exhaustion may be caused by sexual excess, coitus interruptus (withdrawal before ejaculation), excessive masturbation, gonorrhea, heavy petting at frequent intervals without intercourse, or even by moderate masturbation. It should be emphasized that sexual intercourse begins with kissing and necking and continues with all of the phases of petting. It should continue normally to completed coitus, which is the final phase of intercourse. Frequent congestion of the sex organs and their associated glands without safety-valve orgasms and ejaculations should not be expected to have a salutary effect. It does not.

(3) Psychogenic or inhibitory impotence is caused by the effects of impulses from the higher centers (in the cortex or the cerebrum or brain) on the lower centers (in the spinal cord) and through them upon the erectile nerves and the generative organs themselves. Various emotions usually set up the inhibitions. Fear is the most frequent: fear of detection, fear of causing pregnancy, fear of venereal disease, fear that youthful masturbation might cause impotence. Distaste for the partner, great joy over good news, untoward attitude of the woman, and many other disturbing factors may cause temporary psychogenic impotence.[17]

SEXUAL ATTRACTION

It is natural that there should be a strong physical attraction between the sexes. God has so established it. Biologically, it is a part of His plan to assure the continuance of the human race. There is nothing evil per se in this mutual attractiveness.

It is a common complaint of spouses that he or she flirts. A wife tearfully reported that when she and her husband went to a social, he ignored her and acted the fool with every pretty woman present. A husband became irate after he and his wife attended any sort of social affair "because," he said, "she flirts with every

---

[17] Kelly, "Impotence," *The Encyclopedia of Sexual Behavior*, pp. 518-19.

man on the dance floor." Yet, in neither of the above instances was there any evidence that any indiscretion had been committed or the bounds of social etiquette broken. In fact, the husband and the wife each felt only that they were being polite and sociable.

They had not purposely ignored their spouses. The jealousy felt and expressed by the spouses was due to a misunderstanding about the natural attraction between the sexes. In fact, each admitted having experienced this attraction himself but felt that it was sinful and therefore must be repressed—repressed only to explode in a quarrel after every social affair.

After hearing an explanation of the dynamics of the attractiveness between the sexes, its purpose, and also the controls we all must exercise over it, the wife said, "I have been very unfair with my husband. I've been the green-eyed monster sitting apart with a raging fire burning within. I've been fighting against any little attractiveness I've felt for other men, thinking that it was sinful. I understand now and believe that we can have a much happier time with our friends."

THE RELUCTANT LOVER

It is not infrequent that the marriage counselor will hear a wife say, "I don't want him to touch me." "I would be content if he would just leave me alone." "Is sex really necessary to marriage; why can't we just love each other and leave sex out?" This last question was asked by a young brunette of twenty-four. Her case will be a good starting point from which to explore answers to these questions.

This young woman, whom we shall call Arlene, had been engaged several times before she met and married Rex on a sort of rebound from a broken engagement to a man disliked by her mother. In fact, her mother disliked every boy she went with. When Arlene was sixteen, she went steady, and when she broke off with the boy, he very soon ran away and married a young girl. This marriage ended shortly in divorce.

Arlene was brought up in a very strict home. Her father was active and prominent in church affairs. Her brother had not turned out well and was a disappointment to his parents. Consequently, they concentrated their attention and love upon Arlene, telling her that she must make up to the family for the failure of her brother. This included marrying a man of whom her parents approved.

They also made insinuations about sex. Her mother told her, "All men want in marriage is sex," and, "It is disgusting to think that my daughter will have to endure sexual activity."

Arlene enjoyed dating, but not until Rex came along did her mother approve of any of her boy friends. Rex had everything her mother admired—he did not drink or gamble, and he rarely smoked. He had a good profession and a bright future dollar-wise. Arlene said, "It was the best catch I had ever made. Mother was happy. I believed I loved him. And we married. But now I'm not so sure but that I was more concerned about getting married and pleasing mother, rather than marrying a man because I really loved him and wanted to be a wife to him."

Before marriage Arlene also enjoyed petting. She could be "warm and yielding." But after marriage her mother's attitude toward sex came to have more and more influence on her. She also felt quite sure that neither her mother nor her father would condone sex except for the purpose of procreation.

To her relief, and early in the marriage, her husband's profession caused him to go away for several months. Financial problems made it impossible for her to accompany him.

But Arlene had strong sexual desires and soon was dating a man whom she met in a bowling alley. It was not long before they engaged in sexual relations, which she accepted and enjoyed, but because this was contrary to all her parents' teaching, she felt guilty. Without telling her parents about this affair, she told them to their astonishment that she wanted a divorce, that she had never wanted to marry Rex, did not love him, and dreaded his return. She saw a lawyer and wrote to Rex asking him to agree to a divorce.

He would not do this and returned home. Arlene told him about her love affair and that she had engaged in sexual relations with the man several times. Rex said he forgave her and wanted to keep the marriage intact.

They then moved to another part of the country to which he was transferred. Reluctantly she accompanied him. She was equally reluctant as a lover. She yielded passively and only as a matter of duty to his advances. Then she became pregnant.

After the birth of the child she visited her parents and

renewed her relationship with a sweetheart of her teens. He was divorced. He said that he was still in love with her and that if she should ever get a divorce, he would marry her.

She went again to see a lawyer about getting a divorce. But again she did not carry it through and returned to Rex. This time she felt that divorce would bring disgrace on her parents and add to their unhappiness caused by her brother.

But now life with Rex became more and more intolerable. His patience and kindness increased her dislike for him. She began corresponding with the last man. He also visited her with her husband's sanction because she told him that the man was only a childhood friend from home.

The correspondence increased after that, but Arlene would not let her husband see the letters. Finally, the rift between Rex and Arlene became so wide, and her reluctance to express any affection became so intolerable that Rex told her they would have to seek outside help through marriage counseling.

Arlene was very frank in talking with the counselor about her behavior and asked, "Why is sex necessary to a good marriage?" If Rex would not touch me, I would not mind staying married to him."

In analyzing Arlene's case several points must be kept in mind.

First, Arlene was preconditioned by her parents toward rejecting sex as a natural and normal part of married life. This had to be met by an objective discussion of sex, including the threefold aspects of sex as set forth in the Lambeth report on the theology of sexuality. This is an entirely new approach to the subject for most counselees. It enables them to rethink and reevaluate their adverse childhood conditioning. It also presents through the Church and minister authority figures counter to the parents. These counterauthority figures carry considerable moral weight and persuasion with those who hold the Church in respect and consider themselves to be Christians. They are relieved to know that Christian teaching places sex in a reasonable and acceptable place in the whole of life and recognizes its pleasurable and natural expression as morally right. After the interview in which sex in marriage was discussed on this level, the husband reported a decided change in Arlene's response to his love-making. She had lost much of her reluctance.

Second, Arlene's unsatisfied sexual desires, which she would not allow to be met in marriage, drove her into extramarital sexual relations, which had been overlooked in her parents' teaching. They apparently took for granted that she would be as puritanical as they. She had never discussed petting with them ("all my friends engaged in it"), feeling inhibited from bringing up a subject she felt would shock them and end in arguing and perhaps crying.

Third, Arlene had considerable guilt about her extramarital sexual relations, but not regret—except perhaps in the first case. The man left town and gave her a phony address! She then realized that his protestations of love were only to get her to yield and that he had used her. This hurt her pride, and also confirmed her mother's frequent statements that "all men want from a woman is sex."

This affair blocked her relationship with her husband. He was becoming more like her father; in fact, he was very much like her father in his behavior, habits, professional standing, and religious practices. Knowing what she had done, knowing her father would be disappointed in her, she simply could not accept Rex as a husband, sweetheart, and lover. The dynamics of her behavior had to be made clear to her so that she could see Rex again in his true role and herself as his wife and sweetheart. Unsatisfied with Rex, she had fallen victim to the Proverb: "Stolen water is sweet, and bread eaten in secret is pleasant." [18]

Fourth, One of Arlene's problems was ambivalence. She had never taken a firm stand toward making her marriage a success. She was like a little child walking with her father, holding his hand, but stumbling as she looked over her shoulder at attractive lures along the way. She knew that in playing golf one could not hope to make a good score unless one took a proper stance. She was quick to recognize that in her marriage she had failed here. The psychological concept of "set" also enabled her to see her marriage objectively—that is, to perceive her marriage in such a way as to reflect the objective facts pertaining to it. There is an established pattern in Christian marriage. Arlene needed to perceive the environment of her own marriage according to this pattern. She herself added "approach" to stance and set, explaining that she must

---

[18] Proverbs 9:17.

approach her marriage according to the Christian pattern and the positive values in her marriage. These positive values were listed on the greenboard as she named them.

THE PHYSICAL NOT ENOUGH

Mr. and Mrs. Doe were as unhappy as any two individuals who had ever come for counseling. He was twelve years older than she. When they married, she was seventeen, and he was twenty-nine.

She had just finished high school where she majored in secretarial work. She had been an "A" student, particularly good in mathematics, and had had no trouble at all getting a good position with an established business firm. They had been married five years when they came for counseling. She had risen to a very good position that paid about $100 a week. She was attractive, smartly dressed, well poised, and proud of her position.

Mr. Doe was a successful businessman. Before his marriage he had enjoyed life as a bachelor and had had several love affairs. He had been in service where he lived in a very carefree manner.

They had met at a dance and were immediately attracted to each other. At seventeen she was flattered by an older man's attentions. They began to date, and he showered her with gifts and took her dining and dancing.

It might be said here that Mrs. Doe had had a very unhappy childhood. Her parents' living on a farm several miles from neighbors resulted in her having very few playmates. Her mother was sick and nervous; her father was noncommunicative and gave his daughter very little attention. High school was a real boost to her morale. She participated in the various activities, did well in her studies, and was valedictorian of her class. But she had few dates. Since she had not had any companionship through her father with the opposite sex and had not had any sex guidance from her mother, not even menstrual instruction or advice on how to get along with boys, she began having sexual relations at an early age with any boy with whom she happened to be going. But she was never content with the older boys in her group. She was interested in older men—and unconsciously searched for the love and affection she had yearned for and never received from her father. Consequently, when Mr. Doe came into her life, she was swept off her feet. Physically, he was not unlike her father. Also, he was a quiet, serious-minded man like her father. So at seventeen all her pent-up childhood emotions found an outlet in her relations with Mr. Doe. They had sexual relations from their first date.

During the courtship period, as related by both of them, they had nothing really in common except the physical attraction between them. They never discussed the future, having a family, or ultimate goals. Their dating time was spent in petting and intercourse. They took trips together to the beach on weekends posing as man and wife.

After several months of courtship they decided to get married. He gave her a large diamond engagement ring and let a contract for a new house. She told him about her previous sexual experiences, and he told her about his. Each accepted the other without any apparent feeling toward their previous love affairs.

After the excitement of the wedding, honeymoon, and new house wore off, they began finding fault with each other and quarreling. She was dissatisfied with this and that about the house. She fussed because he went hunting on Saturday, which was her day off. He complained about her housekeeping and her dissatisfaction with the new house. She nagged him about his drab clothes, and he nagged her about her extravagance in clothes.

After two years she had a miscarriage which disappointed Mr. Doe, but Mrs. Doe said that she was glad. She did not want to bring a child into the unhappy home atmosphere and was not sure at all the marriage would last—"And what would I do with a child?"

Soon after this she left him for three weeks. They decided to try again to make a go of the marriage. But now she began to refuse to have sexual relations, which would make him angry. Then she would again coerce him into having relations. Uppermost in their minds was either to deny or to demand the physical.

In the counseling both of them came to realize that they were attempting to build their marriage on the physical level of erotic love (eros). They had never discovered each other as friends (philia) or as mature individuals capable of productive, self-giving love (agape). They saw each other only as gratifiers of the basic physical needs—hunger, thirst, and sex.

Although both were church members, they had no conception of Christian marriage. Their church attendance was spasmodic. They had no association with church friends. They had given no thought to Christian ideals and how to enhance the personality.

When Mr. Doe realized the false foundation on which they were trying to build their home, he was genuinely concerned as to how they might correct this situation. He loved her more than she loved him and understood better than she what could be done to bring other factors into the marriage—such as developing good communication and empathy, becoming a giving instead of a receiving self, and showing appreciation and giving affection without its being a prelude to coitus.

Mrs. Doe was not so responsive in the counseling. She was not sure she wanted to be married to him. He was too old and was "settling down." She wanted to go out as they did before their marriage. With her job she knew she could be independent of him financially.

But underneath all of this was a developing sense of guilt and shame because of her premarital sexual relations, not only with her husband, but with others. She had always gone to Sunday School and church as a child and while in high school. Her promiscuity had made her feel very self-conscious and guilty at church. She knew that she had done wrong but could not seem to stop it. Now that she was older, she realized even more the wrong she had done. Her confession, which extended over three interviews, brought her great relief. She came to accept God's forgiveness and to forgive herself. Her personality, released from "the bonds of those sins, which by frailty we have committed," [19] could now develop fully toward a life of self-giving and service to God.

She was now able to reevaluate her marriage. She saw it to be a good marriage and that her husband was a good man, faithful to her. He was proud of her, and she saw that she could be proud of him. Together they could build a happy and successful marriage. But not on the physical level only.

She was not sure that she loved him as a wife should but decided that they both must raise their marriage to the level of love found in true friendship (philia) and then to the level of

---

[19] *The Book of Common Prayer,* p. 223.

mature love (agape) in which each would give all to the other. This they began to do.

At their last interview together they felt that they had really rediscovered each other and their interests. They were communicating along various lines. She had learned about his real goals, and he had learned about hers. They were planning to have a child. They were attending church regularly and enjoying it. A real companionship was developing between them. Sexual relations now occupied a wholesome and proper place in their marriage. It was an expression of mature love in which each found completeness.

Mr. and Mrs. Doe were very much impressed with the whole statement of the Lambeth Conference on marriage, the family, and the theology of sexuality. Sex in marriage took on new meaning for them. They came to realize, also, their responsibility to the Christian community and to society.

THE INVOLVEMENT OF THE WHOLE PERSON IN MARRIAGE

In marriage one cannot isolate the sexual relationship from the rest of the marital relationship. Outside of marriage, of course, sexual relations are usually engaged in without regard to past or future relationships, attitudes, or what have you. But in marriage, coitus involves the whole person—mind, spirit, and body. It is a sort of summation of all that one is as expressed in one's many interests: business, housework, care of children, and plans for the future.

A husband who does not keep his wife informed about his business may cause her considerable anxiety about their security and/or his confidence in her. Likewise a husband should manifest an interest in his wife's daily activities, and she, too, should keep him informed about her household duties or income-producing activities. This mutual exchange of interest inspires mutual confidence which has its influence on the more intimate affectional relationship between husband and wife.

The sexual relation in marriage should be an expression not only of love, but of confidence, trust, and security. It cannot be isolated and treated as a separate relationship without impairing the marriage structure.

THE MINISTER-COUNSELOR AS A PROFESSIONAL

The minister-counselor must learn to deal with sex problems in a professional manner. That is, he must have sufficient scientific knowledge of sex so that he can discuss the subject without becoming emotionally involved. The minister-counselor must feel comfortable in his discussion of sex; otherwise he may produce a serious traumatic experience in the counselee. Sex is so important to everyone, the minister included, that it is easy to be emotionally involved or sexually stimulated in discussing sex problems, especially with young women.

In order to alleviate this involvement the minister must study the problems of sex scientifically until he is able to be objective in the counseling situation. There are many excellent books for him to read, which have been listed at the end of this chapter.

A further suggestion is that he sit down with his wife or a fellow minister and that both individuals first go over and score the Sex Knowledge Inventory, Forms X and Y.[20] Then, with the accompanying manual they should discuss the questions and answers. This will give him confidence and objectivity in discussing sex problems with others.

In beginning such a discussion for the first time the minister may feel self-conscious. He should not mention this to the counselee, for that would make him or her also feel self-conscious, with resulting emotional involvement. Just as the physician must learn to be objective, professional, and scientific in his services, so the minister-counselor must develop counseling skills along the same lines.

The minister-counselor must be familiar enough with sexual deviations not to be shocked when individuals speak of them in their own conjugal relationships. Sex practices vary. Oral contact, mutual masturbation in order to produce orgasm, anal contact, and other practices that may not be understood as normal by the minister must not shock him visibly. He must realize that these are not moral problems if they are mutually acceptable to the couple, but

---

[20] The Sex Knowledge Inventory, Forms X and Y, with manual, may be ordered from Family Life Publications, P.O. Box 6725, College Station, Durham, North Carolina. See J. Kenneth Morris, *Premarital Counseling—A Manual for Ministers* (Englewood Cliffs, N.J.: Prentice-Hall, Inc., 1960), Chap. 9.

are simply means by which they have discovered sexual pleasure. Any sexual practice between husband and wife that is satisfactory to both may be considered acceptable.

COUNSELOR—A FATHER FIGURE

As a father figure the counselor must be careful to maintain an attitude toward the counselee consistent with that of a proper father figure. For example, if a female counselee should "fall in love" with the counselor or show incestuous desires, either expressed (suggesting sexual relations) or unexpressed verbally (evidencing signs of affection), he must be careful not to respond positively. But he must not refuse her in such a way that he gives the impression of rejecting her. He can accept the transference, but respond to it as a proper father should. Mowrer and others suggest that

. . . if the patient's [counselee's] attention is drawn to the possibility that she is trying to get the therapist [counselor] sexually interested in her, not because of her own sexual needs, but in order to neutralize and discredit him as a proper father figure and therefore as an effective therapist, this kind of behavior can be quickly liquidated, new material released, and a great positive step taken toward the patient's self-understanding and recovery.[21]

This kind of response on the part of the counselor is interpretative and conveys to the counselee that the counselor is concerned with helping her to resolve her problems by moving them to the level of a proper interpersonal relationship.

SUMMARY

The modern age is proud of its sophistication, but has not learned the right use of sex. Inadequate, improper, and antiquated knowledge about sex causes more unhappiness in marriage than any other one cause.

---

[21] O. Hobart Mowrer, Bernard H. Light, Zella Luria, and Marjorie P. Zeleny, "Tension Changes During Psychotherapy, with Special Reference to Resistance," in *Psychotherapy Theory and Research,* ed. O. Hobert Mowrer (New York: The Ronald Press Company, 1953), p. 569. Copyright 1953 by The Ronald Press Company.

Family, church, and school constituencies need to cultivate a wholesome attitude toward sex and transmit this to children and teen-agers. Reproduction must be replaced with the concept of pro-creation as a cooperative act with God. The Christian attitude toward sex has been made clear in the New Testament and Church ordinances.

Problems of sexual adjustment in marriage are many but are usually related to the attitude of the individual toward himself and sex. These problems relate to frigidity, failure to reach orgasm, conflicts, menopause, and impotence.

The case of the reluctant lover is cited as an example of counseling with a couple who based their marriage solely on sex. That the physical is not enough is shown in the case of Mr. and Mrs. Doe. These cases emphasize the fact that the whole person is involved in the marriage relationship.

The minister-counselor must see himself as a professional and prepare himself to deal with sexual problems brought to him by counselees. He will find no adequate substitute for scientific sex knowledge as a valuable tool in his ministry. He is also a father figure and in counseling can relieve much anxiety and correct many unwholesome attitudes toward sex as he teaches its right use. But he must be careful not to become emotionally involved while discussing sexual problems.

SUGGESTED READING

Bailey, Derrick Sherwin, *The Mystery of Love and Marriage*. New York: Harper & Row, Publishers, 1952.

———, *Sexual Relation in Christian Thought*. New York: Harper & Row, Publishers, 1959.

Bertocci, Pete A., *The Human Venture in Love, Sex, and Marriage*. New York: Association Press, 1949.

Bowman, Henry A., *A Christian Interpretation of Marriage*, Chap. 3, "Premarital Sexual Relations." Philadelphia: The Westminster Press, 1959.

———, *Marriage for Moderns* (4th ed.). New York: McGraw-Hill Book Company, 1960.

Butterfield, Oliver M., *Planning for Marriage*. Princeton, N.J.: D. Van Nostrand Company, Inc., 1956.

———, *Sex Life In Marriage*. New York: Emerson Books, Inc., 1937.

Ellis, Albert and Albert Abarbanel, eds., *The Encyclopedia of Sexual Behavior*. New York: Hawthorn Books, Inc., 1961. Suggested readings: "Advances in Modern Sex Research," p. 25; "Aging and Sex," p. 75; "Anatomy and Physiology of Sex," p. 110; "Modern Attitudes toward Sex," p. 186; "Autoeroticism," p. 204; "The Case for Chastity and Virginity," p. 247; "Coitus," p. 284; "Contraception," p. 293; "Frigidity," p. 450; "Guilt and Conflict in Relation to Sex," p. 466; "Impotence," p. 515; "Sexual Adjustment in Marriage," p. 710; "Menopause," p. 718; "Anatomy of the Female Orgasm," p. 788; "Sex Drive," p. 939.

Franzblau, Abraham, *The Road to Sexual Maturity*. New York: Simon and Schuster, Inc., 1954.

Greenblat, Bernard R., *A Doctor's Marital Guide for Patients*. Chicago: The Budlong Press, 1957.

Kelly, G. Lombard, *What Teen-agers Want to Know*. Chicago: The Budlong Press, 1962.

Levine, Lena and David Loth, *The Frigid Wife*. New York: Julian Messner, Publishers, Inc., 1962.

Mace, David R., *Whom God Hath Joined*. Philadelphia: The Westminster Press, 1953.

Stone, Abraham and Hanna Stone, *A Marriage Manual* (rev. ed.). New York: Simon and Schuster, Inc., 1952.

Wood, Leland F. and R. L. Dickinson, *Harmony in Marriage* (2nd ed.). New York: Round Table Press, 1949.

Mistakes to Avoid

9 It is trite to say that experience is the best teacher, but, nevertheless, those who have had long experience in counseling have learned some valuable lessons from which those new in counseling can learn, and thus they can avoid repeating their predecessors' mistakes. Some of these mistakes will seem quite obvious to many ministers who would never make them in the first place, but there are others who unwittingly do make these mistakes and wonder why their counseling is not more effective.

UNDERESTIMATING THE WRONGDOING POTENTIAL IN THE BEST OF US

Years ago a young man came to talk with the author about a problem. He was reticent about discussing it, but finally mentioned it. He was a fine young Christian, twenty-two-years-old. He taught in the Sunday School and was very faithful in his church duties. The author, proud of him, looked on him as a model Christian young man. In an awkward fashion he said that he had been out with a girl and they had gone too far in their relationship. Here was where the author failed. He was fearful to ask him to tell him plainly what he mean by "too far." Instead he said something rather meaningless about young people not being careful. He knew the girl, and she, too, was an outstanding Christian. What he was trying to confess, the author, by his manner, refused to permit or understand.

Psychologically speaking, both of these young people were seen with a "halo effect." The author saw them as he wanted them to be and would not see them as they saw themselves and as they really were. The "confession" was lame and ineffective. The counseling was worse than nothing because it showed that the author was unwilling to grasp the meaning of what the youth was trying to tell him. He never saw the girl in counseling. He was trying to avoid the destruction of the picture he had in his mind of this Christian young man and woman, so he was completely inaffectual in helping either of them.

He did know, however, what the young man was trying to tell him. This came to him later—but too late to be of any use. As the reader has surmised, they had engaged in sexual relations. This was known because later there was strong evidence that the girl had become pregnant: she was sent away mysteriously for nearly a year.

How differently the author would handle the same situation now. He would ask for a clear statement of the facts. He would see the girl, if possible, and also her parents. There might have been grounds for a good marriage. At least this could have been explored and the parents counseled.

Since those early, inexperienced, uncertain days the author has long since removed the "halo" from those who come for counseling. He knows too well that many outstanding Christians have been dishonest, unfaithful, and unpredictable in their conduct.

Works of religious piety must not be equated with moral conduct. In a study of the role of self-esteem or security in the total personality, A. H. Maslow found it necessary to study each subject as a whole, functioning, adjusting individual before he could attempt to find out specifically about the self-esteem of the subject. Before any questions were asked specifically about self-esteem, explorations were made to determine the kind of subculture the subject lived in, his general style of adjusting to his main life problems, his hopes for the future, and his ideals, frustrations, and conflicts. Only then was it felt that the psychological meaning of self-esteem for specific lists of behavior could be understood. To quote Maslow:

> We can indicate by example the necessity of this background of understanding for proper interpretations of a specific behavior. *In general, people with low self-esteem tend to be more religious than people with high self-esteem, but obviously there are many other determinants of religiosity as well.* To discover whether, in a specific individual, religious

feeling means a necessity to lean on some other source of strength, one must know the individual's religious training, the various external compulsions for and against religion that play on the subject, whether or not his religious feeling is superficial or deep, whether it is external or sincere. In a word, we must understand what religion means for him as an individual. So a person who goes to church regularly may actually be rated as *less* religious than one who does not go to church at all, because (1) he goes to avoid social isolation, or (2) he goes to please his mother, or (3) religion represents for him not humbleness but a weapon of domination over others, or (4) it marks him as a member of a superior group, or (5) as in Clarence Day's father, "It is good for the ignorant masses and I must play along," . . . or . . . , and so on. He may in a dynamic sense be not at all religious and still behave as if he were. We must obviously know what religion means for him as an individual before we can assay its role in the personality. Sheer behavioral going to church can mean practically anything, and therefore, for us, practically nothing.[1]

A young woman, greatly upset by her sexual promiscuity, came for counseling. She had heard the author speak on Love, Courtship, and Marriage and felt, therefore, that she could discuss her problem with him. She had already been to her own minister, but the "halo effect" had diverted him, as it had once diverted the author, and he refused or did not want to know what she was trying to confess. She went away distressed and perplexed. After several counseling sessions and sex instruction including some "do's and don't's" of dating, she had a better understanding of her problems and seemed capable of controlling her sexual desires until marriage. Later it was reported in the newspaper that she had married.

We frequently read in the newspapers of prominent church members, men and women, who have become involved in various crimes. Some of them, realizing their problems, may have gone to a minister hoping to receive some help, advice, or counseling, only to find that he was either too shocked by their confession or too reticent to accept it at face value to be of any help to them.

RITUALISM AND ETHICAL CONDUCT

The minister-counselor must remember that the professedly religious person may not always exhibit correspondingly

---

[1] A. H. Maslow, *Motivation and Personality* (New York: Harper & Row, Publishers, 1954), pp. 24–25.

moral behavior. He may be a rigid conformist to ritualism, which may actually become for him acts of ethical behavior, but outside of the circumscribed regulations he may show marked deviant behavior—and see no inconsistency between his profession of faith and his acts. A prime warning to the minister-counselor is, therefore, not to allow religiosity in a person to crown him with a "halo" which blinds the counselor to the sins the person would confess and the temptations he may be seeking to overcome.

Confession

When anyone comes for counseling, the minister should be prepared to hear any kind of confession. The counselee may be a prominent community leader and official in his church. A woman from another city, well thought of in the PTA and church, whose honor any number of men, including ministers, would have defended against all odds, discussed with scarcely any evidence of guilt her love affair with a man who visited her regularly in her husband's absence and occupied his place in her bed while her children slept in another room.

Why do these people come to the minister in the first place? What do they expect of him? They know their conduct is unacceptable to society and church. They are not satisfied with themselves. They need guidance in self-understanding and someone who will listen patiently, and not condemn or judge, so that they can both gain some objectivity in relation to their problem and make such an evaluation of their situation as will enable them to resolve its problems in ways acceptable to their own moral integrity, moral integrity instilled in them from childhood. We can help them only if we accept the probability of their wrongdoing even before they speak and, therefore, will not be skeptical or shocked when they tell us what they have done.

Personality structure—Freud

There are various theories of personality structure. While the author would not call himself a disciple of Freud, Freud's description of the personality as being made up of the ego, superego, and id has enough truth in it as we see it in ourselves to assure us that his theory has considerable merit to recommend it.

All of us are conscious of wrongdoing. No thinking person would claim moral perfection. We possess so-called base passions which cause us to be tempted by lust, greed, and falsehood. We spend considerable time combating these temptations. Our social life presents them to us on every hand. The *id* says to us, "Take what you want. If you hate, get revenge: destroy, kill. Fulfill your sex desires wherever and with whomsoever you wish. Dominate those around you and have things going your way. Don't be a panty-waist." The id shouts, *I want*. But over against the id is the *superego,* which includes our conscience, moral sense, loyalties, religious aspirations, and social responsibility, in short our ideals. The superego shouts, *You must not*. The *ego* holds the two in balance. It is constantly striving to control the id and the superego so that as we face reality, we shall conform to what is considered normal behavior. But sometimes the id takes control. And "good" people do things they regret—even things disgusting to themselves. They don't understand how it could have happened. They do not understand these two forces battling within them for control. But these people do not always want to continue in their sins, and so they come to the minister-counselor hoping that somehow he may reinforce the superego—their ideals, the desire to live right. This the minister can do, not by lecturing but by listening and suggesting the many assistances and reinforcements God has provided: a formal confession and absolution, the Holy Communion, and daily prayer and Bible reading. Also he can point out how St. Paul dealt with the problem. He says, "Walk by the Spirit (superego), and do not gratify the desires of the flesh (id)." [2] The ego that is oriented toward God and righteousness listens to the voice of the superego as directed by the Spirit of God and holds in control those base passions of the flesh that are calling, and at times screaming, from the id for release in deviant behavior. In spite of all the ego can do, the id will express itself at times; but the superego, if properly reinforced, will soon orient the ego again. By confession and forgiveness, guilt and shame are removed, and control of the self returns to the ego.

A wife went to her minister and began to tell things her husband was doing which made their marriage a "sorry mess." The husband was well liked by the minister, was one of his good church

---

[2] Galatians 5:16.

members, and was highly respected in the community. The minister told the wife that he did not believe what she was telling him and that unless she told him the truth he could not help her. She left, indignant and disillusioned about the minister, and called the author for an appointment, telling him what she had told her minister and that her minister did not believe what she said about her husband and his sexual abuse of her. The author told her that he would like to talk with her husband and suggested that she ask him to phone for an appointment. When he came, he admitted that what his wife had said was true. Their problem was due to ignorance of what constitutes a wholesome sexual relationship in marriage. They were lent one of the many excellent books on the sexual side of marriage. After two interviews with each spouse, they felt that their marital problem was solved.

A minister called one day about one of the young women members of his congregation. She taught in the Sunday School and came from one of the "best" families. Her mother had been concerned about her dating, and the minister referred her to the author. In the minister's conversation with the author, the minister spoke of her as a "sweet young girl who would never do anything wrong." The mother and daughter came for counseling. The mother was seen first. She believed in her daughter, but felt that she had gotten in with the wrong crowd. She did not think that her daughter had done anything wrong but only that she needed some advice. Her own minister felt that he was too close to the family to become involved in counseling. Next, the young woman was seen alone, while her mother waited. She discussed her dating and realized her mother's concern. Then she told about her petting experiences, petting to orgasm, and also having intercourse. She did not want to continue this sort of behavior. She knew it was unwise and could get her into trouble. She wanted help in understanding herself and her relationships with boys. She also wanted assurance that what she told me would be kept confidential and that her mother would never know. Several interviews followed this one, and her mother came with her each time. Plain talk about sex, petting, and marriage helped her to become objective and realistic about her relationship with boys. She learned the "off limits" in handling boys and talked of her goals in marriage. A follow-up interview six months later showed that she had dropped out of the "bad" crowd and was going with a boy she hoped someday to marry. She was no longer promiscuous and held the intimacies with her sweetheart in bounds—she gave him to understand the "off limits."

Personality structure—Lewin

The personality structure, according to Lewin's topological psychology, is divided into regions, with each possibly self-contained in such a way that there may be no communication between them. Hence, a man may seem to be very religious in all the externals, but may also be an embezzler, there being no communication between the religious "region" of his personality structure and his behavior "region." How true this is of social organisms, also, especially of the family. Here, too, communication can break down between the component "regions," or members—spouses, parents, and children— when, for example, husband and wife show behavior quite inconsistent with their marriage vows. Each may be unfaithful without fully comprehending this as being inconsistent with his sworn loyalty to the other spouse. This inconsistency may also be true of their relationship with the children. Children may then find communication impossible with their parents and show behavior inconsistent with the family standards.

In topological psychology the personality structure is divided into the inner region and the outer, or motor region, which is in contact with the environment.

It is to a certain degree arbitrary where one draws the boundary between the motor-perceptual system and the inner regions, whether for instance one considers the understanding of speech as an event within the boundary zone or within the inner-personal systems. The essential task is to determine the relative position of the regions in question, and the degree of communication between them and their neighboring regions. The same is true of the boundaries between the motor region and the environment. Both determinations depend upon the nature of the person and also upon the momentary state of the life space.[3]

These two regions, inner and motor, react upon each other as the individual seeks to deal adequately with his environment and

---

[3] Kurt Lewin, *Principles of Topological Psychology* (New York: McGraw-Hill Book Company, 1936), p. 178.

the demands made upon him. Lewin gives the following example of the relationship between mother and infant in the life space of the mother:

> As an example of a disagreement between certain functional relations and the topology of the quasi-physical field we shall consider the relationship between mother and infant in the life space of the mother. It seems to me characteristic of this relationship that the mother picks the child up, lays him down, washes him, etc., without asking him. She uses direct bodily force in a dictatorial manner. Thus, the mother controls the infant by her will in a way which is only slightly different from the way in which she controls her own body.
>
> On the other hand the actions of the mother are wholly at the service of the infant. She tries to act entirely according to its needs, i.e., the needs of the child, as the mother understands them, have for her the position of an inner system, that is, of a system which directs the motor region of the mother. It becomes clear that such a representation is meaningful when one considers that the birth of the child does not complete his psychological separation from the mother. The psychological separation in the sense of the freeing of the child from the mother is usually completed only much later. At the same time however the child has to some extent the position of an object in the environment or one may say it has the position of a part of her own body, but a part which is in direct contact with the rest only at certain times, for instance when the child is being fed. The antagonism between functional dependency and bodily separation leads to typical inner conflicts of the mother.[4]

Between husband and wife we have the same kind of motor response as each tries to meet the needs of the other which are communicated both verbally and nonverbally. Where the affect of love is strong, the overt response to those needs are effective. But where the inner region is strongly protected by walls of immaturity and selfishness, the overt response is weak, slow in coming, or may not be evident at all. This is why so many spouses say, "He (she) cares nothing for me or for my feelings." What is meant is, "He does nothing to meet my emotional needs. It is as though there were a psychological barrier between us," as indeed there is a barrier in the inner region of the personality structure of the spouse. Where this condition exists in both spouses, either quarreling and fighting re-

---

[4] Lewin, *Principles of Topological Psychology*, p. 179.

sult, or both sever the emotional bonds between them. Communication becomes impossible.

TAKING THE ACCUSING SPOUSE AT FACE VALUE

It is easy to be overly sympathetic in the first interview with the spouse being seen and before the other spouse has been heard. Naturally, each wishes to present his side in the most favorable light. He wants the counselor to feel that he is right. The inexperienced counselor is very apt to fall into this trap and take an antagonistic attitude toward the other spouse. In order to avoid this, some marriage counseling services are able to provide two counselors for each couple—one for the husband and one for the wife. But generally this is not possible in church-related services. The minister-counselor therefore must see both parties.

Mrs. M had a very serious problem in her marriage and consulted her minister. She accused her husband of infidelity and of various threats against her person. The minister was visibly shocked and began to denounce the husband. This increased the woman's anxiety and resulted in an emotionally charged atmosphere which nearly got out of hand completely. Fortunately, something interrupted the interview. Later, the minister went to see the husband with the intention of "straightening him out." He met with such hasty rejection that he went home, called the man's wife, canceled any further interviews with her saying that he felt incompetent to deal with the problem, and referred her to the author.

When she called for an appointment, one of her first statements was that the minister "had taken sides and sided with me against my husband without even hearing his side."

In her first interview she went over her marital problems and again accused the minister of siding with her "when he had not even heard my husband's side." She said that she knew she had faults and that she had contributed to the unhappiness of their marriage. She continued to accuse her husband of infidelity and of trying to harm her. As she talked, it became more and more evident that here was a neurosis bordering on a psychotic condition with a persecution complex due to her projection upon her husband that he was doing what she had thought of doing and was afraid she might do. She cried and asked desperately for help. She said that she did not really believe he would be unfaithful, but some woman had called him and would not give her name. Recognizing that she needed psychiatric help, I called her husband. He was glad to see me because he was quite anxious about his wife's peculiar behavior and accusations. He loved his wife and children and readily agreed that she should get psychiatric treatment. He felt that this should be explained to her, which was done at her next appointment. She was able to realize her need for treatment, and arrangements were made for it.

It may be added, also, that although this woman accused her husband of many things, her indignation with her minister was really her way of saying that she knew something was wrong with her which was causing her to accuse her husband whom she loved and depended on; having found her own accusations hard to believe, she had gone for help, hoping the minister would not accept these accusations at face value but would discuss them with her husband so that she might get the help she was beginning to realize she needed. Her appeal to her minister, and later to the author, was the cry of a distressed person afraid of the gathering darkness of mental illness.

BEING ALERT TO PROJECTION

The counselor must be alert to projection. It is a rare person who likes to blame himself; therefore, everyone is prone at times to project his own failures and shortcomings upon others, particularly those with whom he may feel himself to be in competition or of whom he is envious. The alcoholic is very apt to project upon his spouse his own deviant behavior and accuse the spouse of doing the very things that he is guilty of.

THE IMPORTANCE OF SEMANTICS

The minister-counselor must be sure that the words used in accusations are correctly understood by the counselee and counselor. The wife of a professional man accused her husband of unfaithfulness. She was intelligent and active in her community. She was proud of her husband's position, but knowing that he had become interested in another woman, she was ready to leave him and expose the whole matter to the community.

Her husband did not love the other woman, but he had become infatuated with her and had met her in another city. When he saw her under clandestine circumstances, however, his loyalty to his wife and children would not allow him to go through with his intentions of staying in a hotel with her. She, too, had moral principles, which made her rather cool in their rendezvous. He kissed her, some awkward moments passed, and both tacitly agreed to leave.

When he came home, he confessed everything to his wife, asking her forgiveness. She accused him of unfaithfulness. In discussing this point, the author asked her what she meant by unfaithfulness, she said that it meant kissing the woman; she had always known that unfaithfulness was a rightful cause for divorce. She was surprised and relieved to know that unfaithfulness, technically speaking, was equivalent to adultery. She did not believe her husband had engaged in sexual relations. She believed him when he said he had only kissed her. But in her mind this meant that he had been unfaithful. They were a happy couple when they knelt together in the church to ask God's forgiveness and to pledge their love to each other anew. Be sure words are understood in their true meaning. It is wise to ask, "Just what do you mean?"

NEUTRALITY ESSENTIAL

The minister-counselor must maintain a neutral position if he is to be of any help to both partners. It is not unusual for one or the other to accuse him of taking sides, and in some cases it may be extremely difficult for him to conceal his sympathy with one of the spouses; still, he must try to be neutral and assure them of his neutrality. This does not mean that he is to be indifferent to either, but rather that he is to be emphatic with each. If they feel that he is trying sincerely to be understanding and helpful, they will work hard to resolve their conflicts.

SPECIAL WARNINGS FOR THE MINISTER-COUNSELOR

There are several warnings for the minister-counselor which may be pointed out.

Recently, a woman told the author that ten years ago he had told her that she should leave her husband then and there. When he looked up her file, he could not find where he had said anything like that; instead he found that she had come at that time expecting him to tell her what she felt she should do, which was to leave her husband, and that whatever the counselor may have said, she felt that that was what he meant. However, she did not leave her husband. Incidentally, had she done so, she would have blamed the counselor! When she consulted the author later, she seemed to be psychotic and was referred to a psychiatrist. At first she resented the suggestion, but finally admitted that perhaps she did need psychiatric treatment and agreed to go—but only in order to get her husband to see the psychiatrist, because, she said, "My husband is really crazy."

Playing God

It is a great temptation to play God. It appeals to one's vanity to have a couple lay their problems before one and ask for his solution. Beware of it! It will be ruinous to your effectiveness as a counselor. Also, it may lead to a lawsuit.

More than one couple has come for counseling saying that they had consulted their minister but that he had not helped them. On inquiry it turned out that he listened briefly to their complaint, gave them his solution, and sent them on their way. They have been told such "solutions" as: "You don't have any real problems, just forgive and forget." "Come to church every Sunday for a month and your problems will resolve themselves." "Say your prayers together and read the Bible." "You increase her allowance." "Give her more love and affection." "Cook the things he likes." A favorite one seems to be: "You are nice kids—go on and be sweethearts. You have no real problems."

One minister of a large church admitted that it inflated his ego to have people in marital trouble bring their problems to him. It was a shock to him when he realized that he was enjoying playing God in trying to direct people's lives. It was encouraging to hear him say that he had learned the real purpose of counseling and now understood that people must solve their own problems and direct their own lives under the influence of the Holy Spirit.

Sitting in judgment

The error of "sitting in judgment" follows from the above. A couple come to the minister and lay before him their conflicts, expecting him to resolve them. The minister who is untrained in counseling techniques responds by sitting before them like a judge, weighing the evidence and giving his decision. Sometimes this is done at one interview.

Many people come to the minister-counselor for a judgment on their marriage, on themselves, or on their spouses. A woman berated the counselor severely because he refused to tell her that her husband was wrong and that she was right. Finally she said, "If you will not tell me whether what he is doing is wrong, tell me that what I am doing is wrong. Why should I come to you if you will not tell me whether I'm right or wrong?" It was explained to her that the work of a counselor is not to judge either of them, but to help them come to their own decision as to whether either is right or wrong. At the end of the interview she seemed well on her way to accepting some of her own actions as the cause of friction with her husband.

A couple was told by a minister that their relationship was so bad they should separate. However, they were not satisfied and came to the author for counseling. Their situation was bad and of long standing, but they could never have worked it out apart. If they had separated, they probably never would have lived together again and may have ended the marriage with a divorce. How could they work out a sexual adjustment separated? But after a number of individual counseling sessions and the reading of several books, coupled with patience and understanding, they did work out their problems, remained together, and established a happy relationship.

It is very easy for the minister to be judgmental and hand down decisions. That is much easier and quicker than counseling. Also, it relieves the minister of exposing himself to situations which may be paralleled in his own marriage and for which he has found no solution. In theory he may know the answers, but in practice he must know and explore the dynamics of the motivations which set spouse against spouse and which destroy marital unity. There is no quick and easy patent remedy for marital difficulties. The minister-counselor who truly loves his people will work with them in counseling to find the happiness they seek.

Allowing counselee to become overdependent

In most counseling situations there is a tendency for the counselee to become overdependent on the counselor. In psychiatric treatment this transfer of affection is sometimes encouraged, but the psychiatrist is capable of redirecting it to its proper affinity. The minister-counselor is cautioned against this.

The inexperienced counselor may enjoy a certain feeling of exhilaration in finding that someone begins to look to him for advice on serious personal and marital problems. It again feeds his latent desire to "play God." It stimulates his will to dominate, which is found in all persons. To be able to direct the lives and set the goals for others and to "solve" their problems gives one a great sense of importance. It inflates the ego and soon gives one a false sense of worth.

Furthermore, to take over the life of another in this manner can lead to very serious consequences. Suppose the mental or emotional state of the counselee deteriorates, resulting in psychiatric treatment and later restoration to normalcy. Then the person may find that the solution given by the minister-counselor to his or her problems were not what were really desirable or best. These are instances in which a lawsuit might well follow.

There are many people who ask the minister for advice. Neurotics, unable to make decisions for themselves, will come to the minister and ask him to tell them what they should do. The author has had such questions asked in all sincerity with the belief that he could give the correct answer or best advice:

"Now that you know the facts, should I get a divorce?"

"I love somone; would I not be right in divorcing my wife and marrying the person I really love?"

"Shall I invest my money in this business?"

"I cannot make up my mind; you must tell me what to do."

The minister-counselor must be on his guard constantly lest he be drawn into giving advice and allowing people to become dependent upon him.

What does the minister do if someone does become overdependent upon him? How can he break the relationship without making the person feel rejected?

The answer lies in two directions. First, as soon as there is evidence of dependency, the counselor should move at once to throwing back on the person the questions he may ask. If he says, "Shall I see my lawyer?" the counselor may reply, "What do you think?" or "How do you feel about it?"

Second, the minister-counselor should find cause for not seeing the person so frequently or discussing matters over the phone. The overdependent neurotic will come as often as the minister will let him or will phone daily and oftener.

It is well to discourage this. One should try to give the counselee a sense of importance by insisting on his making decisions; at the same time one should point out his dependent attitudes and that he cannot lean upon the minister but must find resources within himself on which to depend. As I have pointed out before, each person seeks naturally to enhance his personality. The counselor can best help a counselee do this by recognizing his need to make his own decisions in his life planning. This attitude on the part of the counselor reduces anxiety and produces confidence in the counselee.

A young wife of twenty-eight, who had received psychiatric treatment including shock therapy, came for counseling because her husband had asked for a divorce. She was of small stature, thin, with pallid complexion and wide eyes. The woman was quite nervous. Tears were near the surface, and she wrung her hands constantly as she talked. Her voice was high pitched. She was obviously neurotic.

She came to ask the counselor to tell her what to do. After the interview she showed that she had become dependent upon him and thought of him as her father. She was insistent that he tell her what to do. He began to seek evidences of her own competence and found that she managed money carefully, was a good cook, kept her house properly, and cared for her children. As she began to see that he had confidence in her and that she could talk freely without being criticized, ridiculed, or scolded, the anxiety lessened and she began to be more objective regarding her marriage.

The next time she came she was terribly emaciated. Her husband had taken the children to his family and had moved out of the house. She had stopped eating and was not sleeping. It did not take long for her to realize that she needed hospitalization and asked the counselor to call her physician. He found her in a serious condition of malnutrition. The physician and counselor consulted about her marital problem and agreed that the counseling should continue in the hospital and that the physician would treat her malnutrition.

She responded to this treatment and was able to leave the hospital after nine days. During this period the counselor saw her three times. Emphasis was placed upon restoring self-confidence, helping her gain objectivity in her thinking, and realistic planning. She decided to get legal advice, visit a friend in another city, go to see her husband's family, and bring the children home. She later phoned the counselor to tell him that she had done these things on her own, adding, "I never believed I could make so many decisions and carry out my plans so well. I think I can handle things now." She spoke firmly, unemotionally, even when she said that she now felt her husband was in love with someone else.

There is no question that many neurotics never have a chance to become independent because they can always find someone willing to assume responsibility for them and plan their lives.

Succumbing to flattery

There are those who will come saying, "I've heard so much about you and your ability to help others. You have so much knowledge. And you have helped so many people. I am sure you can tell me what to do. I need your help so dreadfully. I really have no one else to turn to. Et cetera, et cetera."

Certainly it is easy for any minister to realize that a trap is being set for him by such flattery and appeal to his ego, a trap that is getting him to hand down advice from the height of his ego-exalted position.

The author's answer to such counselees is to ignore the flattery no matter how sincere it may seem to be, and to say plainly and firmly, "I never give advice to anyone, nor am I able to solve anyone's problems. However, I shall be glad to help you find what you may consider the best course of action to follow and to resolve your problems in the light of objective thinking and realistic planning. But, I can give you no advice." This is generally accepted by people; they seem to be glad that their ability to make decisions is recognized and that the decisions they make must be their own. Some-times the minister will feel that he knows immediately what the person should do, and although he may be right, it is best not to tell the person, but to help him find it out for himself.

Every person has a need to handle his own life and to make decisions involving himself and his future. And this is his inalien-able right. To take away this right from a person is to degrade his personality and probably to make an enemy of him. The time may come when he will realize that he is carrying out a plan that was not his. We see this, for example, in boys and girls whose parents decide their careers for them, planning their college courses, some-times nagging, cajoling, and forcing them to engage in some career foreign to their basic self-concepts and goals. Some parents may come to the minister to solicit his aid in encouraging a son toward a career for which he had no liking. The author has counseled with embittered men in middle life who were failures because they were not allowed by their parents to enter the profession they wanted, felt they had aptitude for, and would be happy in.

One of the most brilliant men I know is an alcoholic. He comes from a fine family. His father was a professional man of high moral caliber. He recognized his son's capabilities and had in mind a great professional career for him as an engineer. While the boy was in high school, the father began talking up this career and how he himself had always wanted to follow it. His son would not be cheated out of it. When the boy said he thought he would rather be a doctor, the father ridiculed him. When he entered college, his father planned his courses for him. Not knowing how to oppose his father, the boy acquiesced. He got his degree and started on his career—all the while detesting it. He kept thinking of the years in college that he might have used to prepare for the medical profes-sion. To himself he now seemed trapped. He did very poorly in his work. Then he began to resent his father for forcing him into this profession. This made him feel guilty. Bored with work and sick at heart, he began to drink. This turned his father against him. More resentment. More boredom. More alcohol.

Let us not become partners in any schemes to make decisions and plans for another human being without his full and free partici-pation and the recognition that he must decide for himself what he wants to do. Beware of flattery!

Encouraging involvement with the counselee

A woman consulted a minister about her marriage, which was going badly. She was an attractive woman but was neglected by her husband. The minister she consulted had not had a happy marriage himself. At times he and his wife were estranged. The woman had asked him to come to her home saying that she wanted to ask his advice. Although at the time he knew her only very casually, he went to her house. He heard her story. He was attracted to her physically, and he was very sympathetic with her. He went back several times to discuss her problem; at the same time he was becoming emotionally involved with her. They even met away from her home because a relationship had begun to develop which was no longer that between a minister-counselor and his client.

She became more and more confused and felt guilty about the relationship developing between them. It was at this time that she came for counseling and told what had occurred. But after two interviews she never returned. It was learned that the minister who had gone away on vacation had returned and renewed their relationship and that the woman's marital situation had reached the breaking point.

This man made several serious mistakes: (a) He visited alone a woman whom he scarcely knew, instead of asking her to come to his office by appointment. (b) He tried to do counseling in her home, which is seldom, if ever, satisfactory. The neutral, professional atmosphere of the office, with a secretary or the minister's wife outside, is a much more appropriate place. (c) He became subjective, seeing her marriage in terms of his own, and felt sorry for her. Probably he reacted toward her as he should have toward his wife, but had not, and therefore felt guilty. (d) He failed to maintain a strictly professional attitude and distance. Each became emotionally involved with the other. (e) When he realized what was happening, he temporarily withdrew from the situation, but he deliberately re-entered it.

The minister-counselor cannot be too careful in his relationship with women who consult him. He must adhere rigidly to a professional decorum that will maintain a certain barrier between himself and the counselee. This does not mean that he is to be cold and distant, but he must not respond in kind to any flirtation or coquetry, and he should not yield to any play for his sympathy. He must not touch the counselee, except to shake hands. If one should approach him for any kind of physical contact, he should be completely unresponsive emotionally, indicate proper seating, and remove himself to a respectful distance.

SUMMARY

It would indeed be unusual for anyone working in the field of human relations to make no mistakes. Counseling is also an interaction of two or more personalities, and all the emotions are brought into play to be repressed, stifled, or allowed to be expressed in hopes of being understood. The minister, like anyone else in such encounters, can be moved toward, away from, or against the counselee.

The minister wants to believe the best about people, especially those of his own congregation. He is therefore apt to see those who come to him with a "halo effect" and may refuse to "hear" what they want to tell him that is "bad" about themselves. Works of piety and religiosity must not be equated with moral conduct. Therefore, the minister-counselor should be prepared to hear any kind of confession from anyone.

Freud and Lewin, as well as others, have given us much understanding of the personality structure, which can be of great help to the minister in understanding behavior and in helping people cope with as well as understand their moral problems.

In the first interview with either spouse he is very apt to hear many accusations and to shift the blame for the marital unhappiness to the other one. Each spouse will want to appear in the best light with the counselor. The counselor must not accept at face value what one spouse says until both have been seen. The counselor should be neutral. Often the accusation may be the result of projection.

It is also important to use words in their correct meaning and to be sure that counselor and counselee are talking about the same problem. Semantics has a place in counseling.

Special warnings for the minister-counselor may be pointed out, such as playing God, sitting in judgment, allowing the counselee to become overdependent, succumbing to flattery, and becoming emotionally involved with the counselee.

SUGGESTED READING

Brammer, Lawrence M. and Everett L. Shostrom, *Therapeutic Psychology*. Englewood Cliffs, N.J.: Prentice-Hall, Inc., 1960.

Doniger, Simon, ed., *The Minister's Consultation Clinic*. Great Neck, N.Y.: Channel Press, 1955.

Duvall, Sylvanes M., *Men, Women, and Morals*. New York: Association Press, 1952.

Guntrip, Henry, *Psychotherapy and Religion*. New York: Harper & Row, Publishers, 1957.

Outler, Albert C., *Psychotherapy and the Christian Marriage*. New York: Harper & Row, Publishers, 1954.

Communication

10 One of the most common complaints couples bring to the marriage counselor is the lack of communication between husband and wife. It is not always known to them when, why, or how communication broke down. Usually it comes about gradually. Jeff said, "We can't communicate. I don't know how we got to this point in our relations. Recently, I realized that the wires were down between us. Whatever we say leads either to a quarrel or to silence."

Without communication husbands and wives have no way to share their companionship or to show understanding or to give encouragement; their deep emotional feelings will be kept within; they cannot give each other directions toward the goal each must see and work to achieve if the marriage is to be successful. Good communication is therapeutic. It allows for ventilation and emotional relief from stress.

COMMUNICATION—AN ANSWER TO LONELINESS

Most people have experienced the painful feeling of loneliness in the midst of a crowd or while staying in a large city. But it can be equally painful to be in a small group and yet not be a part of it—that is, to be out of communication with the group. This may be experienced in a social group, a committee, or even in one's own family. To be out of communication with those in one's own household can produce a sense of loneliness so great as to cause one to feel rejected and unwanted enough to attempt desperate acts. It may also result in counterrejection of the group so that one becomes isolated, lowering about oneself an invisible wall behind which one may feel safe but unhappy.

Many spouses complain about the breakdown of communication:

"My wife sits night after night looking at TV."

"My husband tells me nothing. He eats supper in silence, then spends the evening before the TV set with a can or two of beer."

"All day I look after the children. At night I want to talk, but my husband calls my conversation chatter. He won't listen. 'Don't bother me with that gab,' he says."

So it goes. No sharing of experiences; no exchange of ideas; no friendly banter.

COMMUNICATION—A HAZARDOUS ADVENTURE

Johnson [1] reminds us that communication is actually a hazardous adventure, the outcome of which may be uncertain and unpredictable. In communication one lays oneself wide open to being misunderstood or criticized or attacked, perhaps physically. And, of course, one sometimes intends to communicate viciously, using words like sharp arrows.

Again, as Johnson says, communication may be distorted by our perception of others.[2] We cannot be sure of how the other person feels toward us—scornful or hostile, bored and inattentive, or resistant and argumentative. Consequently, we speak and act toward others as we perceive them. The shy person finds it difficult to communicate because he perceives others as being superior, hostile, or incapable of understanding him. He may perceive himself as being inferior and therefore afraid to join battle with another in a verbal exchange of ideas.

Spouses often complain that husbands, or wives, do not perceive them as they perceive themselves and therefore that what they say is misinterpreted. Only as spouses are able to perceive each other as persons with whom they can share their deepest feelings can they

---

[1] Paul E. Johnson, *Psychology of Pastoral Care* (Nashville: Abingdon Press, 1953), p. 312.

[2] Johnson, *Psychology of Pastoral Care*, p. 313.

then come to that greater understanding of each other where communication flows evenly and pleasantly. They are then able to share experiences, ideas, and feelings without fear.

Rogers views the counseling sessions as a means of reducing the fears of communicating. As the counselee learns that he can express himself freely to the counselor without fear of attack or misunderstanding, he gains confidence in venturing to communicate with others, especially his spouse. Improved communication is one of the first signs of a change in a spouse and in the marriage relationship. It is a definite indication of personality change. Rogers lists six conditions which must exist if personality change is to occur through the counseling process:

(1) Two persons are in psychological contact.
(2) The first, whom we shall term the client, is in a state of incongruence, being vulnerable or anxious.
(3) The second person, whom we shall term the therapist, is congruent or integrated in the relationship.
(4) The therapist experiences unconditional positive regard for the client.
(5) The therapist experiences an empathic understanding of the client's internal frame of reference and endeavors to communicate this experience to the client.
(6) The communication to the client of the therapist's empathic understanding and unconditional positive regard is to a minimal degree achieved.[3]

As the above conditions exist and continue over a period of time, constructive personality change will occur, and the counselee's ability to communicate will develop.

Sometimes, even after the first interview, couples report an improvement in communication. "For the first time in years we talked without arguing." "We talked until 3:00 A.M. about things we had not been able to discuss at all." "I found myself telling John without crying my feeling about his treatment of me, and he seemed to understand and assured me of his love." Such comments are not unusual after a couple has come to an understanding of communication and each partner experiences a personality change.

---

[3] Carl R. Rogers, "The Necessary and Sufficient Conditions of Therapeutic Personality Change," *Journal of Consulting Psychology*, XXI (1957), 95–103.

COMMUNICATION IN THE COUNSELING PROCESS

In every interview communication takes place. There is a constant interchange of ideas between the two people through verbal and nonverbal symbols. If the counselee has been noncommunicative with his spouse or with the other members of the family, but finds that he can converse with the counselor and have his ideas accepted and his thinking stimulated, he may be so pleased that he may begin to communicate at home. As Jurgen Ruesch points out:

> If at the beginning of therapy, the patient [counselee] was motivated to seek help because of anxiety, fear, anger, guilt, shame, or depression, he gradually learns to seek more fundamental gratifications. One of these is the pleasure of communicating, and the exchange between patient [counselee] and therapist [counselor] may become one of the major incentives not only to continue therapy but to extend gratifying exchange to other people as well.[4]

For the minister-counselor, as well as for the counselee, the counseling process, being an interpersonal relationship, has in it many of the emotional aspects of any other relationship between two persons confronting each other. The minister-counselor is not an isolated individual; he is as much a part of society as the counselee. Both have their involvement in family, community, and religion. In addition, the minister-counselor, because of his vocation, may be much more sensitive than even the professional therapist to certain standards of behavior based upon his religious teachings of right and wrong. He is identified by others as well as by himself as an integral part of the religious system of morality. Therefore, he is apt to feel that breaches of moral standards are threats to him and to the Church and/or society. As a consequence, he might experience anxiety in the counseling process as he seeks to empathize with the counselee and understand his problems.

Whitaker and Malone [5] point out the necessity for understand-

---

[4] Jurgen Ruesch, "General Theory of Communication in Psychiatry," in *American Handbook of Psychiatry*, ed. Silvano Arieti (New York: Basic Books, Inc., 1959), I, 906. © 1959 by Basic Books, Inc.

[5] Carl A. Whitaker and Thomas P. Malone, "Anxiety and Psychotherapy," in *Identity and Anxiety*, eds. Maurice R. Stein, Arthur J. Vidich, and David Manning White (New York: The Free Press of Glencoe, Inc., 1960), pp. 166ff.

ing the role of anxiety in both counselor and counselee in the process of psychotherapy or counseling in order to clarify the problems of the interpersonal dynamics of emotion. Anxiety arises out of interpersonal relationships that may give rise to feelings of being rejected, feelings which in turn may result in intrapersonal disorganization of the emotions, producing fear and uncertainty about the future. Many counselees are both anxious and afraid because some interpersonal relationship has broken down. If the counselor has similar anxieties either because some significant relationship of his own has broken down, or because the counselee reminds him of a significant relationship in which he does not feel secure, the counselor will also experience anxiety and fear in the counseling process.

Whether this is an advantage or disadvantage depends upon the counselor's degree of objectivity. He can empathize with his client in an "I know" relationship, giving him such support to enable the counselee to become organized in a new relationship with the counselor; this in turn encourages the counselee to recognize and develop his potentials as a person. In other words the counselee becomes intrapersonally organized. As a result, the counselor, too, is helped to bring about his own intrapersonal organization.

A counselee can gain great confidence in the area of communication under the skill of an understanding, appreciative counselor. Both spouses in turn often find a new understanding and a new appreciation of each other as the result of successful marriage counseling and thereby "extend gratifying exchange" to each other.

AUTHORITARIAN COMMUNICATION

"We cannot discuss anything. Paul makes all the plans, then tells me what he has decided. He will buy things, maybe a car or a piece of land, then tells me he has done it. I want to help him plan. I want to know when he is buying something. I'm no child." The wife spoke with deep resentment. She loved her husband and wanted to share his life—his everyday, out-of-the-home life. She was interested in all his activities, but he shut her out by cutting the wires of communication.

Paul did not realize that he was following a family pattern. His father and grandfather had been uncommunicative at home about business affairs. "My dad never told mother any of his business affairs. He always said that women know nothing about business. Anyway, if you tell them too much they worry, or they want to tell you what to do. Dad always said, 'Don't take your business home.' So I don't."

The counselor discussed with him the relationship between his parents and how he felt about it, especially how it related to his wife's needs as an adult for sharing in the planning of their family affairs and how it affected her as a member of the family. He had not considered how his noncommunicativeness related to his wife's needs, but only how it concerned him as the authority figure in the family. He was responsible for the family and felt that it was his duty, as he had heard his father say, to direct and control all the family affairs. But when he began to think of his wife as a partner with a need to share with him in these affairs, he also began to discuss things with her. He had not realized, for example, that she did not know what insurance he had, if any, or savings, or even how much his income was. As he revealed these things to her, he found in her a new person—a very mature person who could discuss matters intelligently. But more, he found that she was very proud of him and appreciative of his business sense. As the barrier to communication about these matters was removed, other matters came into their conversations, enriching their companionship immeasurably.

In the above illustration the husband's lack of communication showed a feeling of authority and a disdain for the opinion of his wife in the larger affairs of the family, especially those involving business. But there are also those spouses who hold themselves aloof and superior to the other, resulting in their giving detailed directions and/or commands. They may be kind and considerate in all the family relationships, but everything is centered in themselves. Communication flows in only one direction, from the one in authority to the other members of the family.

Philip was not mean to his family, though he was described as a "hard" man. According to his income, he provided well for them, but when he came home, a silence fell. No one spoke unless he asked a question. His wife, Sara, went about cooking and serving supper silently and noiselessly. Meals were eaten mainly in silence. The questions he addressed to others were answered politely but briefly.

No opinions were asked for or given. He made all the plans for everyone, which no one dared question. He sometimes told of his work or related some amusing incident. He showed interest in the children's school work. There was nothing rude or unkind in his attitude or behavior, but the only communication was really from him, with practically no recognition of anyone else's opinions.

Right always

Ellen was always right. It made little difference about the subject. If politics was the subject, her position was the only logical one to take; if child training, she alone had the correct methods. She told everyone what to do and when to do it. She was continually after the children about eating, dressing, and picking up their toys. If her husband did not lay the paper down folded after reading, he was scolded. The house had to be in perfect order all the time. Dishes had to be washed immediately after each meal and the kitchen put in order. If her husband protested, she would argue her point that the way she kept house was the only way and the correct way. Children had to be disciplined every waking moment. She changed their clothes three times a day, according to her husband. The washing machine ran continuously. "She is driving us all crazy," her husband exclaimed when he came for counseling. "No matter what I say or do it is the wrong thing."

When Ellen came, the reason for her authoritative attitude was apparent. She was thin, nervous, talked rapidly, and cried a little, saying, "No one cooperates with me." Ellen was a neurotic. She felt safe only in a situation which she controlled. Any disorder upset her. Everything had to be in its proper place at all times. She had to control the conversation because she felt insecure if her opinions did not prevail.

Her neuroticism affected the affectional relationship between her and her husband. Affection had to be shown on her terms and at her convenience—it was never spontaneous. Conditions for sexual relations had to be just right, and when agreeable to her. She made no attempt to meet her husband's sexual needs.

Ellen's behavior to some degree is typical of the neurotic spouse. Neurotic behavior may stem from some known or unknown fear and anxiety. It may be acquired from a neurotic parent. According to Ellen's description, her mother was evidently a neurotic and unhappy person. She overemphasized the type of behavior exhibited by Ellen. Thus Ellen had a fear of failing as a housewife in her mother's eyes. If she failed to clean house, even though sick, she felt guilty. If she was proved wrong in some opinion, she felt she had failed and had let herself down. In telling about her child-training tactics, she expressed fear lest the children grow up to be delinquents and bring disgrace upon the family (primarily meaning herself for failure as a mother).

She was referred to her physician for a thorough examination. She was found to have an overactive thyroid condition. She made some improvement in counseling, but her anxiety reactions were so strongly fixed that she was referred for psychiatric treatment.

Neuroticism

Neuroticism has not been proven to be hereditary; however, there is ample evidence from many studies [6] that it may be induced in a person by the neurotic behavior of those who create the home environment. In the words of Dollard and Miller,[7] "Neurotic conflicts are taught by parents and learned by children." Coleman [8] is of the opinion that biological heredity does not play a primary role per se in the development of the psychoneuroses, but rather that tension, produced by an undesirable early environment leads to neurosis. Freud [9] and many psychologists have found that serious emotional conflicts in the child result in neurotic behavior when the child grows up and is faced with the problem of adjusting to an adult milieu. For example, such an adult when angered (anger being an expression of aggression in frustrating situations) may

---

[6] See Burdett H. McNeel and T. E. Dancey, "The Personality of the Successful Soldier," *American Journal of Psychiatry*, CII (November 1945), 337–42; Jack G. Sheps, "Psychiatric Study of Successful Soldiers," *Journal of the American Medical Association*, CXXVI (1944), 271–73.

[7] John Dollard and Neal E. Miller, *Personality and Psychotherapy* (New York: McGraw-Hill Book Company, 1950), p. 127.

[8] James C. Coleman, *Abnormal Psychology and Modern Life* (Chicago: Scott, Foresman & Company, 1950), p. 211.

[9] Sigmund Freud, *The Problem of Anxiety* (New York: W. W. Norton & Company, Inc., 1936), p. 91.

lose all sense of selectivity, sulk, and go into rages or tantrums without ascertaining in the first place whether the social situation is one in which anger is appropriate. This sort of random behavior or lack of selectivity in other situations is characteristic of the neurotic and is traceable to childhood situations in which the parental attitude to the aggressive behavior of the child was generally negative and repressive.[10]

Many neurotic men and women, however, can be helped through counseling and become willing to learn more acceptable patterns of behavior. One wife who had been a meticulous housekeeper did a bit of reality testing by going home, kicking off her shoes in the living room, and leaving them there! Nothing happened! Instead of vacuuming the apartment daily, she let it go, and again nothing happened. She now has found time to do other things. On the other hand, there was the neurotic wife whose house was always in perfect order—but whose husband left! She ended up with a beautifully clean house and no husband!

Of course, there are also neurotic husbands. They react to the environment similarly to the neurotic wife. Wives of neurotic husbands describe their behavior in much the same way: he is bossy; he expects me to wait on him like a maid; the children get on his nerves, and he yells at them; he has no patience; he cries like a baby over his frustrations—"I thought I married a man, not a child"; he won't allow me to express any opinions of my own if different from his; he is always right; he's a know-it-all; everybody's stupid: his boss, his customers, pedestrians, my family, and friends.

Some neurotics are so insecure and have built up such strong defenses that they can be helped only through prolonged psychiatric or psychological treatment and should be referred if and when they come for counseling. There are others, however, who are able to recognize their neurosis and cooperate in learning new and better ways of relating to the persons in their environment. As already pointed out (page 219), they learn in counseling how to communicate in an exchange of ideas without feeling that they must be authoritative and always right. This is one of the distinct advantages of good counseling procedure.

---

[10] Dollard and Miller, *Personality and Psychotherapy*, p. 151.

Reaction-sensitivity

In all interpersonal relationships an individual reacts unconsciously to the reaction of another individual with whom he may be conversing or working. This is known as reaction-sensitivity or being sensitive to the reaction we provoke in others, by the cues we put forth. For example, if we meet a person who has just experienced grief, we unconsciously avoid making some flippant remark. We take into account the person's feelings and how our words and actions would affect him.

But there are those whose reaction-sensitivity may be very weak. They say the inappropriate words, or they act without regard for the feelings of others. In the marriage relationship this can be a constant source of friction. The wrong cue can set up a violent reaction in the other partner. With sadistic self-righteousness one husband would bring up the wife's infidelity. It took him a long time to understand his motives and to learn to be sensitive to her feelings. In another case the husband was an alcoholic who had found sobriety, become a hard worker, saved his money, and taken good care of his family, but his wife would give him unmerciful tongue lashings by reminding him of his past. She seemed completely insensitive to his reactions to her cues. Many other examples could be cited. Those couples who find themselves in a constant state of friction and mutual irritation may lack reaction-sensitivity.

However, the learning process can help one to become sensitive to cue-producing responses. Let us take, for example, a woman who learns to drive an automobile when past her teens. Up to this time she has ridden in the family car with little knowledge or concern about its mechanical efficiency, but after learning to drive she gradually becomes sensitive to the normal purring of the motor and the smooth running noise of the car. Thus she is anticipant of any strange noise and reacts to it immediately by becoming apprehensive and stopping at a filling station to ascertain the trouble. She is reaction-sensitive to the operating noises of the car. Or we may take a mother and her infant. There may be considerable commotion in the living room where the mother and family are watching television. The mother suddenly leaves the room. She has heard a sound from the baby which no one else heard. She is reaction-sensitive to her child's cries.[11]

Cameron defines reaction-sensitivity as

. . . a selective readiness-to-react to certain components of a stimulating situation and not to others, which is the result of one's having acquired a system of related attitudes and responses.[12]

A person can develop reaction-sensitivity to the cue-producing responses in another person by understanding the critical points in the other's behavior pattern and by anticipating the reaction that certain cues produce.[13] It can be devastating momentarily to a wife who is trying both to find relief from her guilt due to infidelity and to acquire a new self-concept to have her husband remind her of her infidelity by some thoughtless remark or behavior. His thoughtlessness can cause her to burst into tears or a rage, which may be followed by a period of discouragement. To develop reaction-sensitivity to the emotional responses of others one must

(1)   Learn more about himself and the impact of his personality on others, particularly his spouse and children
(2)   Understand his own feelings and emotional reactions to the significant persons in his environment
(3)   Become more sensitive to the ways people communicate with others —verbal and nonverbal
(4)   Think in terms of how the other person feels and learn to detect subtle meanings in the cues, that is, in the words and actions of others
(5)   Learn how to convey understanding and confidence to others [14]

The degree of discomfort and irritability may increase when one expects a certain behavior pattern to be followed, yet finds it disconfirmed.[15] For example, a husband usually had a few drinks before coming home from work on Saturday afternoons. This al-

---

[11] Norman Cameron, *The Psychology of Behavior Disorders* (Houghton Mifflin Company, 1947), p. 66.

[12] Cameron, *The Psychology of Behavior Disorders,* p. 66.

[13] Dollard & Miller, *Personality and Psychotherapy,* p. 121.

[14] Lawrence M. Brammer and Everett L. Shostrom, *Therapeutic Psychology* (Englewood Cliffs, N.J.: Prentice-Hall, Inc., 1960), p. 408.

[15] J. Merrill Corksmith and Elliot Aronson, "Some Hedonic Consequences of the Confirmation and Discomfirmation of Expectancies," *Journal of Abnormal and Social Psychology,* LXVI (1963), 151–56.

ways upset the wife, and a storm of words was the standard greeting. Occasionally, he would not drink at all, expecting his wife to be pleased. On the contrary. Her rage would then begin even before he had approached near enough for her to smell his breath and before she could detect any odor of alcohol; she would grow violent, accusing him of drinking vodka so she could not smell it, and then become more enraged, thinking that he was lying. Even on those few occasions that she was convinced he had not had a drink, she was angry because her accusations were false. At times she was apparently more upset by her expectations being disconfirmed than by their being confirmed.

Since the counselee must develop his reaction-sensitivity in reality-testing situations, progress should be noted between interviews. The signs of development may be slow at first and manifested only spasmodically and uncertainly toward his spouse, but with practice they will become more constant. The development will also include others in an ever-widening circle, resulting in the improvement of all interpersonal relationships.

Reaction-sensitivity is basic to the development of skills in interpersonal relationships.

HOSTILE AND DESTRUCTIVE COMMUNICATION

Lack of communication also reveals a lack of trust or a fear of the reaction of one's spouse. Let us take for example the man who always takes issue with what his wife says—always ready to argue or to point out a weakness in his wife's statements. His words may be like sharp arrows that pierce her self-confidence, making her afraid to venture any opinion. Communication between them ceases.

Jack had a sharp tongue. His wife complained that his ridicule and sarcasm were more than she could take. He seemed to delight in making her cry. He used the same method on her mother. He and his wife could discuss nothing because he always found some way to make fun of her opinions. He was a patient in a hospital when his wife came for counseling. She dreaded his return home and was contemplating taking out separation papers while he was in the hospital. After talking with them, it was evident that they loved each other and what they really wanted was to find a way to communicate. Jack felt guilty when he said cutting things to his wife—and yet he continued to say them. He had been a soldier, and before the war their life together had been happy. It was after he returned home that the situation changed.

He said, "This mean habit of making fun of my wife and of others started during the war. I was a sharp shooter and often hid in trees or other places of concealment and would snipe off the enemy. It was mean business, but I liked it. I was good at it. I had always been a shy person. I never seemed to be able to be one of the bunch. This way I was the bunch. I called the shots."

"So when you came home," I replied, "you continued to be a sharp shooter."

"How do you mean?"

"You answer the question. Do you always need a rifle to cut another down?"

"Gee, I never thought of it that way. I see what you mean. I snipe at people with words. I have learned to hurt with words."

It did not take Jack long to see that he was still the sharp shooter—still hiding within a wall of his own making and taking verbal shots at his wife, her mother, and others. In his case his insight into his behavior was sufficient for him to restore communication with his wife. Both found a new companionship, and the marriage was strengthened.

Talking down

Helen was quite upset when she came for her first interview. She was a highly intelligent young woman, twenty-five years old, a college graduate, and quite successful as a secretary before her marriage. Bill, her husband, had finished high school at seventeen and joined the army. He had worked himself up to a technical sergeant and was proud of his grade. They had been married only a short time, but the relationship between them had become very strained.

"He resents everything I say because I am better educated than he is. He accuses me of talking down to him." "Well, do you?" the counselor asked. Helen admitted that sometimes she did. "But," she said, "when he makes statements which I know are not correct, why shouldn't I express my opinion and tell him what I know is the true situation, whatever it may be. I have a college degree. I held a good position before I married. Am I to forget all that and go back to a high school level? I can't do it, and I won't do it. I'm proud of what I have accomplished."

Certainly she could not move backward. She was right in refusing to surrender her own prestige and self-esteem. Obviously her education and position meant a great deal to her and should have been a valuable asset to the marriage partnership.

When Bill came for his first interview, he haltingly told about his dislike for school, which began before he entered high school. By the time he was nearing his last year in high school, he became very impatient to be done with it. "No more school for me!" So he finished and joined the army. He was a forceful lad, aggressive and self-confident. He made a good soldier. When he became a technical sergeant, he met Helen. They fell in love and married.

Here were two individuals, each successful in his own field and each proud of his accomplishments, but each putting different values on the other's achievements. To Helen a sergeant's grade meant little. There were sergeants aplenty, some with less education than Bill. To her, a good physique, forceful personality, and strong voice were all the requirements needed for the position, whereas she saw her field as one requiring a high education, broad knowledge, skill in secretarial work, and intellectual acumen. She was proud of Bill in some ways—he was handsome, and she liked to be seen with him. He was her "man." But when he spoke incorrect English, she felt embarrassed and ill at ease. Also, she wanted him to go to Officer Candidate School. She disliked being an enlisted man's wife. If he became an officer, she felt she could overlook his educational deficiency. He would have status, and so would she—more commensurate with her education.

With all her education Helen did not realize that whenever she displayed her superior knowledge, it made Bill feel inferior and inadequate. It was this that made him angry and started arguments. "If you're so damn smart, why did you marry a dumb cluck like me?" he would fling at her. She would cry and say, "I'm only trying to help you." To which he would hurl, "To hell with your help."

But both recognized their need for each other. They loved each other and hoped to be blessed with children. They were happy in each other's company as long as Helen would "stay off that intellectual stuff. She makes me feel so inadequate."

It was necessary for Helen to understand the dynamics of his resentment. He would not have had her go back and undo her education. He was really proud of her when out with others. She seemed superior and finished. He sometimes wondered how he had attracted such an intellectual woman to be his mate. He wanted her as she was, but he resented her criticism of him. He needed her approval of his good traits. He had a strong sense of morality and high ideals of personal conduct. His military record was exemplary, but Helen had given him no credit for this. When he was in uniform, she could think only of how soon he could change his sergeant's insignia for a second lieutenant's gold bar. She never told him she was proud of him and his military record. Now she had to learn to appreciate him as he was and to give him credit for what he had accomplished. She also had to learn to offer her opinions, when divergent from his, in such a way as not to demolish his: to use such expressions as, "What do you think of this point?" rather than "Here is the real crux of the matter." Or, "What you say is quite right, but had you thought of this factor?" "You have good down-to-earth ideas, but there are those who might disagree. . . ." We went over many phrases she might use which would not deflate him and yet would allow her to express herself. She also came to realize that she could not force him to go to OCS, but might be able to encourage him in that direction by building up and reinforcing his pride in himself as a soldier and leader of men. He seemed to be good officer material, but he was not yet motivated to apply for OCS.

When he and the counselor discussed this question, he felt that his dislike for school had been so strong that the mere thought of going to school again frightened him. It now became necessary to dissociate his adolescent dislike for school from school as a stepping stone to real achievement in his chosen military profession. He had never really made a sound appraisal of education and its value to the individual. Now he began to ventilate his early feelings toward school. He had never been a good reader; consequently, he had found it difficult to keep up with his assignments. He failed many subjects largely because of this. He was told about reading clinics. In fact, there was one available in the city, as well as private teachers. This appealed to him and also answered a long-time unanswered question: Why did he do poorly in school and dislike studying? That he had never learned to read well was not due to lack of intellectual ability. One could see his relief and awakening interest in school. He also realized that he and Helen were unequal, not intellectually, but in the amount of knowledge each had gained. He could accept this. He felt he could appreciate her college education as an asset to their marriage and not as a deflation of his own ego. He began to see how he could use Helen as a tutor in his future studies without degrading himself.

Subsequent interviews showed steady progress and better teamwork. He made plans to apply for OCS.

Symbiosis

In biology symbiosis is a situation where two organisms live together for mutual satisfaction. However, in psychology, it refers to parasitism, which is antagonistic symbiosis.

Erich Fromm [16] uses symbiosis to describe a condition in which a person depends upon others, not for cooperative mutual support and affection but for exploitation and the satisfaction of neurotic needs, e.g., the sadistic wit dependent upon his stooge. The stooge equally depends upon the wit—perhaps financially. Both "profit," but the "profit" is neurotic.

The spouse who makes a doormat of the marriage partner displays sadistic domination. A husband and wife whom I saw a number of times in counseling were both neurotic. Each attempted to destroy the other one by the use of ridicule and sarcasm. The husband was the more hostile and destructive. His attacks on his wife would prod her to the point of hysterical weeping, he showing no sympathy or understanding in response. Afterwards he would make a lame apology, but never would say that he was sorry—yet he showed feelings of guilt when telling about these episodes.

The wife would retaliate by vicious sarcasm and ridicule—

---

[16] Horace B. English and Ava Champney English, *A Comprehensive Dictionary of Psychological and Psychoanalytical Terms* (New York: David McKay Co., Inc., 1958), p. 538.

sometime provoking him to anger and abuse. In their sexual relations she accused him of mauling and raping her—fighting him off as long as she could, then submitting passively. Here we have symbiosis expressed as masochistic submission.

A husband whose wife was taking various drugs came to realize that he was partly responsible because he derived some satisfaction in the fact that although he had access to anything he might want, he had "too much character" to take anything. When his wife would take the drugs, his friends commiserated with him and would say, "I don't see how you endure this," all of which gave him feelings of exaltation. He had actually done or said things to his wife which he knew would cause her to take the drugs, and he did nothing to help her—except have her committed to a hospital several times; each time he was overwhelmed by the concern and solicitude of his friends and neighbors, again finding satisfaction for his neurotic needs at the expense of his wife.

A father who was jealous of his son took delight in making fun of him, belittling and criticizing him in such a manner that in comparison the father emerged from the encounter as "perfect" and the son as a dumb stooge.

All too frequent this type of symbiotic communication shows up between husband and wife. When out for a social evening, one may try to be the wit, using the other for a stooge. They may try to laugh it off as "fun" but inside each knows it to be sadistic and intended to hurt.

COMMUNICATION—A WAY TO SHARE

While communication may be nonverbal as well as verbal, let us consider it now on the level of intellectual sharing, or the exchange of views, ideas, and ideals. The personality is enhanced as it is challenged intellectually to expand the mental processes involved in thinking. It is this which makes conversation stimulating. We often describe people as good conversationalists. This does not mean good story tellers because conversation means an interchange of ideas and sentiments. Without this interchange, or thesis and antithesis, there can be no meeting of minds, or arrival at a synthesis. Nor does this mean that a good conversation needs to end in agreement. Often there can be no agreement, but only mutual understanding and respect for the ideas expressed. A man complained that his wife was dull—she offered him no stimulating conversation. The notorious Becky Sharpe never failed in communication. Her attraction to men lay as much in her witty conversation as in her seductive charms. Husbands and wives should be as entertaining with each other after marriage as before.

Laura Capon Fermi readily admitted that she was not the intellectual equal of her famous husband, Enrico Fermi, at least not in the realm of physics and mathematics, but she was intellectually stimulating to him in their everyday life together. Communication was a process of sharing their innermost thoughts and feelings. His genius never overshadowed her position as a wife, mother, and companion.

A wife may not necessarily be able to discuss her husband's specialty—but she can be an interested listener and "tease" him lightly in the area of his special knowledge, doing it in such a manner as to boost his ego and show her pride in his knowledge. And, of course, the same must be said of the husband whose wife has pursued some specialized field of knowledge. So many wives today follow careers outside the home that it is all the more important for husbands to share in and show respect for their knowledge. Each can stimulate the other intellectually and benefit from the other's learning.

Here is a danger in television. It can be very distracting and interfere with family talk. Some homes report that there is seldom a time when the family can engage in conversation because of the demoralizing effect of television. Some families set limits on when the set may be turned on; they refuse to allow the home to be invaded daily and nightly by these "outsiders" who enter and monopolize the family hearth, even to instructing the family in morals.

COMMUNICATION—A SHARING OF ONE'S SELF

Jesus said, "For out of the abundance of the heart the mouth speaks." [17] Words are symbols which we string together to express our thoughts, ideas, and feelings. It is out of

---

[17] Matthew 12:34.

our store of knowledge, experience, wisdom, and education that we set forth before others by spoken and written words our inner selves. We seek to share our selves in friendly or hostile fashion by gestures and by the tone of voice in which our words are carried. We have various expressions commonly used to describe how we say words: "spit out words," "words like sharp arrows," "melting words," "Words . . . a great wind," [18] "His speech was smoother than butter," [19] "Words of my groaning," [20] "cutting words." We thus use words as weapons of defense or aggression, and as means of deceit or praise.

Words are means by which the ego declares itself and may stand or fall as the consequence.

Husbands and wives do not always appreciate the importance of what they say to each other. Verbal communication, as already shown, can be authoritative or destructive and can do great harm to the personality growth of others.

The author has used the following explanation with good results to impress upon couples the importance of understanding the source of words and ideas in the art of communication. For example, we have a husband and wife in the process of verbal communication. Having been reared in different families with different traditions, customs, extent of knowledge, ways of meeting crises, and perhaps different educational advantages, each spouse is dependent on his store of knowledge, experience, wisdom, and education in expressing himself—his thoughts, feelings, and ideals. He uses words with the connotations he learned when he heard them. Truly, it is "out of the abundance of the heart the mouth speaks." Therefore, to understand what is spoken by another, one must know something of the emotional content out of which the mouth speaks and which in turn is rooted in the knowledge, experience, wisdom, and education of that individual.

To ridicule and belittle the ideas of one's spouse because they do not seem reasonable is to deflate the ego—it is to cast aspersions on all that the ego stands. It seeks to demolish the very foundations of the self. On the other hand, to appreciate—although in disagreement—the ideas of one's spouse is to show respect and

---

[18] Job 8:2.
[19] Psalms 22:1.
[20] Psalms 55:21.

admiration for the ego and the heritage on which it seeks to enhance itself.

Many couples have reported marked improvement in communication as a result of the above simple, but meaningful, explanation.

SUMMARY

Communication is one way by which husbands and wives share their companionship, show understanding, and give encouragement. Without it deep emotional feelings will be "bottled up" inside." Good communication is therapeutic. Through communication they give to each other directions toward the goal they have chosen for their marriage.

Where there is no communication, one can be very lonely and feel isolated from a group or one's family.

Yet communication is actually a hazardous adventure for the outcome may be unpredictable, and one lays oneself open to being misunderstood, criticized, or attacked. Also, one may use communication to attack viciously. Perception may distort the meaning of others. The counseling sessions are means of reducing the fears of communicating and lead to better communication between spouses.

Authoritarian communication is one-way. It does not allow an interchange of ideas, but rather shows disdain for the opinions of others in the family. The one who speaks with authority may be neurotic and therefore must be right always in his attempt to control the environment. Many neurotic men and women can be helped through counseling and become willing to learn more acceptable patterns of behavior. They learn how to communicate without being authoritative.

Reaction-sensitivity is essential to pleasant give and take in any conversation. We refrain from using cues which create crises with those we respect and wish to keep as close friends. But in many marriages sensitivity to the reaction of one's spouse to certain cues is dead, resulting in hurt feelings and conflict.

Words can be used like sharp arrows to pierce another's self-confidence and produce fear and anxiety. Talking down to another can so deflate his ego that he will feel inferior and become resentful.

Symbiosis is a condition in which a person depends upon another, not for cooperative mutual support and affection but for exploitation and the satisfaction of neurotic needs, e.g., the spouse who makes a doormat of the marriage partner and seeks to destroy him by ridicule and sarcasm, especially in a social group.

Communication between husband and wife can be a way to share in the exchange of views, ideas, and ideals. Each personality is enhanced as it is challenged intellectually to expand the mental processes involved in thinking, which make conversation stimulating.

Words are symbols that we string together to express our thoughts, ideas, and feelings. It is out of our store of knowledge, experience, wisdom, and education that we set forth before others by spoken and written words our inner selves. One seeks to share himself in friendly or hostile fashion by gestures and by the tone of voice in which one's words are carried. Words thus become means by which the ego declares itself. To appreciate the ideas of one's spouse is to show respect and admiration for the ego and the heritage on which it seeks to enhance itself.

SUGGESTED READING

Cameron, Norman, *The Psychology of Behavior Disorders,* Chap. 4. Boston: Houghton Mifflin Company, 1947.

Fermi, Laura Capon, *Atoms in the Family.* Chicago: University of Chicago Press, 1954.

Howe, Reuel L., *The Miracle of Dialogue.* New York: The Seabury Press, 1963.

Johnson, Paul E., *Psychology of Pastoral Care,* pp. 310–30. Nashville: Abingdon Press, 1953.

Reconstruction
vs. Dissolution

11 Not every marriage can be saved. The minister-counselor may feel that the marriage relationship is indissoluble and therefore he should not be involved in a situation where divorce is inevitable. Let us not here debate the indissolubility of marriage. There is general agreement that divorce is not always the best solution, and in some cases it is not a solution at all to the problems of the individuals concerned. The marriage, whether of a short or long duration, has taken place; two or more persons have spent a few or many years together. These years form a part of their life history and cannot be set aside or wiped off the slate. They are a part of each person's life history as long as he lives regardless of whether or not he remains in the marriage or whether it is dissolved and he marries again.

There are those who never remarry and spend seemingly endless years of loneliness. Some fall into indiscretions and immoralities, which add to their unhappiness. Before a person seeks a divorce, he should set down very carefully the pros and cons of this action, going over them with a counselor. If the person is a member of a church, he should seek the counsel of his minister. But the minister must prepare himself to counsel with the person in order to help him arrive at a decision which will be acceptable to him and with which he will feel comfortable in his own conscience and in his relationship to God. Too many people have rushed into divorce and later regretted it. Some divorced couples have returned to each other and remarried.

The position of the Protestant churches is not uniform, but

all recognize that there are circumstances which justify a divorce. Of course, there are couples whom every minister has probably encountered who take the position that they will get a divorce regardless of their church's position. But even in such cases they need counseling and understanding. The minister-counselor, though he may disagree entirely with their arguments, must still counsel with them as members of the church for whom he bears a spiritual responsibility.

THE REDEMPTIVE POWER OF GOD

The minister-counselor must never forget that those who come to him for counseling are seeking redemption from the Egypt of their environment, which has become dark and oppressive. This is particularly true of those who come for marriage counseling. Because of pride and fear and because of ignorance of where to go for help, many people delay seeking help until they are driven by desperation. They are crying for redemption from the bondage of loneliness, fear of losing their family, and insecurity.

Often there lurks behind all this desperation a growing, destroying guilt complex, which turns innocent stimuli into evil machinations, setting up a syndrome of frightening symptoms. The minister-counselor can offer such persons the availability of the redemptive power of God in the life of the individual. God knows the darkness of sin, failure, guilt, and fear, not because He has experienced these but because He is all light and by contrast knows how black thick darkness can be in a human life. He lived this life in Jesus Christ. Therefore, His empathic understanding of loneliness, grief, and guilt enables one to trust His redemptive power. He saves us to the uttermost from those forces within us which bind and destroy our personalities.

To help a counselee toward an understanding of the redemptive power of God in his life is the special privilege of the minister-counselor.

As pointed out elsewhere, the family is a community. The Christian family is a cell of the Kingdom of God. Therefore, the family, also, must understand and experience the redemptive power of God. Sin destroys families as well as individuals. Wrongdoing can overshadow a family with black clouds of fear, suspicion, and insecurity. Hence the minister-counselor is called on at times to counsel with the parents and children, and sometimes the in-laws, in order to help them know God's redemptive power —His redemptive outreach—available within the family constellation. Only if the family makes rational use of personal devotion, family prayer, and church attendance can God's guidance be felt when the family seeks to rebuild as a cell of the Kingdom of God. There is no magic in any of this—that is why it is a "rational use." Every minister has had the disappointment of discovering that what he and the community considered a model Christian home was in reality hiding moral failures in one or more areas of interest. The family must find its commitment to the Christian way of life and through its members dedicate itself to that end.

THE FAMILY—A REDEMPTIVE COMMUNITY

The family not only must be redeemed but it also must become redemptive. Those who sin and those who experience failure need to find forgiveness, acceptance, and restoration within the family. In the case of the son of the illegitimate father (page 175), we see clearly the result of rejection extending into the next generation. No one is perfect. No one escapes sin or failure. All need the forgiveness, acceptance, restoration, and support of those within the family. In the Christian family the members have an opportunity to reveal to the erring one God's love and forgiveness. This was one of the results of the counseling in the case of a family in which two daughters were counseled in addition to the parents.

I have found the following line of thought helpful in explaining the family as a redemptive community: St. John [1] tells us that "the word became flesh and dwelt among us, full of grace and truth; we have beheld his glory, glory as of the only Son from the Father." The glory which the disciples beheld was not a halo, nor did Jesus go about in bright and radiant garments. The glory they saw and experienced was His love, compassion, empathic understanding, healing power, and forgiveness. This glory of God

---

[1] John 1:14.

can be shown to others only as they see it in our lives, beginning first between husband and wife and parents and children.

Perhaps this is where our Christian families break down: there is no understanding of the role of husband and wife in showing to each other the glory of God.

THE CAPACITY TO FORGIVE

Many couples have come for counseling for whom divorce seemed at first glance to be the only solution, but the counselor did not underestimate the ability of a person to forgive. The following case is typical of many:

A couple, whom we shall call Bill and Susan, went to a lawyer after the husband discovered his wife had been having extramarital sexual relations. The husband wanted a divorce. The wife blamed her husband for what had happened, saying that if he had been more attentive and less indifferent sexually she would never have sought love from someone else. The couple had three children. The lawyer tried to help them to a reconciliation, and when he realized that the recriminations on both sides were getting more and more bitter, he asked them if they would at least, for the sake of the children, consult a marriage counselor. They agreed and came to the author.

At the first interview there seemed to be very little left in the marriage on which to begin reconstruction—except, and this was very important, they were willing to consult a marriage counselor. There was enough doubt on their part to cause them to take this step before pursuing a divorce further.

Bill was greatly confused. It was a terrific blow to him when he learned that his wife had engaged in extramarital sexual relations with a certain man not once but several times. It made him angry. His first impulse was to shoot the man. His family, whom he told, persuaded him not to do that, but to get a divorce and take the children; they were outraged at what his wife had done. But in the second interview Bill said, "I love my wife. I don't know how she could have done what she did. But I love her. My parents are making it very hard on me. They think I'm a fool to stay with my wife. I don't know what to do."

The counselor sought to get him to realize that he must make his own decision and take the responsibility for it regardless of his parents' attitude; that his life and that of his wife and children were his responsibility and not his parents'; that the counselor would not tell him what to do, but would help him decide what he really wanted to do and what in his own eyes he should do. The first step seemed to be to reassure him that the counselor had full confidence in his ability to make this decision and to plan his life either in this marriage or in divorce.

In the meantime, Susan was also coming for counseling. She was very guilt-conscious and cried considerably in the first interview. Talking with a minister for the first time since her affair made her feel very guilty and ashamed. But as the counselor listened patiently and empathically to her story, and without any emotional response but with a noncondemnatory attitude, Susan became calm and began to reach out for some constructive help. It was pointed out to her that the Church offered to her the privilege of Confession and Absolution whenever she felt ready for it.

In her next interview she said she felt better about herself but did not believe that she had any love for Bill. They had quarreled a lot, and each had a quick temper.

The origin of their tempers was discussed with each of them, going back to their childhood. Each was a spoiled only child who had temper tantrums in childhood. As they came to understand that disagreements between them produced crises similar to those which provoked the childhood temper tantrums and that they were following a well-known psychological pattern of reverting to childish modes of behavior at such times, they began to exercise control over their tempers, which did much to improve the home atmosphere.

One day Susan said she had been thinking about Confession and Absolution and wanted to know more about it. How it is practiced in the Episcopal Curch was carefully explained.

CONFESSION AND ABSOLUTION

There is no prescribed form of private Confession and Absolution officially set forth by the Episcopal Church, but individual ministers have devised forms and methods generally following ancient confessional practices.

Perhaps most Protestant ministers today, at least those in the old established churches, realize the need for hearing confessions and either pronouncing absolution or saying a prayer which gives the penitent the assurance of God's love and forgiveness.

In counseling, where confession is so general, the author has followed a plan which seems to produce the desired results by bringing great relief to a person seeking release from a guilty conscience.

First, the person is allowed and encouraged in the counseling session to talk out his wrongdoing as he sees it and feels it. He is assured that what he says is to be held in strict confidence and is never to be discussed outside the counselor's office. Details of the offense are not to be embellished but merely to be stated plainly and frankly. Questions may be asked to clarify some point or to encourage the counselee to be more explicit—but this must not be mere probing. Nor should the person be forced by questions to reveal details which would only increase his shame and not add to the value of the confession.

After the problem has been discussed, it is explained to the counselee that the Church offers a formal Confession which may be made in the office, but preferably in the church building before the altar. In the Episcopal Church this would be at the Communion rail. The minister would put on his vestments and be seated inside the Communion rail. The penitent would come forward and kneel at the rail facing the altar. Or, if done in the office, the penitent would kneel at the desk and the minister stand near.

THE NEW LIFE IN CHRIST

After carefully explaining the practice of Confession and Absolution, the Christian concept of its results, which is a new life in Christ, should be made clear. This finds a ready reception by one who has struggled long and hard with deviant behavior resulting in guilt and shame—some for 5, 10, or 30 years or more. To find that they can be free from this anxiety gives them great hope and courage and of course releases new energies to cope with their everyday problems. The minister has here a "remedy" for guilt which the Christian is eager for and more than ready to accept when it is presented to him as a part of the gospel which he already believes but probably has never appropriated fully in his own life.

Let us consider a case of an unrepentant wife and then come back to Susan.

THE UNREPENTANT WIFE

Eloise had been happily married several years and was the mother of several children when a man, whom we shall call Frank, crossed her path. He was attractive, sociable, and a free spender. He also was married, the father of several children, and several years older than Eloise. She had occasion to visit his place of business from time to time and so they became acquainted.

One day he came and sat with her as she had coffee in the establishment. Then again and again he would join her. A friendship developed. One day he offered to take her home in his car. She demurred slightly, then accepted. Another day he made the same offer but this time they went out to lunch together and then he took her home. He next proposed going out to a quiet place where they parked. She let him kiss and fondle her. Their next meeting was in a motel room, and from then on for several weeks they went to various motels and engaged in sexual relations.

Eloise enjoyed the excitement of these clandestine rendezvous, and since her husband was away a great deal and she had a reliable maid who would stay all night, she seemed to lose her bearings completely.

One day, however, Eloise's husband, Doug, was surprised to hear from a friend that he had seen her at a certain motel in a nearby town. Doug said nothing about it to his wife, but in making inquiries of the maid he found that Eloise had been spending the night out at times when he had assumed she was at home.

Finally, he faced her with the information he had acquired. At first she denied everything. But he persisted in his interrogation until she admitted the whole affair. It was a serious blow to Doug who became distracted: his trust in his wife had been betrayed since she had been unfaithful; yet he did not want a divorce but did not know if he could continue to live with her. At the same time he wanted to kill the man.

They came for counseling soon after. Doug was like a man

who had been ill for months. He had cried a lot, especially at night. He no longer slept with his wife. He ate scarcely at all. All interest in his work was gone. One day he met the man by chance and attacked him—the man only defended himself and left.

Doug related what had happened with considerable emotion. He did not want a divorce; he loved his wife, children, and home; he had a good position. He had "run around" some before marriage, and he knew his wife had had sexual relations with another man before her engagement to Doug, but this he accepted. They had both told each other of their premarital sexual activities. But, "before marriage was one thing. Marriage is another. I've looked at no other woman since marriage. I would never engage in love-making and intercourse with another woman. I swore to be faithful to my wife and I always will be. How could she do this thing?"

When Eloise began counseling, she told practically the same story as Doug, but with little emotional content. She said that she enjoyed the experience and blamed Doug for it. "If he had shown more love and had not neglected me, I never would have done it. I don't blame myself. Doug is to blame." Again she expressed her love for Frank and appreciation for his love and concern for her happiness. "He understands me."

It was not until the third interview with Eloise that she became emotional. She cried during most of the session. "If Doug had only been half as loving and thoughtful several months ago as he is now, it would never have happened. But I don't feel bad about it, except I'm sorry I hurt Doug. I believe God has forgiven me."

Doug in an interview said that he felt that he had forgiven Eloise, but that he did not feel that she was sorry. "She even talks as if she still loves the man. Even tells me how nice he was to her, and how kind. I can't take that. I hate him. What shall I do?"

Doug wanted to prosecute Frank and discussed it with an attorney, but was advised that there was no evidence unless Eloise would agree to testify and list the motels where they had stayed. This Eloise flatly refused to do. Doug felt that she was thereby choosing the man in preference to himself.

Doug then offered her a divorce. This she did not want, nor would she agree to a separation. She also stated that Frank did not want to divorce his wife either. Doug would say repeatedly, "I cannot live with her this way. I can't go on knowing she cares more for Frank than she does for me and our children."

Eloise was afraid to face the consequences of true repentance. She did not want to say, in fact had not yet admitted, that she had sinned, that is, done anything morally wrong. She said, "I only regret that I hurt Doug and the children." Then one day she said, "I know what I did was wrong, but I'm not sorry I did it." Looking at it objectively without seeing herself involved in it, Eloise, like King David, could say that an unfaithful spouse has committed a sin, but shuns hearing the words of Nathan, "Thou art the man"; and shuns saying to herself, "I have sinned by my own fault, my own grievous fault." One must accept the full moral responsibility for one's acts before there can be any true repentance and sorrow for one's immoral acts. So long as Eloise blamed Doug for what she did, repentance had no meaning for her or for Doug. In saying that God had forgiven her, she was merely saying that she had rationalized her actions to the point where she could blame Doug and where her conscience would not trouble her. Her hurt was to see Doug hurt. It was a feeling of pity for one who had brought this upon himself.

Doug's love for Eloise seemed genuine and mature. He said repeatedly that he would do anything to help her and to keep the family together. He wanted to forgive her, but felt that to say it in words was not sufficient. "She is not sorry for what she did, and will not say that it was wrong. She does not realize and will not believe what others say, that this man has had affairs before. She thinks he is a fine person! How can she think this of a man who steps out on his own wife and causes a woman to step out on her husband?"

In one of the interviews Eloise mentioned this phase of the problem, but her answer was, "I don't know. I don't believe he has had other affairs. He said that he loved me. I loved him. I would feel different if I knew that he had been with other women."

"What do you mean?" she was asked.

"If I were just one woman among several he had claimed to love and had sex relations with, then I. . . ." She burst into tears. After a few moments she continued. "But I can't believe that. It is not true. He said I was the only one."

No, Eloise could not see herself in the role of one among several members of his Don Juan conquests. To do so would shatter her self-image, and her defenses. What she did then would not be in answer to Frank's love but solely in answer to his physical desires which he could and had satisfied with others. This would have been devastating to her personality ideal and her belief in herself as a wife and mother.

There was very good evidence that Frank had had other affairs; in fact, it was said that he had been transferred from another branch office to his present one because of this kind of behavior. When Doug threatened to go to Frank's boss and tell him what had happened, thereby hoping to learn something of Frank's past, Eloise left home. To learn the truth about Frank would have been overwhelming.

Eloise refused to "die" to her relationship with Frank in order to live in a new relationship with Doug. It was better, she felt, to try to stay on the hilltop of self-justification than to walk in the valley of the shadow of death. But the way of redemption lies in the valley. To reach the pinnacle of a good relationship with Doug and to forgive and accept herself as God's forgiven and accepted child, she must like all of us someday walk in that valley and acknowledge and confess herself to be a sinner in God's holy eyes. It is not easy for anyone. But there is no other way. God Himself, in the person of Jesus, walked in that valley carrying his Cross. When Eloise comes to understand this mystery and that it is for her that He walks there today (for the Cross is eternally in the present), then she will find redemption and peace. Doug will then be able to forgive, accept, and restore her to her place as his faithful wife. She will have become a new creature.

DYING AND RISING

To die and rise again is the gospel. To know how to die with Christ and to nail one's sins to the Cross, to be justified by faith in Jesus Christ, and therefore to die with Him so that one may rise with Him here and now to a new life as a new creature is the eternal Word the minister-counselor can share with those who come as Susan did to find release from their sins and failures! The minister-counselor must not preach a sermon on this to the counselee but must share with him what it has meant to him and to others to find this new life and to become a new creature. Unless the minister-counselor can do this for the counselee, he may find that his ministry in counseling is not unique but similar to that of the secular counselor.

THE UNIQUE HELP OF THE MINISTER-COUNSELOR

Again, the question is: Why do people come to a minister for counseling? There are other counselors and in many cases better-trained counselors. Why did Bill and Susan (see page 241) come to the author when their marriage was almost on the rocks when they could have gone to a social agency? The answer is: They came because they hoped that he would use a Christian technique in dealing with their problem; they wanted to know how their marriage and a possible divorce would appear in the eyes of God and His Church. They believed the Church might have a solution to their many marital problems.

As Susan listened to the counselor who shared briefly with her his experiences of forgiveness, of dying and rising, and of finding a new life in Christ, her face lit up with the light of joy and hope.

"When God forgives," the counselor said, "He sets your sins from you as far as East is from West, never again to remember them against you. They are covered over with His own blanket of love. When you make your confession and receive Absolution, you will have done all that anyone can do in this life. You will then have told the Christian fellowship represented in the person of the minister what you did. You will have told God audibly in the presence of His ordained representative what you did. And with the full authority of his ordination, he will assure you of God's forgiveness, acceptance, and restoration. You will be free. You will rise from your knees a new creature. One who no longer does what you did. You will literally rise again to walk in newness of life: not the old Susan who committed adultery, but the new Susan who is loyal and faithful to her husband and her marriage vows."

Susan, as many others have done, accepted this, but Eloise did not and lost her marriage, and lost Frank too.

Susan made her confession and entered upon a new life in Christ. Bill, seeing the change in her, was able not only to forgive her, but to accept and restore her to her place in the family. Together they began to reconstruct their marriage in accord with Christian ideals and practices.

SELF-FORGIVENESS

There was one step further Susan had to go. Could she forgive herself?

This is one of the hardest things a person has to do. Counselees have said, "I know God has forgiven me, and my wife (or husband) has forgiven me, but I still blame myself. I still hate myself for what I did. I don't seem to be able to forgive myself."

An approach to this problem is to ask the counselee, "What is your worth to God?" This may be a hard question for him to answer. It is only by going at it from various angles that the answer finally comes: "God came in the person of Jesus Christ to die for me that through faith in Him I might be justified before God."

"Then your worth to God is inestimable. No one can put a price tag on you, because there is no possible way to arrive at your value as a person created in the spiritual and moral image of God Himself. If that be so, and you accept it, how can you not then forgive yourself, you who are worth so much to God and whom He has forgiven?"

It was not easy for Susan to move on to this level of spiritual insight, but she ultimately did. And when she did, things began to happen in her marriage. Not only did her attitude toward her husband and children change, but his attitude toward her changed. The atmosphere of the home became more conducive to congeniality.

After several more interviews the idea of divorce was dissipated. Both said they no longer wanted a divorce. This was not an easy case to bring to a successful conclusion. At times it was frustrating to the couple and to the counselor. There were times when progress seemed nil. In fact, at one point it seemed that there was no way to rebuild the marriage. The role of the counselor is not an easy one; there are times when he is greatly discouraged. But the minister-counselor must never forget that One greater than he is present. Many a time he prays silently in the counseling session for the guidance of the Holy Spirit and is rewarded by seeing open up some avenue of approach which may lead to an adequate handling of the particular problem under discussion.

THE MAGNIFICENT CHALLENGE

No person can have a more magnificent challenge presented him than he may have when his spouse has violated the marriage bond, repented, and asked forgiveness. Then it is that the husband or wife becomes a redemptive agent to share with God in the rehabilitation of the other one. The deviant behavior of which one is guilty may have been expressed in unfaithfulness, alcoholism, addiction, lying, stealing, sexual behavior in the marital relationship unacceptable to the other spouse, physical cruelty, and many other offensive actions which may have imperiled the marriage.

True repentance requires humility and genuine sorrow for what one has done. No one is perfect. No one should sit in judgment on another. Even Jesus did not judge the woman taken in adultery; [2] he showed remarkable empathic identification. He understood her humility. His answer was simply, "Neither do I condemn you; go, and do not sin again." In these few words he conveyed to her his forgiveness, understanding, and confidence in her ability to become a new person.

There is scarcely a marriage problem which does not require repentance and forgiveness. Since most of the couples who come to the minister-counselor are already oriented toward Christian teaching and principles, they want a Christian interpretation of their behavior and redemption. They respond readily to this, and many who had left the Church return to become active participants in faith and practice.

When a spouse repents, the other one must forgive, accept, and restore him once more to the relationship which existed before the deviant behavior took place. Then follow the years of redemptive activity—maintaining a relationship which will strengthen his ability to resist temptation, control temper, attain sobriety, or whatever may have been the offensive acts.

---

[2] John 8:3–11.

Three meanings of forgiveness

The author has found it very helpful in counseling to point out three meanings of forgiveness:

To cover over.   Forgiveness means to cover over the sins, mistakes, and failures of the past with a blanket of love. "Love covers a multitude of sins." [3] Where there is mature love for one's spouse, the capacity to forgive is unlimited, and the dead past with its dead sins is covered over with love.

To separate one from one's sins.   This is expressed by the Psalmist, "As far as the East is from the West, so far does he (God) remove our transgressions from us." [4] He no longer identifies or associates them with us. So in our forgiveness, we too should no longer identify the sins of the past with the new creature (the repentant, forgiven spouse) of the present. It is true that the past is a part of his life history. He did do those things; but they belong to the old Henry (Sue) not to the new, for he no longer does them. They are not consistent with the new emerging personality.

To let go.   God lets go the past with its dead sins, mistakes, and failures, and He lets it stay gone! Many husbands and wives have said in counseling, "Why does he (she) always bring up the past? I've said I was sorry. But let me make one little mistake and he (she) goes back to what I did years ago. Can't he (she) ever forget?" It is not a matter of forgetting but of putting the matter in its true perspective in the light of the spouse's present behavior pattern. We do not forget, and there will be incidents occurring which will cause us to recall the past, but we must be able to be objective and say to ourselves, "Yes. That did happen. But that was the old Henry (Sue), not the one I know now." And with that one should let go the past and let it stay gone.

As a spouse adopts this attitude, he becomes a redemptive agent working with God in the creation of a new personality or, we may say, in the rehabilitation of a child of God whose personality has been damaged by sins, mistakes, and failures.

---

[3] I Peter 4:8.
[4] Psalm 103:12.

The case of Bud and Agnes

The challenge to become such a redemptive agent faced Bud when his beautiful wife Agnes confronted him with the fact that she was pregnant by another man. They had been married several years and had three children. When Bud came for counseling, he broke down as soon as he entered the office and began to sob out what had happened. When she told him, he was so stunned that he could say nothing. He turned pale and almost collapsed, according to Agnes. Theirs had been a happy marriage. He had been extremely busy getting a new business started; he realized that he had not given Agnes and the children the attention they should have, but he had no idea that his wife was seeing another man. "I felt the world was coming to an end," Bud said. "I could not believe she was serious . . . Yet I knew she was speaking the truth. I knew that men stepped out on their wives . . . but I had not. I ran around some before marriage, but never once after marriage . . . I can't understand it. What am I to do? What can I do? What of the child?"

The problems were overwhelming for him. Agnes came also for counseling. She was confused by it all. She could give no valid explanation for her actions and was very emotional. For several interviews she and Bud, seen separately, could only go over and over their dilemma: could they continue in the marriage, or should they dissolve it? Each time they came back to the fact that they loved each other and their children. One day each one said that they had reached two decisions: we love each other, and we want to keep the marriage.

Then Bud was confronted with the question, "Can I ever forgive her?" Several interviews were required for him to explore with the counselor the meaning of love, and love's capacity to forgive—for where there is mature love, its capacity to forgive is unlimited.

One day both came together. Bud said, "I have forgiven Agnes. I believe now that she is truly sorry. I love her and cannot give her up. Our children need us, and we must make a home for them. I know that Agnes and I need each other. I cannot live without her." Agnes expressed the same ideas. This did not conclude the counseling. There was still the problem of the child Agnes was carrying.

Bud next began to look toward the future and his part as a

redemptive agent. He was eager to learn how he could give Agnes the love and support she would need in realizing that he had forgiven, accepted, and restored her to her place as his wife and sweetheart. Bud began to learn the requirement of true forgiveness on the level of mature love.[5]

This led to his empathic identification with Agnes as he attempted to understand her problems and the anguish of her guilt and shame. After all, it was she who was carrying the child of another man. She was the unfaithful wife, the untrue mother. In one of her interviews she broke down and berated herself for her failures as a wife and mother. She had thought of suicide and a few days before had taken an overdose of sleeping tablets. He rushed her to a hospital where she was treated and discharged. This frightened them greatly. As Bud came to understand Agnes empathically, tears came into his eyes as he said, "What a burden she carries! How can I help her?"

In thinking of how he could help, Bud had to understand her needs. They had resumed sexual relations, and this had helped them to achieve a very close and satisfying love relationship. Agnes had been afraid lest Bud would reject her as a sex partner and also lest the guilt of her unfaithfulness would be a barrier to her giving herself to Bud and reaching a climax. The next step for Bud was to assure Agnes that the marriage was secure. This he did, not only by words but by making plans for their future together and especially for their three children. Along with this assurance went the expression of his love for her through affection, communication, and giving her the attention she needed. They began to plan more recreational activities together as a family. This increased attention and the assurance of his love for her gradually led Agnes to be less self-depreciative and to acquire again her self-esteem. She began to realize that she was a worthwhile person, not only to God but to her husband. In the end Agnes was well on her way to self-actualization as a wife, mother, member of the Church, and citizen.

In the course of the interviews the time came when Agnes wished to make a confession and receive Absolution. This was not done until the purpose of Confession and Absolution was clearly

---

[5] See J. Kenneth Morris, *Premarital Counseling—A Manual for Ministers* (Englewood Cliffs, N.J.: Prentice-Hall, Inc., 1960), for a discussion on the three levels of love: eros, philia, and agape.

understood by her and she felt the need for them. The assurance this gave her of God's love for her and the meaning of His forgiveness as explained above enabled her to move on to the forgiveness of herself. But until she could forgive herself and accept herself as a new creature in Christ Jesus, she could not, of course, achieve self-esteem and self-realization.

Then came Bud's challenge to be a redemptive agent together with God and give Agnes continuing love and support through all the years ahead. This I believe he can do. Is not this a magnificent challenge?

What of the baby? In order to avoid any possible identification of this case with any actual persons, I shall answer this question as follows:

I have dealt with couples who have kept the illegitimate child and come to love that child as their very own, guarding well the secret all their lives. Other couples have put the child up for adoption, feeling that this unwanted child would be unloved and always a threat to the marriage. They too have made a good adjustment. In any case the child is blameless and a husband can acquire, as many do, a deep love for the child and come to accept it as his own.

HOSEA AND HIS UNFAITHFUL WIFE

The story of Hosea in the Old Testament is of great help to men like Bud, for Hosea's wife was not only unfaithful to him, but actually went to live with her paramour. Gomer had already borne Hosea a child. Hosea still loved her, which puzzled him, because she had violated and broken the marriage bond. Why should he love her? Why should he care? But like one obsessed with an overpowering feeling of concern he found himself making plans to go and bring her back according to the custom of his time.

Hosea was a country man, so he loaded on his donkey the price of her redemption, five bushels of barley and $150 in silver coinage (shekels) of that day.

Hosea's act becomes meaningful when one recalls the kind of man he was, a gentle, sensitive soul of unquestioned integrity, whose personal life had not been smirched or weakened by moral compromise.[6]

---

[6] Harold Cook Phillips, *Hosea,* Interpreter's Bible (Nashville: Abingdon Press, 1956), VI, 596.

He set off on his sad and painful mission.

Why does he do this? Gomer does not merit it. She has not asked forgiveness. She has not sent for him. Yet out of this experience Hosea makes a great discovery: God also loves his people though neither do they merit it! Hosea and every husband who loves his wife deeply is one with God in forgiving and redeeming. Wives of unfaithful husbands need to know this story too. Forgiveness and redemption are found only in love (agape). Such love is self-giving and is not satisfied until the loved one is brought back, accepted, and restored.

So Hosea brought Gomer back. He forgave, accepted, and restored her as his wife, and she bore him other sons and daughters. He accepted the challenge of her redemption and helped her to be the loyal wife and true mother she really wanted to be. He forgave the past: he let it go, and stay gone!

Bud, and many husbands and wives, have learned this, and both spouses have found a fuller and deeper meaning to their love and their marriage.

The question may be raised: Suppose Gomer had not asked forgiveness because she did not want to come back to her husband? The minister-counselor will encounter husbands and wives who do not want the forgiveness of their spouses. They do not want to reunite, desiring only a divorce. The counselor must accept this, because it is not his province to say what must be done. He can only help the counselee to a conclusion acceptable to his conscience and trust that it may be acceptable to God. Again it must be emphasized that all marriages cannot be saved. However, such a person in coming to a minister may be seeking the forgiveness of God—otherwise, why would he come? There may have been circumstances in the marriage which produced such stress upon the relationship that one party—or even both—sought solace, comfort, and relief from someone else. As a result one may be overcome with regret for the sins committed. The minister must help such a one find peace with God and the redemptive love of Christian fellowship in the Church.

ONE'S LIFE HISTORY

One day, after several interviews, Fred said that he was troubled about a love affair his wife had had with a boy she was engaged to before she met him. As a matter of fact, it was soon after meeting Fred that she broke her engagement to the boy and returned his ring; later she became engaged to Fred whom she married. Although married for 15 years Fred said, "If that man should appear on the scene today, I believe Janis would be interested in him all over again. In fact, I would not be surprised if she said she still loves him."

"Why do you say that?" the counselor asked.

"Well, she has mentioned him a number of times during our marriage and since we have not been getting on too well together. I have been wondering how she feels about him and what she might do should he come around. I don't know where he is, or even if Janis knows, or what he does. But lately I keep thinking about it."

It was naturally on his mind because his marriage had become quite unstable; he and his wife had discussed the possibility of a divorce, and it was on the suggestion of a friend that they saw a marriage counselor before they took any definite steps. The prior love affair of his wife loomed up as a threat to his marriage. The more unstable his marriage became the greater became this threat.

"When Janis fell in love with the boy, did you know her?"

"No, they had been engaged several months before we met."

"Then her interest in him could have had no connection with you; in fact she did not even know you. That was a part of her life you could not have shared. And she shared it with someone you did not know."

As Fred and the counselor discussed the basic fact that Janis's life history had been taking shape for many years before their paths crossed, Fred began to see the necessity for accepting the affair without its being a present threat.

One's spouse's life history must be taken into account in working out marital adjustments in order that one may view realistically the present day problems. Fred had to see that he must accept Janis's whole life history, including her prior love affair and engagement as having actually happened and that Janis had had every right to love the man and be engaged to him. Furthermore, he had to see that it was only natural for her to recall from time to time the man's name and the experiences they had shared together. She could not and should not repress them or in any way attempt to blot them out beyond her power to recall them.

As the counseling proceeded, Fred remarked, "Well, you know, I have often thought of a girl I was in love with when I was only seventeen or eighteen and she was sixteen. Lately, I have been recalling some of the incidents of that relationship, which has made me feel guilty of being disloyal to my wife. I have tried to forget the girl. But we thought we were very much in love. Then she went off to school and was soon in love with another boy whom she married."

"Then, why do you recall all of this now some 19 years later? And, indeed, you seem a bit emotional about it."

"I've never talked about it before. I wouldn't mention it to Janis. I really loved that girl. As you say, it is part of my life history, and there is nothing now for me to do except accept it as such. But if I told Janis, she might see it as a threat to our marriage, just as I likewise have seen her affair as a threat. Now I understand that both of these incidents belong to each of us. They are a part of us."

The importance of these premarital love affairs must not be overlooked in counseling. The author has found that it helps individuals to gain a better perspective of their own marriage when they realize that they cannot segment their spouse's life history and choose only those portions which are pleasing to them. There must be recognition of the fact that what a person is today is the result of environmental forces from the time the person was born, if not from the time of conception, for there is strong evidence that the embryo and fetus are affected by the external environment.

As interesting as these early influences may be, they are not so much our concern here as those later environmental forces which influence our attitudes, traits, and behavior patterns in adulthood. It is not necessary that spouses reveal to each other all the environmental factors before marriage, nor all their experiences, but only those which affect the marriage relationship. For example, if a wife knows the manner in which her husband's father dealt with financial problems, it will help her to understand why her husband deals with them in much the same manner.

Tim's father never discussed financial or business matters at home. His mother knew nothing about the family finances. When Tim married, he followed his father's pattern. In counseling, Tim's wife showed considerable insecurity simply because, as she expressed it, "I don't know where we stand financially. Tim has never told me anything about our finances. In my family Dad always discussed finances with mother and sometimes with the older children, and this helped us to understand why we could not do things we wanted to do."

When Tim came to understand the two family patterns, that the only reason he did not keep his wife informed on money matters was that his father had set the pattern, and that his father-in-law had set a different one, he was quick to change. He realized the advantage of helping his wife feel secure and saw also that if she understood his financial position, she would be able to manage her part of the family budget more wisely.

There are other experiences which are of little value to a marriage when shared. Let us take the case of premarital sexual relations with others prior to engagement. While it is true that these experiences belong to one's life history, nothing is gained by sharing them with one's future spouse. They are not related to the present situation, unless of course they are affecting the present relationship. Then it may be necessary to reveal them to one's spouse, but only after consulting a marriage counselor and after the spouse has been prepared to receive this "confession" and to accept it as a part of the other's total life history. Generally speaking, what happened to a spouse before engagement, so long as it was not of a criminal nature which might later be discovered, is really not any concern of the other partner.

As we have said, there are incidents in everyone's life before marriage which play a part in the marriage—early love affairs, broken engagements, disappointments, and family squabbles. To understand the individual one must take a longitudinal view of his life history and not a cross-sectional view.

The longitudinal view

The longitudinal view looks from where one's spouse now is—at twenty-five, thirty-five, or fifty years of age—down the corridor of years to his birth so far as the incidents in his life history are known to one, realizing that he cannot go back over his life and relive it. His personality today is the product of all that has taken place in the yesterdays. Those incidents and experiences must be accepted. Some of them form cherished memories, some are recalled with shame. No one is perfect. Anyone who looks for a perfect spouse or marries believing he has found one is headed for disappointment. As unpleasant experiences of former years are made known, either intentionally revealed by one's spouse or inadvertently discovered, one must realize that these are only segments of the life history, which the longitudinal view accepts along with the spouse's good experiences. They are to be accepted in love. Mature love overlooks the 40 per cent of unpleasant incidents in one's life history in order to appreciate the 60 per cent of good and wholesome incidents. Even when one feels this is reversed, with 60 per cent bad and only 40 per cent good, it is still possible for love to forgive and become a strengthening agent to encourage a person to achieve his best according to his potentialities. The longitudinal view can do much to help a person understand another and to help work out a good marital relationship.

The cross-sectional view

Many people, however, are prone to highlight segmental behavior of their spouses. They take a cross-sectional view and magnify some past incident in the life history out of all proportion to the whole. That is what Fred was doing in regard to Janis's early love affair. The crisis of marital discord caused him to "blow up" that early incident to where he was visualizing her girlhood sweetheart returning and carrying her off! He had also begun to take a cross section out of his own early life and try to relive it again! Impossible.

A young man's father and mother had filed for divorce but, after counseling, had dropped the suit and were reunited. This young man was resentful toward his father for past cruelty to his mother and himself, and refused to accept him in the home. He took a cross-sectional view of his father's life, picking out only the unpleasant incidents and humiliating experiences and magnifying them to such a point that he could see none of the good traits in his father.

As he and the counselor analysed the situation, he began to realize that all of those incidents, as painful as they were, were only segments of his father's life history and not the whole of it. Even as he himself had unlovely segments in his life and would not want them picked out and magnified, but would rather have his life viewed longitudinally, so he must try to see and understand his father.

"After all," said the counselor in summarizing, "your father is not the man he was. He has made remarkable changes in his life and has asked forgiveness of your mother and of you. He is now going in a new direction, but to reach his goal of a good, stable, trustworthy husband and father, he needs your belief in him and appreciation of him. All that happened in the past is admitted. It is factual. He knows that you and your mother know it. But the good things in his past life and his present behavior are also factual. They, too, are a part of his life history and must be appreciated."

The son said, "I feel better about him now. I was really hard on him. Do you think God will forgive me?"

"Yes, if you are genuinely sorry, God will forgive you. But will you forgive yourself?"

This was not easy for him to work through for he was conscientious and religious-minded. But as he came to look at himself longitudinally and appreciate his good traits, he realized that it was unfair to God who had forgiven him and to himself to pick out this recent cross section of his life and let it overshadow the whole, including the many happy past occasions in the father-son relationship.

A longitudinal study of one's life under the guidance of a minister-counselor can be of great help to a person by enabling him to see his life history as a continuing process, ever changing to meet new challenges, sometimes heading into dead-end streets, at times taking on bad habits, again striving to reach high goals of achievement, but always involving the same person and a child of God: one whom God loves and whom the Holy Spirit is ever ready to guide toward the fulfillment of the purpose God has planned for that life. Self-acceptance as a worthwhile person in God's sight and the acknowledgment that much of his life has been good will enable him to plan so that the rest of his life may be better and he may reach the end with a sense of having accomplished worthwhile goals.

Making over one's spouse

No one is perfect, and no one is likely to come up to all the expectations of one's spouse. A friend may be considered a reasonably "perfect" individual, but one does not live in the intimacy of marriage with a friend. And it is in the marriage relationships that one's real self is more completely revealed than in any other.

The romance of courtship puts a "halo" over a person, which may shine brighter as the marriage date approaches, only to diminish suddenly and sometimes to disappear completely soon after the marriage. This is due to the fact that before marriage there are very definite goals to be considered—the conjugal union of the man and woman, a lasting companionship, and the establishment of a family. Nothing is allowed to thwart the attainment of these objectives. Therefore, whatever may be unacceptable to the other partner is fairly well inhibited from expression by word or behavior.

However, after the solemnization of the marriage has set up a legal relationship, there is less need for one to inhibit any sort of speech or behavior. The long pent-up and repressed words and acts can now be overtly revealed. The thoughtful lover may change into a selfish domineering husband. The sweet, demure "girl of his dreams" may become a clever, scheming wife who puts a price tag on conjugal affection.

As they settle down to the routine of married life, each becomes more and more confirmed in his ways. If the other spouse complains, it only causes the tense situation between them to crystallize.

Sometimes one spouse decides to make over the other one. There are ways to help people change their behavior patterns, and many a wife or husband has changed his whole personality after living with his spouse for a time. But the change is more apt to come in response to new stimuli provided by the spouse in his reaction in the interpersonal relationships than by direct urging, nagging, or suggestion. To set out to make one's spouse over into a preconceived stereotype of the kind of person one thinks the spouse should become is sure to provoke resentment and opposition. It is playing God with the personality of another person, which no one has a right to do.

A personality relieved of its fears, anxieties, resentments, and feelings of inferiority and inadequacy will strive to enhance itself and become the kind of self God in His wisdom would have it be. By trying to understand the source of a wife's or husband's fears and anxieties, one can do much to release the energies needed for the enhancement of the personality, thereby seeing her or him become a better-adjusted individual in the environment of the family. He or she may not become the stereotype the other desired, but may become a person who expresses in the marriage relationship the essence of mature love and companionship.

Ned and Emily presented a case in point. When Emily came for her first interview, she sat down wearily, saying. "I'm completely worn out. I'll never be able to make Ned into the man I want him to be. For 10 years I've struggled to make him over. It can't be done!"

"What is it you want him to be?" the counselor asked.

"I want him to be more responsible around the house; to get a better job. He's not earning all he could in his profession. I want him to go out more, we just stay at home."

Emily had been trying a direct approach. She ridiculed, nagged, and cajoled. Ned was "fed up with it."

"I'm ready to quit," he said. "I've begged her to stay off my back. She's a regular hellcat. Says I'm no good because I won't seek another job. I like what I'm doing. She blames me because I like to read at night. I play with the children, but she thinks that is all I should do. Calls me a lousy father. Well, maybe I am. But she is a sorry mother. She lets the servant raise the kids while she plays bridge. But if she doesn't get off my back, she's going to wake up some morning and I'll be gone."

Emily and Ned were both well educated and well read. They lived comfortably but with very little real companionship.

Emily was quick to see the fallacy of her approach. Ned readily admitted that he could change and would like to but that he would not be forced by Emily into changing. His life was his and he would "live it as I damn well please."

The more Emily cajoled him, the more he stiffened, so Emily decided she would have to change her tactics if the marriage was to be saved. She was helped to see that first she must understand Ned's life history, which in turn would enable her to understand his behavior pattern.

Ned and I went over his life history very carefully. His father had died when he was five years of age. His mother worked, and he had been reared by a grandmother and a maiden aunt with whom he lived alternately until he went off to college. There was no man for him to identify with, no man to set before him a father and husband's role. Being shuttled between two households made him feel insecure. He found it easy to shirk responsibility. His grandmother was severe and his aunt lax. When his mother visited them, she tried unsuccessfully to exercise discipline but only added to Ned's confusion.

Emily, by her actions, had actually come on to the scene as another woman in the same category with his grandmother, aunt, and mother. Her methods provoked emotional crises which resulted in the renewal of Ned's juvenile patterns of behavior.

According to both of them, before their marriage they had enjoyed a fine relationship. Ned seemed to want to do whatever Emily suggested. She was equally willing to give in to his suggestions. Soon after marriage, she became more and more insistent that he set his life to a mold she had brought to the marriage.

As Emily came to a better understanding of Ned, she decided that she would forget about her mold and would encourage Ned to develop his own potentialities as a husband and father.

One day, after several interviews with each of them, Ned said, "Emily certainly has changed. She doesn't jump on me any more for reading, or for not playing with the children. She hasn't even asked me to do anything around the house—not even to mow the lawn [which Emily had said was growing up in weeds]. What a relief to have her off my back!"

At a later interview Emily reported that Ned and she had spent an evening just talking "like we did before we were married" and that Ned had been playing with the children before supper and had brought home a football which he and the two boys were throwing. "Believe it or not," she said, "he finally mowed the yard without my saying anything, and the boys helped him!"

"And what did you say about all this?"

"I told him how happy I was to see him and the boys having such a good time together. And I told him the yard looked beautiful and that I was proud of him."

Emily gave up trying to make Ned over; instead, she began creating an atmosphere conducive to the enhancement of Ned's personality as a unique individual; along with it, she, herself, found an environment conducive to the enhancement of her personality.

To know and appreciate the life history of one's spouse gives one a perspective in meeting the many problems which arise in working out a good marital relationship. No two people are alike. There are no stereotypes that fit any two people. Every one is entitled to an opportunity to be himself, and if given a fair chance will more often than not be a good husband or wife and parent.

One's life history flows on from conception to death like a river meandering among familiar and strange environments and subject to all kinds of hazards. It can be controlled and directed, but to stop its flow or change its course abruptly will cause overflowing of its banks, and destruction.

WEAVING A PATTERN FOR A CHRISTIAN MARRIAGE

Lester and Jackie had been married only a short time. There were no children; though each wanted children, they thought it best to postpone having any until they themselves felt that their own adjustment to each other had been made. But almost from the beginning of their marriage there had been friction. He had been brought up in a home in which the father dominated and she in a home in which the mother dominated. Lester and Jackie pulled not with but against each other. There was no conception of partnership but only of competition. Each was overcritical of the other.

One day a real breakthrough came when Jackie announced to the counselor at the first of the interview, "I believe we are beginning to weave together." Asked to explain, she said in substance, "Well, to weave a piece of cloth there must be the warp and the woof. You can do nothing with either; you must have both, and a design to go by. We have had no pattern. We've gotten the strands all tangled up. Each of us seems to be following a different pattern —or maybe no pattern." In order to clarify this line of thought to see what a discussion of the weaving process could provide in helping Lester and Jackie to weave the pattern of a happy and successful marriage, the greenboard was used. She was to take this up later, with Lester, and the counselor was to go over it with him also in his next interview. This was done with immediate response from Lester in a cooperative effort with Jackie. (Since the author had once worked for several years among Japanese weavers of silk brocades on hand looms, he was familiar with the process.) The following was developed in the interview:

The design

Before one starts to weave, one must have in mind the design. This may be discussed with the weaver or selected from a number of designs already drawn. For example, in Christian marriage we have a design which God has given to us in the Bible. We find it described in various places in the Old and New Testaments, e.g., Gen. 1:27, 28; 2:23, 24; I Cor. 7:2–5; 13:4–8, 13; Eph. 5:22–33.[7] We may say then that the design for a Christian marriage is given to us by God through scriptural teaching.

The artist

The next step is to find an artist who will draw and paint the design in color according to the specifications. In Christian marriage the artist is the Church and one might also say the social structure in which one lives, which includes the State. Thus the Christian concept of marriage is the product of several artists and varies somewhat from culture to culture, even among Christians.

The pattern

After the design had been drawn in color, pattern cards must be made. These are perforated cards linked together which go on the loom. They engage pegs on a revolving drum, which picks up the different colored threads on the warp as the shuttle is shot through to weave the design. The working pattern to weave a Christian marriage is the marriage service, or in the Protestant Episcopal Church, The Declaration of Intention (page 313) together with The Form of Solemnization of Matrimony.[8] Also, we must include in this pattern the statements on marriage drawn up by representative churches.[9] The pattern is a good one, well tried and proven, and if truly followed, should result in a happy and successful marriage.

---

[7] A larger list for Scripture references pertaining to marriage may be found in Morris, *Premarital Counseling—A Manual for Ministers,* pp. 204–6.

[8] *The Book of Common Prayer,* p. 300.

[9] Such statements may be found in the Appendix to Morris, *Premarital Counseling—A Manual for Ministers.* Statements are by The Protestant Episcopal Church, the Methodist Church, the Presbyterian Church in the United States, and The United Lutheran Church in America.

The material

To spend one's life weaving cheap and weak material would hardly be considered economical, and the weaving of a good marriage is a daily task year in and year out. Therefore, one should be sure that the material for the weaving is the finest available. This is where preparation for marriage is of prime importance. It is woefully lacking in our American religious and educational institutions. Many of our young people fall in love and marry without any conception of a goal, design, or pattern. They just get married.

But our problem in the marriage-counseling session concerns two people who are married for better or worse. What can they do about the material? Actually, in the case of Lester and Jackie, there was good material, but not recognized as such. On the positive side, both were college graduates, held good positions, and were personable. On the negative side, they belonged to different churches about which they quarreled; one was from a broken home, the other a family in which "there had never been the disgrace of divorce"; she was not sure of the right use of sex in marriage, which made sexual adjustment difficult; his mother interfered; her parents were overprotective. During the counseling much improvement was made in correcting these negative elements so that one might say the material was reasonably good and with proper use could be woven into a very stable and satisfying marriage with much happiness for both partners. Had they been thoroughly prepared for marriage they might have chosen different partners, but couples must deal with where they are, not where they might have been. There is no way to go back and do it over. And as has already been said, divorce is not usually an answer.

The weaving

Weaving takes place only while the loom is being operated. In marriage not much can be woven if there is no communication or if one partner withdraws, pouts, and gives the other one "the silent treatment." No sexual adjustment can be made if the sexual relationship is on a "buying and selling" or "punishment and reward basis." The loom of marriage is kept in motion as each spouse reaches out to the other in sacrificial, steadfast, and mature love.

This reaching out must be an ongoing process affecting every area of the marital relationship.

As these thoughts of weaving were shared between Lester and Jackie and discussed with them separately and together in the counseling, they began to weave what should become in later years a beautiful example of Christian marriage.

CREATIVITY—THE KEY TO REHABILITATION

Alan came for counseling with the following brief description from a referral agency: alcoholic, psychopathic, immature, promiscuous. He was indeed such a person. He had received treatment in two institutions with no improvement. When first seen in counseling, he was drinking periodically and keeping a woman and her two children. His wife had consulted a lawyer concerning a separation and possibly a divorce, but because she still loved her husband and wanted to save the marriage if possible, she came for counseling; later her husband came.

He was a very likeable person and in spite of his behavior held a responsible job. In fact, he had worked regularly in his job for 15 years and was in line for promotion. He would have been promoted already had he not been absent so often because of his drinking. To be able to hold such a position raised the question of the correctness of the diagnosis given above.

Alan's self-image was very disturbing to him. He had begun drinking at about seventeen years of age. Instead of going to college he joined the army. After serving his enlistment period, he returned home, married, and got the position he now held. A few years prior to coming for counseling his drinking began to increase, and he had his first affair with a woman since his marriage. He experienced considerable remorse from which he sought escape in alcohol, but soon after he became involved with the present woman. He had stopped attending church, although at one time he had been on the official board.

He was very sincere in describing his behavior and expressed a strong desire to create for himself a new self-image.

He took four positive steps toward that end: he stopped drinking, began attending AA, cut loose from the woman, and began attending church with his wife and children. At first Alan felt strange going to church, knowing that others present knew something of the kind of life he had been leading. Thus, to declare himself a new person was not easy to do. But he expressed it somewhat in these words, "After all it is my life. I know what I want to be. If I seem hypocritical to others now, I can only hope that in time they will recognize the change in me."

His wife, who had been nagging him about his former behavior, stopped doing so. She forgave him and accepted him as he now presented himself: a new person. Of course she was filled with doubts at times but persisted in believing that he had changed.

Before coming for counseling Alan had bought a house which was in considerable need of repair. It was in a more desirable part of town than where he was living. His wife complained that he had been dawdling in fixing it up. Months went by with nothing done. She was anxious to move.

Now the interesting part here is that as Alan began to reshape his self-image, his interest in repairing the house increased. It came to symbolize, unconsciously to him, the repairing and rebuilding of his own character and personality. He got off from work at 4:30 P.M. and went each day from his job to the house and worked until dark. As it was, he had two or three hours to work on the house. On weekends the family went together to work so that it became a family project. Alan was an excellent carpenter and cabinetmaker. In early fall the house was completed, and the family moved in.

He turned an old garage into a cabinet shop where his creative activity with wood, which he said he "loves to touch and make into useful things," continued. He found new interests in church and community and was greatly pleased when asked to join a civic club through which he began working with boys.

A function of counseling is to help individuals realize their creative ability and begin to express creativity in daily life. Life is very dull, drab, and uninteresting for countless people. This is particularly true of those who are tied to a machine or a production line where they endlessly repeat a manual act. They are starved for romanticism, creativity, and the zest for living. In many cases both husband and wife work, often on different shifts. Their recreational hours together are few. Some have very shallow resources for intellectual stimulation. They are bored. Is there any wonder that they are subject to flirtations, clandestine affairs, alcoholic indulgence? The counselor can often find in the counselee latent potentialities for creative work and with imagination can indicate ways in which such activity may be developed: a workshop such as Alan has, scouting, night school, extension courses, fishing, camping, photography, and many, many other activities. Creativity is the answer to boredom and the key to the rehabilitation of the personality.

COUNSELING THE REMARRIED-DIVORCED

Divorce may not be an answer to marital storm and tumult, the only result being another unhappy marriage. But couples do get divorces, and one or both partners may marry again. Soon, however, when the glow of the honeymoon has faded, and they settle down to the routine of married life, the trouble in the first marriage may begin all over again. It is as though the quarrels of the first marriage had been taped and were now being played back with the names of the former spouses changed to those of the present ones. Soon they may be seeking another divorce. There are individuals who may be described as divorce prone: getting out of one marriage and into another, as though playing some sort of game.

Can remarried divorced people, having difficulty in the second, third, or later marriage, be helped to settle down into a stable marriage? Some may be helped, but in the author's counseling experience he has found many of these people to be immature, selfish, and neurotic. Prolonged therapy may help a few. Of course there are cases of a first marriage which should never have taken place. The couple was mismatched and the odds against a successful marriage were too great. Divorcees of such a marriage have a chance for success in a second marriage equal to that of couples marrying for the first time. This statement, however, must be qualified. If either spouse in the first marriage was neurotic and therefore married a partner selected on the basis of a neurotic quest, that individual might marry the same kind of partner in the second or third marriage. There are many variables to be considered in multiple marriages.

In counseling such couples, it is best to begin with the first marriage, the causes for the marriage and its breakup. The same procedure is followed with the second marriage and on down to the present marriage. A fairly well-defined marriage pattern may begin to form. In the process of counseling, the parental marriages of each spouse and childhood conditioning are also discussed.

Mr. and Mrs. Wheat were each on the point of a third divorce. They were a well-to-do couple with ample income. They occupied separate bedrooms. Besides an occasional meal together they were merely living in the same house. They entertained lavishly, traveled a great deal, and enjoyed a life of leisure. This marriage had lasted 10 years, longer than any of the previous ones.

The wife's main complaint was that she was tired of her husband—he bored her. Also she had rejected him as a sex partner because "sex wears me out. It takes weeks for me to recover my strength [sic] after intercourse." They had many quarrels about finances. She felt that all he wanted was her money. Because she was wealthier than he, she thought that he was jealous of her independence. Also, he could not understand her attitude toward sex and threatened to get a mistress.

In reviewing their previous marriages there had been similar problems. There had always been money on each side, and always conflicts over the use of it. There had always been sexual maladjustment which finally precipitated a divorce.

Mr. Wheat treated sex as a man's privilege. To him it was never an expression of mature love and trust. He had never understood the woman's sexual needs, with the result that in each marriage his wife had rejected him.

Mrs. Wheat had no factual knowledge about sex, and her attitude was considerably warped. It had always been distasteful, a duty to be performed. She was cold and frigid. Her mother was the same. Mrs. Wheat grew up in her mother's second marriage.

This couple came for counseling because some years before they had been confirmed in the Episcopal Church and had come under the influences both of its teaching on the sanctity of marriage as a lifelong union, and of the canon requiring that a couple finding their marriage threatened by dissolution should seek first the counsel of a minister. They were also older and less interested than formerly in another marriage if this one could be saved. They sincerely wanted to resolve their difficulties.

Mrs. Wheat became a good student in the study and understanding of love and sex. Seeing this as an area vital to a good relationship with her husband, she became open minded after the second interview on the subject. She read books the counselor recommended and was soon willing to have her husband back in her bedroom. Mr. Wheat learned to be gentle, loving, and patient. It was a relief to Mrs. Wheat to find that she no longer became tired after coitus.

With the sexual problem finally resolved, the other problems with a surprisingly small amount of counseling seemed to resolve themselves. The financial difficulties were not nearly so important as they had seemed.

Toward the conclusion of the counseling they planned a trip abroad as a second honeymoon—or was it the fourth!

All multiple marriages are not as easy to save as that one. Mrs. McCarma was in her third marriage and Mr. McCarma in his second. There were nine children involved. Mrs. McCarma was a pious but promiscuous neurotic of thirty-five. She flirted with anything wearing trousers, drank to be sociable but occasionally to excess, and had a temper which enabled her to express her feelings with profanity that the proverbial trooper would admire. Her complaints against her three husbands were much the same; if recorded, one record would have served for each case: Husband No. 1 drank, ran around, beat her up, neglected his responsibilities at home, was lazy and crazy. Husbands Nos. 2 and 3 were the same. Yet all three husbands held good positions and provided well for the family. There were children by all three.

I knew only husband No. 3, Mr. McCarma. He enjoyed his drinks, but said he could not bear to hear his wife's vicious tongue unless he was well fortified. His temper and profanity matched hers exactly, resulting in fist fights and throwing anything that was handy. On one occasion he knocked her down the front steps. The children usually witnessed, or heard, their quarrels and fights.

Mr. McCarma stayed at home as little as possible. When drinking, he accused his wife of having affairs with other men and questioned the paternity of the children. Before he and Mrs. McCarma married, while she was still the wife of her second husband, they took trips together. He would recall these incidents and accuse her of dating other men when he was away.

Counseling continued with this couple for over a year, but with no success. Neither one would give up drinking, which always resulted in a quarrel and often a fight. The wife had various complaints of pains and illnesses, and was in and out of hospitals. Her doctor and the counselor urged her to have psychiatric treatment, but this she rejected strongly. Her husband tried for a while to change his behavior pattern, but met with no encouragement from his wife. The marriage finally ended in divorce. Will each marry again? Probably. Will their next marriage be successful? Very unlikely. Each will probably marry again the same type of individual and the recording of the conflicts in the first marriage experienced in the second and third marriages can again be listened to in the fourth. The neurotic who has never resolved his inner conflicts will continue to marry the type of person on whom he can displace them. Because of projection he never looks within to discover his guilt and the reasons for his unconscious conflict with his spouse.

There are couples whose marriages are hopeless. They reach the point of no return. Perhaps if they had sought help in time, the marriage might have been saved.

FINDING A BASIS
ON WHICH TO REBUILD A MARRIAGE

We have seen how a couple first bent on divorce were able to find a basis on which to rebuild their marriage. In some cases divorce papers have already been taken out when, through the advice of family or friends, couples have sought counseling. Some have, like Bill and Susan, discovered that they really did not want a divorce but were seeking a way to solve their problems and reconstruct their marriage on a more stable foundation.

MISMATCHED COUPLES

Some couples should never have married and if they had had premarital counseling may not have become husband and wife. Their personalities conflict to such a degree that they are unable to find any satisfactory basis on which to build their marriage. The counselor will note these conditions in the initial interviews as he studies the background information.

Artificiality

There are women who are natural brunettes who become artificial blondes. They attract men who like blondes and marry. Later on, perhaps several years after marriage, they decide to let their hair resume its natural color. They become brunettes. But the husband did not marry a brunette; in fact, he has never been attracted to brunettes. He finds that he is no longer interested in his wife and may begin to be interested in a blonde in the office.

Women should be cautious about changing the natural color of their hair. A blonde wife after several years of marriage decided to surprise her husband by becoming a brunette. He was duly surprised and for a while, went along with it—but not for long. They began to have quarrels over many trivialities they had not had before. He began to stay out late. Sexual relations became less frequent. Finally they came for counseling.

It was soon evident that their marital unhappiness coincided with the wife's becoming a brunette. She decided immediately to go back to her natural color, but considerable damage had already been done to the marriage. He had become involved with a blonde and now wanted a divorce. There were no children. The wife tried unsuccessfully to keep the marriage but was unable to win her husband back.

I would not want the reader to draw the conclusion that the only problem in these marriages was artificial hair dyes, but the changing of the natural color of the hair may be a contributing cause of marital discord.

Another wife would not allow her hair to turn gray naturally, but kept it dyed the dark brown it had been when she married. Her husband liked her hair this color. He did not want to admit her age (or his either!). But time does not stand still. When she was about fifty-five, she was hospitalized for a long period and was unable to keep her hair dyed. Her husband was shocked to find that his wife was a gray-haired woman! Although he wanted her to redye it, she refused, and he was brought to face the reality of aging. But it took him some time to accept it and become adjusted to it. How much better it would have been had she allowed nature to take its course and he had seen her hair gradually turn gray.

Forced marriages

Some couples like Eric and Madge are forced into marriage. Their families were very distressed when Madge told them she was pregnant. She and Eric started going steady when both were in high school. She was only fourteen when they began dating, and he was seventeen. They engaged in intercourse almost from their first date, but Madge did not become pregnant until she was sixteen. During all this period they had dated in order to pet. They could hardly have called it love. In fact, when Madge became pregnant, they were beginning to tire of each other. There was another boy to whom Madge was becoming attracted. Undoubtedly, had she not become pregnant, she and Eric would have soon broken up.

Faced with the pregnancy, the two families decided there was no solution except marriage. They kept the cause of marriage a secret. The couple had a civil ceremony, the actual date of which was reported to friends as having been two or three months earlier and kept secret. But, as Madge said, "This really fooled no one."

Although the families decided to help the couple and to enable Eric to finish high school, the young people had already begun to dislike each other. Being forced into marriage emphasized their growing dislike for each other. They soon began to quarrel. It was necessary financially for them to live with one of the parents— so often the case in young marriages. This created more friction. The in-laws became critical and domineering.

Even so, they tried to make a go of the marriage for several years. Eric finished high school and got a very good job. Madge took some correspondence courses and completed what she felt was the equivalent of high school. They separated on two or three occasions—before coming for counseling. They were also separated at that time. Divorce for them, however, seemed the only solution. They did not love each other. When together, there was continual turmoil. Madge resented the years "I was cheated out of."

There are also couples, not teenagers, who engaged in sexual relations and believe that morally they are bound to each other and should be married, even though they may not love each other. Carl and Frances had been striving for several years to make a go of their marriage. They did not love each other and were very unhappy. They had never told their families the real reason for their marriage. They went through a formal engagement and a church wedding, but there was no romance in it for either. They were doing what they felt was the only thing that could balance off their premarital sexual behavior. Their families were upset by their quarreling and could not understand them. Finally, a friend persuaded them to seek the help of a marriage counselor.

Both of them faced the issue squarely, admitting their premarital relations and their feeling at that time that marriage alone could make morally right what they had done. The marriage turned out to be a mere formality. After marriage both soon became indifferent to coitus, which, when they came for counseling, was very infrequent and without even its premarital physical enjoyment.

Relief of conscience came to them as each talked out their guilt feelings, but there was clearly no basis on which to build a true marriage—indeed there had been no true marriage: the essential elements had never been present. Divorce was the only solution.

These mismatched couples are the unhappy flotsam of the marriage market, a great problem in our society today.

Age differential

There are couples mismatched because of a large age differential. A woman married a man many years her senior. As their ages increased, she became aware of the fact that she was married to an "old man." She turned against him, flirted with younger men, and was ready to seek a divorce. In fact, she had consulted a lawyer when they came for counseling. It took many sessions before she was able to feel better about his age, and that his age was also involved in her concern for the children, for if it had not been for the children, she probably would have gotten a divorce.

Alcoholism

Howard and Salley had a problem which many minister-counselors must deal with. He was an alcoholic. He had been given every treatment available—private institutions, veterans hospital, state hospital, psychiatric treatment, counseling, and A.A. He was also diagnosed as psychopathic. One psychiatrist said, "He will end up in one of two institutions: the state hospital or the state penitentiary. There is no other permanent custodial care for him which he can afford."

The wife and children, mistreated and poorly supported, were facing a very doubtful future. After much counseling and after exhausting every means of help for Howard, it was decided that divorce was the only solution for Salley and the children.

After the divorce the whole atmosphere of the home changed. Salley got a good position as a secretary and a woman to care for the children. Her family helped some for a while. The children are now in their teens. Salley's position in the commercial world has improved through the years. She has done a remarkable job in rearing her family and is highly respected in the community.

Another similar case where it was necessary for the wife to obtain a divorce has also proved that divorce may sometimes be the best and only solution. This woman has reared her children, worked, returned to college, and obtained a postgraduate degree.

One of the unhappy cases brought to the author was that of a man who had been divorced and had the custody of three children. His second wife had been a single woman who was in her thirties when they started dating. The woman was deeply religious, and they belonged to the same denomination. Also, she was eager for marriage, realizing her chances for matrimony were lessening each year.

But this man did not appeal to her. She liked his children, but he was far from the sort of person she had always hoped to marry. He was several years older than she and far more sophisticated in the ways of the world and in man-woman relationships. On their third date the man persuaded her to have intercourse. He said it was necessary to determine if they were sexually compatible. Afterwards, she was so overcome by guilt that she came near to having a nervous breakdown and was under a physician's care for several months. The man was very much concerned and attentive during this period. Soon after, they began having intercourse frequently. Each time it was followed by days of depression for the woman. The man had not yet asked her to marry him, and she became afraid that he might not.

Finally, she brought up the subject. Reluctantly, he agreed on marriage. Here again there was no love between them. However, they married and had a child. But they were not happy. Marital friction became the rule. She became frigid and did not want him to "touch her." He would go into rages and strike her. They quarreled about the children. He accused her of neglecting his children by his former wife.

They had been married about five stormy years when they came for counseling. But after several months of interviews with each of them, during which time she had him arrested on two occasions for mistreatment, it was obvious that this marriage could not be saved. Finally, the counseling was terminated, and she obtained a divorce on grounds of physical cruelty. At last report he was a carefree Casanova with his parents caring for his children, and she a disillusioned woman working and caring for her child. Probably neither will marry again.

These marriages in which divorce seems to be the only solution must be dealt with by the minister-counselor with broad-mindedness and sympathy. The minister will not condone the immoralities, brutality, alcoholism, and other forms of misbehavior, but he is still responsible for helping these people to try to straighten out their lives. They are fully aware of the mess they have made. They do not need condemning and lecturing; they need loving support and understanding so that they can accept themselves again and feel comfortable with themselves, with other people, and with God. Surely this is pastoral care in its noblest meaning.

SUPPORTIVE THERAPY FOLLOWING DIVORCE

Divorce is a crisis for the persons involved in it. Following a divorce many adjustments must be made. If children are involved, they too face many problems of adjustment. If the parties to a divorce belong to the minister-counselor's church and both continue to attend that church, there will occur some strained and embarrassing situations. It often happens that one of the divorced persons may transfer to another church, especially if they live in a city where there are several churches of their denomination. In other cases a church of another denomination may be chosen.

This is just one of the many problems caused by divorce. The minister-counselor must try to help the divorced to continue his religious life and to find a congenial church home where he feels he can worship and be active.

Much depends also on the congregation involved. Here we would hope to see the Church as a redemptive agent working cooperatively with the minister in helping the divorced adjust.

For sometime, even for years after a divorce, the minister may be called on for counseling. A period of loneliness often develops along with a feeling of self-consciousness. There will be times of temptation. There are men who will prey upon young divorcees and exploit their loneliness. This is also experienced by young widows. If the minister has revealed in his counseling that he understands these problems and is ready and willing to listen to his parishioners discuss these problems, he can be a real source of comfort and strength.

Meredith was very lonely after her divorce. She was young, beautiful, and intelligent. Men sought her out and asked for dates. Although she had dated many men before her marriage, and had had the experience of marriage, she was unprepared for the aggressiveness of the male following her divorce. Single and married men made "passes." Some boldly invited her to spend the weekend with them at a beach or in the mountains. "They seem to think I'm available to any man who asks me. I am lonely." She finally said, "I don't know how long I can resist. What am I to do?"

In the counseling this problem was faced unemotionally as a natural and practical one. She was a young woman of high ideals and a fine feeling of self-esteem, but she had the natural desires of a young woman, and in her marriage she and her husband had been sexually well adjusted. She had strong sexual feelings. She said, "To be perfectly honest, I want a man. But I am afraid of what I may do. I know sex relations out of marriage are not right. What does the Bible mean when it says, 'It is better to marry, than to be aflame with passion'?" [10]

She herself supplied the answer, and with it expressed her decision, "I will be more careful about the men I date, and I will be more careful about my own behavior. I have gone farther at times than I should have, which no doubt led my dates to think they could take me. I want to marry again, but I want to marry

---

[10] I Corinthians 7:9.

the right kind of man next time with whom I can be really happy and raise a family. I must think of that and not let my present loneliness and sex desire get the better of me and spoil my future." She had found a good motivation for decorous behavior.

Several years later Meredith came for premarital counseling. She had become engaged to a fine man. One of the first things she said was, "Do you remember our talk the last time I was here? I shall never cease being grateful for the decision I made that day. The man I'm marrying has never suggested that we go all the way. I can marry with a free conscience." They have been married several years and have four children.

The divorced person needs a minister whom he can trust and with whom he feels free to counsel about any problem. The pastor can be to him a strong stabilizing influence.

SUMMARY

The minister-counselor may have strong conviction about the indissolubility of marriage, but he must realize that all marriages cannot be saved. While divorce may not be the best solution, there are cases in which it appears to those involved to be the only solution.

But the minister must appreciate the fact that those who bring their marital problems to him believe that he may be an instrument of redemption. He is one of God's redemptive agents to interpret to others God's redemptive power in the life of the individual. The family, a redemptive community, has its responsibility in the process of redeeming the individual. The capacity of a person to forgive in love should never be underestimated.

Through Confession and Absolution the minister has a special means of helping the repentant to experience and accept God's forgiveness and find a new life in Christ. Dying and rising is a common experience through which the minister can help the counselee to learn its significance for the Christian. When one has understood this, self-forgiveness follows.

When a spouse has sinned against the marriage and is repentant, the other spouse is faced with a magnificent challenge to share with God in his rehabilitation.

One's life history must be viewed longitudinally and not cross-sectionally. A cross-sectional view highlights certain incidents and judges by them, but the longitudinal view sees life as a whole.

Some marriage partners believe they can make over their spouses according to a preconceived mold or stereotype. This seldom is successful and may be very damaging. But a husband and wife with full appreciation of the other's potentialities and limitations can encourage each to achieve his best. Couples can learn to weave together a beautiful pattern of Christian marriage.

A function of counseling is to help individuals discover their creative ability and begin to express creativity in daily life. Those who are bored with a routine mechanical job may find life very dull and drab. In seeking some excitement they may drink to excess or form illicit relations with the opposite sex. The key to their rehabilitation lies in creative activity.

Those individuals who have been married and divorced several times are usually immature, selfish, and neurotic. Some can be helped through prolonged therapy and may settle down in a stable marriage. In counseling these couples it is suggested that a review of previous marriages be undertaken to determine the behavior pattern which has been set up.

Some couples are mismatched and may never be able to work out a satisfactory marriage. The counselor will note in the initial interviews any indications of their condition which may grow out of some unattractiveness caused by artificiality, forced marriage, age differential, or alcoholism. The minister must deal with such couples with broadmindedness and sympathy.

SUGGESTED READING

Baber, Ray E., *Marriage and the Family* (2nd ed.), Chaps. 13, 14. New York: McGraw-Hill Book Company, 1953.

Bergler, Edmund, *Unhappy Marriage and Divorce*. New York: International Universities Press, Inc., 1946.

Genné, William Henry and Elizabeth Steel Genné, eds., *Foundations for Christian Family Policy*. Proceedings of the North American Conference on Church and Family, April 30–May 5, 1961, Secs. 3 and 4. New York: Department of Family Life, National Council of Churches of Christ in the U.S.A.

May, Rollo, *The Art of Counseling*, Chap. 9, "Morals and Counseling," Nashville: Abingdon Press, 1939.

The Dynamics
of Motivation

12

One of the aims of counseling is to help the counselee to become motivated to carry out his decisions and to achieve self-actualization. Therefore, energies must be released through counseling which will begin to propel the person toward the goals he has set for himself.

A NEW SELF-IMAGE

A step toward self-actualization is taken when the counselor helps the counselee acquire a new self-image, one of the major goals of counseling [1]—A *new* self-image, because so many who come for counseling have distorted and ugly ones. They may see themselves as inferior, disgusting, loathsome failures. Self-depreciation is prominent, and often they are depressed. A person in this condition is already defeated in his attack upon life's problems. He lacks incentive. He lacks motivation. All of his emotional energy is directed toward defensive mechanisms and rationalizations as he attempts to defend his behavior.

The concept of self is a learned attribute, a progressive concept starting from birth and differentiating steadily through childhood and adolescence like an unfolding spiral. For example, one of the earliest manifestations of the self is the negativistic attitude of the two-year-old child when he begins to realize that he has an individuality of his own

---

[1] Lawrence M. Brammer and Everrett L. Shostrom, *Therapeutic Psychology* (Englewood Cliffs, N.J.: Prentice-Hall, Inc., 1960), p. 29.

with pressing and distinctive needs and powers. This growing awareness of himself as an unique person is his concept of self. This self takes on various subjective attributes in the form of "I am" (his nature), "I can" (his capacities), "I should or should not" (his values), and "I want to be" (his aspirations).

When the individual perceives himself as behaving in a manner consistent with his picture of himself, he generally experiences feelings of adequacy, security, and worth. If he acts in a manner different from the way he defines himself, he experiences what is known as "threat" and feels insecure, inadequate, or worthless. The individual, if he perceives no other alternative, may then defend himself against this threat or inconsistency via one of the commonly described "defense mechanisms." [2]

Everyone has some kind of self-image. He sees himself as the kind of person he thinks himself to be. It is not necessarily the image others see. It is as though he possesses a camera or lens through which he sees himself with the coloring removed, for the colors are there to help others see him as he wants to appear to them.

Thus, when the author asked the genial, smiling, self-confident Sunday School teacher to describe herself as she saw herself, it was to have her reveal the kind of self-image stated above. She had recently given up her Sunday School class. "I just couldn't face those children another Sunday. I felt like in their innocence they could see the kind of person I really was. I felt all undressed before them. For the same reason I stopped singing in the choir."

She and her husband had begun to quarrel a great deal. She had started drinking. At the club she had flirted with a man who took her outside and frightened her with his intimate petting. This sort of thing had happened on several occasions. She realized that this behavior was not consistent with her early training or with her ideals of womanhood. Her self-image was badly spoiled. She was full of self-blame and self-depreciation.

How was she to be motivated toward becoming the kind of person she wanted to be?

First, of course, was the fact that she realized what was happening and came for help. She was open, frank, and cooperative in the counseling, which extended over several sessions. Her husband also came for counseling because he, too, had become alarmed over his wife's changing behavior pattern. He felt that he was partly

---

[2] Brammer and Shostrom, *Therapeutic Psychology,* p. 37.

to blame because he was away a good deal of the time, and they had no children. He knew his wife was lonesome, but his work required him to be away several days and nights a week. He had scolded her for her drinking; because of her flirtations he had threatened her with divorce.

"The primary question is," the counselor said, "why does she do these things?" Also, "Does she feel safe and secure in your love?"

When her behavior pattern first began to change, he would fuss and then give her the "silent treatment" for the next day or so. On two occasions he had slapped her, and she had cursed him. He was asked if his treatment was getting results. He said that conditions were getting worse and worse.

It was explained to him how his wife felt about herself. This came to him as both a surprise and a relief. He wanted to know what he could do to help her. He decided to say no more about her drinking and flirtations, to try to avoid for a while social functions where these things would most likely happen, and to try to rearrange his schedule to allow him more time, especially nights, at home. He said that he felt that his boss would cooperate with him in this matter.

In the interviews with each one, the counselor drew a diagram on the greenboard of Maslow's hierarchy of needs, explaining it as he drew it.[3] Briefly it was pointed out that among our basic physiological needs is sex. This need was not being met in their marriage. Each had admitted that sexual relations had become infrequent and unsatisfying. They agreed to try and work out a better relationship, but not merely a physical one. Their sex life was to be an expression of their love, confidence, companionship, homemaking and, indeed, a summing up of their whole relationship with each other as husband and wife.

He realized that he must show her more love and affection at all times. They had stopped being affectionate through the day, when he left for work, and when he returned. They decided to bring romance back into the marriage by doing little things for each other such as they did before marriage, little surprises and attentions that each knew the other one liked. For the time being

---

[3] See J. Kenneth Morris, *Premarital Counseling—A Manual for Ministers* (Englewood Cliffs, N.J.: Prentice-Hall, Inc., 1960), Chap. 7.

they decided to avoid controversial subjects, that is, until they could learn to communicate without getting angry.

As they came to show and express their love, each one began to feel secure in that love and that in turn enriched their love for each other. Feeling secure and loved, her self-esteem returned, and his was enhanced. Her self-image began to take on once more its true characteristics that it had before her behavior pattern changed.

She began to achieve self-actualization and to become the kind of person which her inner drives were striving to make her. She realized that she could be a Sunday School teacher with pride, sing again in the choir, take her place in community affairs, and make her home a place to be proud of—a true haven of happiness and of peace.[4]

Her self-image gradually changed in subsequent interviews to one in which she saw herself once more as the kind of person she could admire and live with comfortably. Her behavior changed accordingly. As Rogers expresses it:

Any behavior which formerly seemed out of control is now experienced as part of self, and within the boundaries of conscious control. In general, the behavior is more adjustive and socially more sound, because the hypotheses upon which it is based are more realistic.

Thus therapy produces a change in personality organization and structure, and a change in behavior, both of which are relatively permanent. It is not necessarily a reorganization which will serve for a lifetime. It may still deny to awareness certain aspects of experience, may still exhibit certain patterns of defensive behavior. There is little likelihood that any therapy is in this sense complete. Under new stresses of a certain sort, the client may find it necessary to seek further therapy, to achieve further reorganization of self. But whether there be one or more series of therapeutic interviews, the essential outcome is a more broadly based structure of self, an inclusion of a greater proportion of experience as a part of self, and a more comfortable and realistic adjustment to life.[5]

Thus, her drinking and flirting ceased. She returned to her religious activities. The renewal or re-creation of her self-image was a big step in motivating her toward self-actualization. The

---

[4] *The Book of Common Prayer*, p. 303.

[5] Carl R. Rogers, *Client-centered Therapy* (Boston: Houghton Mifflin Company, 1951), p. 195.

cooperation and understanding of her husband was also a prime factor. He himself benefited as much as she because he became more interested in his work, which could mean advancement and future success.

MOTIVATION ACHIEVED IN THREE WAYS

In the above illustration motivation toward the desired result was achieved in three ways:

Acceptance

The counselor accepted the person or self as presented to him by the counselee, without blame or censure. This relieved the woman's anxiety and enabled her to look at herself objectively and evaluate her distorted self-image.

Changing the emotional environment

The husband understood his wife's problem as she saw it, not just as he saw it. To change the emotional environment he had to develop empathic identification and see reality in their relationship as his wife saw it. (See pages 21–23.) What was real to his wife was reality so far as she was concerned, whether or not it was real to him. We do not always perceive objects, events, or statements as others do, but whatever we perceive a thing to be, that is reality to us. For example, one morning I looked out the window and saw what I perceived to be a large brown dog curled up in the corner of my neighbor's porch. I thought to myself that I had not heard they had a dog and began wondering what kind of dog it was. Later, when I looked from another window, I saw clearly that what I had perceived to be a dog was actually a pile of clothing of some sort, but until then, I had accepted the dog as reality and if challenged would have defended my perception because I saw it with my own eyes. Two people may listen to the same political speech and each have a different perception of the kind of person the speaker is. Parents may perceive their children's behavior differently and by responding accordingly may cause confusion among them. Rogers states the proposition: "The organism reacts to the field as it is experienced and perceived." The perceptual field is, for the individual, "reality." [6] Therefore, in seeking to understand others one should try first to accept their perceptual field and then encourage them to move from there toward the acceptance of reality of the emotional environment as it actually is.

The husband, with this in mind, had to learn by doing how to express both his love for his wife and his understanding of her problem so that he could give her a sense of security and self-esteem as a person worthy of his love. This change in the emotional environment released her from the binding cords of anxiety, fear, and self-depreciation so that she could reach toward self-actualization.

Instruction

In order to help the wife understand what had happened to her personality and to inspire confidence in her ability to develop her potentialities, the counselor used an illustration which has been of much help to others in the learning process.

In this illustration, he uses a sponge. The sponge is a beautiful organism which God has made to grow and develop according to its peculiar innate potentialities. As a sponge in the ocean it is flexible in swaying with the currents—it bends easily this way and that, but it never relinquishes its God-given characteristics of being a sponge, beautifully shaped and textured. It is a blessing to its environment and a joy to those who behold its beauty.

So likewise we, having the God-given characteristics of personality, are creatures made in the moral and spiritual image of God: made to love and be loved; made for fellowship with Him and our fellow man; made to be flexible so that we can give and take in the struggles in our environment, as passions and emotions stir from within and conflicts assault us from without. If we are in an emotional environment which gives us security, love, and self-esteem, our personalities will flower into self-actualization according to our potentialities.

Next the counselor takes the sponge and binds it round with a cord. No longer is it a thing of beauty. It is all out of shape. Distorted. Warped. This is not what God intended! It cannot now

---

[6] Rogers, *Cilent-centered Therapy*, p. 484.

sway easily and freely with the currents of the ocean. It is no longer flexible.

So it is with a personality that is bound round with insecurity, fear, anxiety, hate, self-depreciation, and self-disgust. It, too, becomes ill-shaped, warped, and ugly. It can become so rigid in its defensive mechanism and so tightly bound that it may break in the currents of stress and strain, the result being mental illness. How can it be freed?

The sponge is then unbound. It is free again. And we see something very wonderful take place. Slowly the sponge begins to resume its normal and beautiful shape! Once more it is flexible! Once more its colors and texture are seen plainly!

The same is true of our personalities when they are released from the binding cords of insecurity, fear, hate, self-recrimination, and self-disgust. Their innate potentialities of enhancement toward self-actualization reassert themselves.

SELF-ACTUALIZATION

Maslow points out that

Self-actualization, the coming to full development and actuality of the potentialities of the organism, is more akin to growth and maturation than it is to habit formation or association via reward, that is, it is not acquired from without but is rather an unfolding from within of what is, in subtle sense, already there. Spontaneity at the self-actualizing level—being healthy, natural—is unmotivated; indeed it is the contradiction of motivation.[7]

The true self-image of one as a worthwhile person in the eyes of God and man is formed once again. The minister-counselor must have a strong and sound faith in the ability of the individual to develop his true potentialities when set free.

This conviction that the innate potentialities in the individual, when set free, will enhance the personality is shared by many others. Rogers states in another of his propositions: The organism has one basic tendency and striving—to actualize, maintain, and enhance

---

[7] A. H. Maslow, *Motivation and Personality* (New York: Harper & Row, Publishers, 1954), p. 296.

the experiencing organism.[8] A person moves in different directions: toward self-maintenance, maturation, self-actualization, greater independence or self-responsibility, and socialization.[9]

Various passages of Scripture could be cited in support of the above: ". . . You will know the truth and the truth will make you free . . . So if the Son makes you free, you will be free indeed." [10] "When you were slaves of sin, you were freed in regard to righteousness. But then what return did you get from the things of which you are now ashamed? The end of those things is death. But now that you have been set free from sin and have become slaves of God, the return you get is sanctification and its end, eternal life. For the wages of sin is death, but the free gift of God is eternal life in Christ Jesus our Lord." [11] "For the law of the Spirit of life in Christ Jesus has set me free from the law of sin and death." [12] The story of the raising of Lazarus is particularly appropriate when taken as the raising of man from spiritual and moral death—defeatism in the struggle with life. There is no passage more dramatic than that where Jesus says, "Unbind him, and let him go." [13] In mentioning these passages, and there are many others, I do not intend even to suggest that the minister-counselor use them to sermonize in the counseling process. If he does, he may fail completely in his efforts to enable the counselee to become free. The use of Scripture has its rightful place in counseling, but it lies in giving inferred support and assurance to the counselee—not in preaching to him. Each minister-counselor will have to work this out for himself. Perhaps the best suggestion is that he be so thoroughly converted himself to Christian faith and practice that they will infuse naturally his whole approach to counseling.

---

[8] Rogers, *Client-centered Therapy*, p. 488.

[9] See A. Angyal, *Foundations for a Science of Personality* (Cambridge, Mass.: Harvard University Press, 1941), pp. 32–50; Kurt Goldstein, *Human Nature in the Light of Psychopathology* (Cambridge, Mass.: Harvard University Press, 1940), p. 69; O. Hobart Mowrer and Clyde Kluckhohn, "A Dynamic Theory of Personality," Chap. 3 in J. McV. Hunt, *Personality and the Behavior Disorders* (New York: The Ronald Press Company, 1944), I, 74; Harry Stack Sullivan, *Conceptions of Modern Psychiatry* (New York: W. W. Norton & Company, Inc., 1953), p. 48; Karen Horney, ed., *Are You Considering Psychoanalysis* (New York: W. W. Norton & Company, Inc., 1946), p. 175.

[10] John 8:32, 36.

[11] Romans 6:20–23.

[12] Romans 8:2.

[13] John 11:44*b*.

In the case of the young woman, being a Christian she appreciated the assurance given her from Scripture and felt that now she once again had a faith restored. Religion was for her the challenge to creative living. She was motivated by acceptance, by changing the emotional environment, and by the learning process.

INTERNALIZATION OF VALUES

Let us take another case in motivation. This case brings out a very important factor, namely internalization of values. People behave according to the moral values they have internalized. That is, they have accepted values based on those basic religious and philosophical convictions, good or bad, by which they attempt to deal with life's problems. These convictions may or may not be rational from another's point of view, but they form the framework in which the individual operates. Hence the old problem of words versus deeds, the profession of a creed versus one's manner of life. The syndrome is well expressed in a well-known prayer to be said following a religious service: "Grant, O Lord, that what we have said with our lips, we may believe in our hearts, and practice in our lives." Total church membership in the United States, compiled from reports of 254 religious bodies, totals 117,946,002.[14] This equals 63.4 per cent of the estimated population. But no one would claim that these people are anything more than professing Christians. From the author's experience, and others say the same, it is estimated that only 33.3 per cent of the youth and adult membership can be considered to have internalized the religious and philosophical tenets of their faith so that in moral crises they act according to their Christian beliefs.

A great deal of religious practice is concerned with the externals of ritual and respectability: wearing one's best clothes to attend church, women wearing hats in church, attending at least once on Sunday, sitting properly or kneeling for prayer, giving an offering, ushering, receiving Communion, etc., according to the custom of one's own church. All these acts are external and can be performed by anyone, and much of the ritual may become

---

[14] Benson Y. Landis, ed., *Yearbook of American Churches* (Office of Publication and Distribution, National Council of Churches of Christ in the U.S.A., 1964), p. 280.

mechanical. All these acts have ethical value for the individual only as they express or are the counterpart of his internalized values of his faith.

Andrew and Patti were a delightful young couple with three children. They had been married about seven years when they came for counseling. They were separated. The crisis of separation sent them in haste for help with their marriage. Each one declared his love for the other. Each also asked, "What has happened to us? We were not brought up to live as we have been doing for the past two or three years." Andrew said, "Why, I teach in the Sunday School." Patti said, "I help in the nursery at Sunday School. We have always gone to church."

As each one in separate interviews related their problems, it became more and more apparent that these two young people had always attended church from the time they were small children. They had memorized Scripture passages and prayers, had been confirmed, and received Communion regularly. But in their teens they had done uncritically whatever their "gang" did. Andrew engaged in sexual relations, gambled a bit, and began drinking. He felt guilty but "not too guilty," he said. Patti went with a rather fast crowd, engaged in heavy petting, and "did everything one could do, and not go all the way," she said. She and Andrew engaged in premarital sexual relations. She felt guilty about this, but did not stop.

They were married in the church and soon were quite active. But they fell in with a group of friends who began to encourage them to visit the night spots. Here they all drank alcoholic beverages and danced in very intimate embraces with each other. Andrew became jealous and began to accuse Patti of being intimate with other men. Once he was infuriated because she went out of the dance hall with a man. Yet, Andrew himself was doing the same thing with girls. Patti accused him in return. One night he had sexual relations with a girl and told Patti "if that is what you want, go ahead. I've had mine." Then when Patti did—Andrew left.

"What has happened to us?" they both cried. The answer each came to discover was: They had never internalized their religious values. They knew intellectually what Christian values were. They knew the Ten Commandments and many Scripture verses. But these had never become a strong enough part of their inner conscience, the superego, to combat successfully the demands of the id. Patti and Andrew were weak in the face of the group, which in reality set their moral values for them; therefore, they accepted and began to live by those values. Moral standards are not always appropriated by our young people from Sunday School and Church, but rather from the group with which they become identified. Andrew and Patti came to understand this and, with mutual forgiveness, were reunited.

But how were they to internalize the moral and spiritual values on which they now desired to build their marriage?

Reevaluation

They had to reevaluate the course they had been following. This each one did in the personal interviews and in a terminal interview together. Under the permissive and nonjudgmental atmosphere of counseling each saw himself as he really was, and the self-image was not an appealing one to him or to her. As they thought back over their Christian learning compared with their manner of life, it was apparent that as St. Paul says, they "had not so learned Christ." [15] A recognition of this problem set in motion the will to solve it, and to bring their behavior into agreement with Christian teaching.

Changing to another group

They recognized the influence of the group as the real basis for their moral standards. They wished now to inculcate and follow Christian standards; therefore, they had to find a group which upheld these standards. Although they had been active in their church, they had not identified with any group or couples in the church. The group they identified with had been business, neighborhood, and casual acquaintances—a nest of "honky-tonk society." In order to break into another group, and since this couple were interested in a church group, it was necessary that they attend the church activities which would introduce them into a congenial group. Here is where the minister-counselor can be of great assistance to such a couple by making a point of introducing

---

[15] Ephesians 4:20.

them to other couples in the church in their age bracket. He can also help them develop with others, common interests.

Living the Christian life

"Expression deepens impression" is an old adage which is quite applicable here. As said before, this couple had learned many Bible verses, but like so many people they had never given expression to their meaning in their own personal and everyday lives. They knew well the saying of Jesus, "You shall love your neighbor as yourself," [16] but had never applied this to each other. In fact, when it was rephrased, "You shall love your husband (wife) as you love yourself," both expressed surprise, saying, "I never thought of it as meaning that!" And they then included their children. Several other sayings of Jesus were mentioned and rephrased: "And as you wish that your husband (wife) would do to you, do so to him (her)." [17] There are many other scriptural passages that could be cited. One other, as rephrased, is particularly applicable to the marriage relationship and to Andrew and Patti: "Judge not your husband (wife), and you will not be judged by him (her); condemn not your husband (wife), and you will be forgiven by him (her); give yourself—your love, trust, faith, interest—to your husband (wife), and it will be given to you; good measures, pressed down, shaken together, running over will be put into your lap. For the measure you give to your husband (wife) will be the measure you get back from him (her)." [18]

The goal—a Christian marriage

As Andrew and Patti continued to put into practice their Christian training, they were motivated more and more toward achieving the realization of their new goal—a Christian marriage.

Motivation requires the recognition and acceptance of a goal worth striving for. Here again, intellectualizing is not sufficient to motivate one to make the sacrifices necessary to achieve the goal. However, there must be a felt need to know the essentials of a Christian (or a Jewish, or a "good") marriage—a cognitive need—

---

[16] Matthew 22:39.
[17] Luke 6:31.
[18] Luke 6:37.

which motivates a person to examine what Scripture, the church, or the community sets as a norm for this kind of marriage. One definition as already pointed out is found in the Declaration of Intention. (See Appendix I, page 313.)

CHRISTIAN FAMILY IDEALS

The Lambeth Conference of 1958 set forth the following statement for the Anglican Communion:

Family life has never been so exposed to the acids of carelessness and selfishness as now, nor has the world ever had greater the need of the gifts family life can make. Some of the gifts are:

In a true family, children learn that there is one God. They learn it first from their parents, and from the disciplined and thoughtful obedience parents and children alike pay to the same God. Parents who force on a child an obedience they are not willing to accept equally for themselves are committing one of the depeest offences of family life, for they are giving to their child a false view of the one God who rules over all life and in whose will is our peace.

In a true family, children learn what love and judgement mean, for a family ideally is a society in which all bear common pain and share common grief, and all give and receive equally of love.

In a true family, children learn, little by little, how to be free; they practice how to make the choices life requires of them, within the protection of loving concern and watchful care.

In a true family, children learn the essential standards of judgement —how to tell the important things, how to distinguish the true and the excellent and the right, how to speak rightly and listen with courteous love.

In a true family, children learn how to accept themselves and, in time, how to accept others on the same basis; for membership in a family comes not by earning it nor buying it, nor is it given only to those who deserve it. Like life itself and the grace of God, it comes without deserving; and the self-acceptance of healthy childhood is a previous preparation for a humane and tolerant manhood.

In a true family, children learn how to be themselves, in true individuality, and how to accept others in their equally true individuality, with patience and kindness.

Of such qualities is a true family made. To bear witness to these things is part of the vocation of a Christian family in our society. In that society, sympathetic to its good influences, critical of, or resistant to, its unwholesome influences, the truly Christian home should be salt and leaven. To be this it has to be sure of itself and of its basis in the will of God and the Gospel.

Such a home is the one place where Christians can live by the Gospel, as they cannot fully do in a society where other sanctions come in. The marks of "living by the Gospel" are the care of each for other, the value set on persons for their own sake without regard to merit or demerit, to success or failure. While there is this warm understanding and love there is both freedom and responsibility. Each member feels free to be himself. This sense of freedom is one of the marks of a Christian in the world—all too rarely found in Church or in society.[19]

The Methodist Church has defined the Christian family in the following terms:

A Christian family is one in which parents so live the Christian life and practice the presence of God that children come to accept God as the greatest reality of life.

A Christian family is one in which each member is accepted and respected as a person having sacred worth.

A Christian family is one that seeks to bring every member into the Christian way of living.

A Christian family is one that accepts the responsibility of worship and instruction to the end of developing the spiritual life of each person.

A Christian family is one that manifests a faith in God, observes daily prayer and grace at meals, is committed to behavior in keeping with Christian ideals for family relations, community life, and national and world citizenship.[20]

The Presbyterian Church in the United States makes the following statement:

A true and lasting marriage can be achieved only when its physical bonds are reinforced and sanctified by a variety of moral and spiritual ties: respect, affection, common ideas and interests, the unselfish wish of each partner for the other's welfare in all things, and a mutual sharing of the common joys, griefs, opportunities and burdens of the home. This

---

19 *The* Lambeth *Conference, 1958* (London: The Trustees of the Society for Promoting Christian Knowledge, 1958; New York: The Seabury Press, 1958), pp. 2.151, 2.152. © 1958 by The Seabury Press.

20 *Doctrines and Discipline of the Methodist Church 1960* (Nashville, Tenn.: The Methodist Publishing House, 1960), p. 692. Copyright © 1960 by Board of Publication of the Methodist Church, Inc.

means that both faithfulness and unfaithfulness in marriage must be conceived in spiritual as well as physical terms.

But, while both physical and spiritual fidelity are vital, and while both are essential to the attainment of marriage at its best, husbands and wives should bear in mind that human weakness and frailty may manifest themselves in this realm as in all others. They should, therefore, cultivate the Christian graces of understanding, patience, generosity, repentance and forgiveness. They should remember that just as other human relationships can survive imperfections, so can marriage. Our Lord's command to forgive and, if need be, to forgive repeatedly, is especially applicable in this intimate and delicate relationship. The offending partner should not look upon the forgiveness of the other as license to keep on sinning but should regard this forgiveness as a summons to repentance and as the ground of re-establishing harmony within the union.[21]

The above descriptions of Christian marriage will hold no doubt for all Christian churches. A Christian couple whose marriage has been disrupted by dissension should reexamine—indeed, in many cases it will be a first examination—the essentials of a true marriage as defined by their church. If their way of life has not produced for them happiness and success in their marriage, they may come to feel cognitive need to learn what a Christian marriage entails.

In the case of Andrew and Patti, as in many other cases, gaining insight into the failure of their marriage created in them a need to find out the essentials of a good marriage. This they did. And with it came recognition and acceptance of the basic principles of Christian marriage and family living. They thus set toward the realization of these principles in their own marriage. Having recognized and accepted a worthwhile goal, they were motivated to move toward it.

FAILURES AND FRUSTRATIONS IN REACHING GOALS

Failures and frustrations in reaching one's goal can be so discouraging as to cause one to give up the struggle as hopeless. But if one gains insight into and understands the dynamics of one's

---

[21] *Minutes of the Ninety-ninth General Assembly of the Presbyterian Church in the United States,* p. 70. Statement added to paragraph 376 at the Ninety-ninth General Assembly, 1959.

failures and frustrations, then one may be motivated to make a new effort toward reaching the goal. Hope brings a new release of energy.

Kurt Lewin [22] in his analysis of conflict situations is of help to couples in understanding their failures and frustrations as they seek to reach their goals. Valence is Lewin's term for attraction to, or repulsion from, a goal. Vector represents the strength (by arrow length) and the direction of a force. Of course, these are psychological, not physical forces. Their strength and direction are determined by the individual's perception of his environment. Conflict is produced by the opposition of approximately equally strong field forces. The field of force indicates which force would exist at each point in the field if the individual (or couple) involved were at that point.

When a couple such as Andrew and Patti married, everything went well for a year or more. Without any particular planning and no premarital counseling they had no clearly defined goals for their marriage and consequently no plans for reaching them. Marriage was accepted as a normal relationship out of which would come children. They believed that their marriage would encounter the ups and downs seen in other marriages—those of their parents, in movies, and in novels—but would somehow continue, and with luck, be a happy one. Going to church together, engaging in activities of mutual interest, and visiting friends and relatives made them feel that their marriage was a good one. But they were merely drifting or coasting on the excitement of their new relationship.

Two positive valences

Their temporary daily goals were for the most part positive ones (Fig. 12.1): Shall we go to the movies or stay home and watch television? The conflict as to which valence would prevail was not severe. G represents the goals. The arrow represents the vector and indicates by its length the strength of the force and its direction. The couple decide to go to the movies, but finding it a poor

---

[22] Kurt Lewin, *A Dynamic Theory of Personality* (New York: McGraw-Hill Book Company, 1945); also, the author is indebted to McGraw-Hill Book Company for permission to use material and diagrams in this section adapted from Richard A. King, ed., *Readings for an Introduction to Psychology* (New York: McGraw-Hill Book Company, 1961), pp. 97–100.

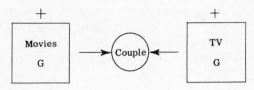

FIG. 12.1
Two Positive Valences

one, they may wish they had stayed home. Thus, after a choice is made, oscillation may occur.

Positive and negative valences

There will also be goals which will have both a positive and a negative valance. For example (Fig. 12.2) the couple may wish very much to have their own apartment, but because of insufficient

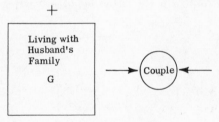

FIG. 12.2
Positive and Negative Valences

income and ample room at Andrew's home, they can live there without paying rent (a reward) but suffering the loss of some freedom in beginning their marriage (a punishment). There may be considerable oscillation as they come to a decision, and even after their decision is made to live with Andrew's parents, they may wish to leave. They move physically toward the goal, but with mental reservations. If their decision proves a very unsatisfactory one, they may find it advantageous to their marriage to move in spite of the hardships involved.

Marriage problems are seldom simple ones. They are generally complex. A constellation of forces is directed toward the couple, individually and collectively. In the above situation many factors might indicate the desirability of the positive elements (rewards) in the goal: no rent to pay, companionship for wife when husband is absent, no furniture to buy, and the family car to use. Likewise, the negative elements (punishments) would be present showing the undesirability of the goals: loss of some independence, danger of friction with Andrew's parents, possible interference on the part of his parents, creation of he-who-pays-the-piper-calls-the-dance situation. Such a constellation of forces may produce such a strain on a young couple as to cause them much ambivalence and great unhappiness. What may at first appear a rather simple problem with an easy solution may be weighted with serious consequences, multiplying its complexity.

Barriers

There are of course barriers between the individual or couple and the goal. The barrier may have a strong positive valence (Fig. 12.3) as, for example, in the situation of a marriage in which the

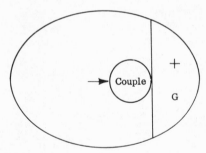

FIG. 12.3
Barrier with Strong Positive Valence

husband is seeking a college degree. The wife works. The barriers are the years of study for the husband, the work of the wife, and the cares and the responsibility of family support. But the barriers become a challenge as they keep in sight the goal defined, chosen, and desired.

For some couples the barriers of time, knowledge, learning, and experience present a positive valence toward achieving a successful marriage. A couple span the years ahead momentarily as they look toward and plan for the education of the children, owning their home, or financial success. To overcome the barrier they may read and study in the fields of child training, insurance, and business success. They find many thrills as they grow and mature together in moving toward their goal.

Then again a couple may run into a barrier with a strong negative valence which prevents them reaching their goal of a happy and successful marriage (Fig. 12.4). In the case of Andrew and

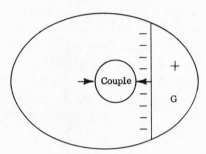

FIG. 12.4
Barrier with Strong Negative Valence

Patti, this barrier turned out to be their friends. At first their friends were those they had known before marriage and with whom they grew up. The barrier possessed a positive valence. But after two or three years, because of Andrew's job and the neighborhood in which they lived, they began to form other friendships. These friends were outside the Church and enjoyed night spots, drinking parties, gambling, and flirtations between couples. Gradually these friends drew Andrew and Patti away from their former friends and from their church activities. They were also pulling Andrew and Patti apart. When drinking they quarreled. Each flirted with others. Andrew "stepped out" on Patti. Patti became involved with the husband of one of her friends. They felt embarrassed to go to church. The barrier, "friends," came to acquire a negative valence. Friends were now making it impossible for Andrew and Patti to reach their goal. Andrew was handicapped in his job by worrying about Patti. He was sure that she was having an affair. Patti felt the same about Andrew's behavior. A considerable amount of conflict was present. In one of the counseling sessions Andrew exclaimed, "I just wish we could move to another part of the country where no one knows us and we knew no one and could live in peace!" In terms of Lewin's analysis of conflict, he had reached the point where the barrier seemed insurmountable, and he wished to go out of the field entirely. As a matter of fact, Patti did, temporarily. She left for more than a week, and Andrew did not know where she was.

In another case the barrier was a mother-in-law who interfered so much in the marriage that severe conflict arose between the couple. The barrier came to have a negative valence. When the couple came for counseling, the marriage was a very unhappy one; they both felt completely frustrated in trying to deal with the dominating mother. Here, also, they expressed a desire to move out of the field—"move so far away she cannot ever visit us or phone us, and if she writes we won't answer." However, this did not prove necessary. She went so far as to forge her son's name on a check, although she prided herself on having high ethical standards. The couple made good the check, but the mother was so overcome with shame that she could not face them. This gave the couple an opportunity to look objectively upon the whole in-law relationship and to realize that if they were to achieve a happy marriage, they must put their marriage first [23] and end her interference. This they did, gently but firmly, in a well-written letter. She accepted the new situation, and the barrier with its negative valence was removed. The husband said, "I feel that I have grown up more in the past month than in all the previous years."

Let us consider a conflict situation in which there are two negative valences. Mr. and Mrs. Ray had been married 20 years. There were three children, ages eighteen, sixteen, and twelve. When they came for counseling, the marriage had been deteriorating for several years owing to Mr. Ray's neglect of his family and his increased affluence which permitted him to go on long hunting and fishing trips, as well as attending conventions where he sought and found exciting adventures with the opposite sex. This behavior pattern and neglect of his family caused severe conflict between husband and wife. The home itself took on a negative valence for the former. Consequently, he avoided being at home as much as possible. Mrs. Ray also came to see the home only as a place (field force) of unhappiness. She began to hate the house and town and

---

[23] See Morris, *Premarital Counseling*, pp. 149ff, for further discussion on this basic principle in marriage and in-law relationship.

felt strongly the talk of the neighbors, saying, "All I want is to take the children and leave. I can't stand this another day. I just want a divorce."

But while each expressed a desire for a divorce, because of its negative valence neither one would take the necessary steps to secure it. For him, divorce would endanger his escapades with other women by making him liable to a forced marriage; being married gave him protection under the law. Furthermore, he loved his children and felt that he should maintain a home for them. He was very proud of his ability to give his children the best of everything: cars, boats, country club, clothes. According to both his was the biggest and mostly costly house in the town. He boasted about it to her disgust. She said it was "nothing but his ego. 'Look what I can do. Nobody else in this town can do this!' " For her, divorce presented the problem of the children. "I'm not able to take on the full responsibility of the children. They need a man." Divorce would mean uprooting them and moving to another town because she felt she could never remain in that town where her husband had his business. "I feel weak all over when I think about moving." Also, she said that her family did not believe in divorce and for her to get one would bring disgrace upon them. So for Mr. and Mrs. Ray divorce was a negative valance.

They were now between two negative valences (Fig. 12.5): the home and divorce, both unacceptable to them. In such situations, as for example that of a child (C) who is forced by threat of punish-

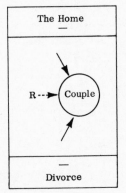

FIG. 12.5
Barrier with Two Negative Valences

ment to do a task he does not want to do, the resultant (R) causes the subject to move sidewise out of the field, unless other circumstances prevent it. The couple (C), Mr. and Mrs. Ray, were also moved sidewise. They were unable to move completely out of the field so they agreed to a mutual (not legal) separation, and Mr. Ray moved to an apartment.

Now both of them had to learn to adjust to an unresolved conflict if they were to find happiness. This particular couple discontinued counseling, feeling that they could now work out their problems. Another couple who obtained a legal separation did continue the counseling and finally became adjusted to the new situation.

However, there are individuals who become trapped in a conflict situation. These unfortunate persons do not seek counseling (perhaps do not know that it is available), and since the situation becomes hopeless, they withdraw and attempt to build a wall be-

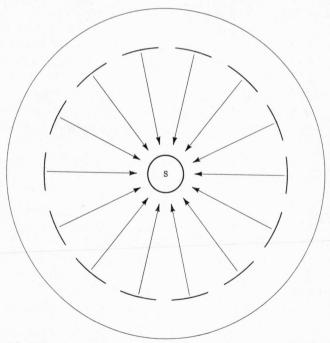

FIG. 12.6

Surrounding the Self with Barriers of Negative Valences

tween themselves and the situation, "a sort of encysting of the self" (Fig. 12.6). They are surrounded by barriers with negative valences.

TEACHING—A FUNCTION OF COUNSELING

Teaching, as a function of counseling, is implicit in what has been said on the subject of motivation. Goals must be clearly defined, chosen, and desired.

Clearly defined goals

Unless a goal is clearly defined, one cannot move along specific and constructive lines to achieve it. This was the major problem in the case of Allen and Sadie. Allen dropped out of college in his first year to take a job. This was a great disappointment to Sadie. They had married in high school, but the finances of Allen's college education had been worked out satisfactorily so that he could have continued had he wanted to. When they came for counseling, the marriage relationship was strained almost to the point of a separation. It soon became obvious that Allen had no clearly defined goal regarding a profession. He was visionary and wanted to get to the top quick, which meant for him the accumulation of wealth. How was this to be accomplished? This he did not know. Consequently, he was frustrated. In the short space of a few months he had had several jobs, all low paying and insufficient for their financial needs. Each time he came for counseling, he wanted to be something else: a business man (no particular business), a real estate broker, a technician in a factory, an athletic director, a salesman (of anything), or a TV repairman. Aptitude testing showed that he could probably become an athletic director in a high school if he went back to college and majored in physical education.

In the counseling, it became clear that Allen's orientation in his present environment proved to him that he was floundering hopelessly because his goal was indeterminate, unclear, and intangible.[24] How can one move toward an indefinite goal? Indeter-

---

[24] Compare Kurt Lewin, *Principles of Topological Psychology* (New York: McGraw-Hill Book Company, 1936), p. 39; Ernest R. Hilgard, *Theories for Learning,* Chap. 8, "Lewin's Field Theory" (New York: Appleton-Century-Crofts, 1948, 1956), pp. 258–89.

minateness only leads to frustration and failure. Once a goal is defined in terms of one's capabilities, then, and only then, does it come into focus as something one can choose.

Choosing the goal

The next step is to choose the goal. This requires that an appraisal be made of one's abilities to realize the goal.

The road to goal achievement is strewn with the wreckage of the vain efforts and failures of men and women who set out to reach goals without possessing the intelligence, ability, and training necessary. Many of these people received no vocational testing and guidance to determine their aptitudes, nor to help them understand their real likes and capabilities. Some had their goals chosen for them by their parents, who sought to relive their lives through their children. Each person must choose his own goal, his profession, his personality achievement, his attitudinal set or orientation toward the value judgments he accepts for himself, his marriage ideal, and the integration of the values he holds for his marriage and which he seeks to realize. Of couse, this last goal must be chosen by both spouses if it is to be realized.

Most couples accept their marriage ideal from what may be termed the norm in their culture or among their friends. This is generally a stereotype that is portrayed in multitudinous familial cartoons: indifference, competition, meekness, flirting, overspending, quarreling, fighting, and selfishness. But these are not characteristics of the Christian or of a good marriage. Children who grow up in an atmosphere of bickering, quarreling, and lack of affection may accept marriage to be that kind of relationship and duplicate it in their own marriage. The stereotype is so well fixed in the minds of young people that many marry with the idea that if things get too bad they can get a divorce. And with thousands marrying with no preparation and instruction for marriage, the stereotype seems to become more startlingly silhouetted against the societal sky.

Therefore, as in all areas of conscious personality growth and development, goals must be clearly defined and carefully chosen according to one's potentialities, so also in marriage a couple must know and choose their goals wisely, not sentimentally, or by chance.

Desiring the goal

However, even to know and to choose a goal are not sufficient to realize a goal. Behind the choice there must be conviction and determination—a deep, inner desire to achieve the goal. It is this desire which backs the motivating power enough to energize and propel one over all the barriers he may have to surmount in order to reach the goal. It is this longing for the goal, which gives one his set and stance. That is the reason why a couple should have ample time in their engagement to get to know each other's ideals and goals in life. Marriage is a partnership—and in Christian marriage we must add a third one—God—to the partnership. Teamwork in marriage calls for a united effort and, as children are added, all must pull together. Pride in the family and loyalty to its standards give to children a feeling of security and sense of accomplishment.

A goal, clearly defined, wisely chosen, and greatly desired, whether it be for oneself or for one's marriage, can be achieved with patience, persistence, and hard work. The barriers that must be surmounted will possess positive valences, daily presenting new challenges.

Teaching essential

Many couples, while saying they want a Christian or good marriage, do not have a clearly conceptualized ideal of what the goal implies. They must be taught. As indicated throughout this manual, teaching is an important phase of marriage counseling.

Individuals do not understand the dynamics of their behavior. Once this is made clear to them, some are quick to gain insight and to set about learning a new behavior pattern. Teaching and explaining the dynamics of behavior and motivation prove very helpful to the counselee in his attempt to deal adequately with his conflicts and frustrations.

The minister-counselor must give information and must correct misinformation. This is particularly true in regard to sex knowledge, as we have pointed out in Chapter VIII. Because a couple have been married a long time and have children does not mean that they are well informed on sex knowledge. Other areas in which the minister-counselor must be prepared to give information are economics, family budgets, child training, personality growth and development, religion and the Church, community resources, and on many other subjects already discussed. The minister is not expected be be an expert in all these fields and should not hesitate to refer a counselee or couple for expert advice when needed.

It is essential, according to their particular needs, to instruct individuals and couples in

(1) The meaning of either a Christian marriage or a good marriage

(2) The basis for good interpersonal relationships

(3) The right use of sex, including sex anatomy, because some sexual maladjustment is due to lack of factual sex knowledge

(4) The essentials for building a happy marriage—affection, appreciation, and consistency [25]

(5) The characteristics of a successful marriage—handling finances, getting along with in-laws, cultivating mutual friends, using leisure and recreational outlets

(6) Alcoholism

(7) The dynamics of various behavior patterns

(8) Character disorders

It should be emphasized that the teaching phase of counseling must not turn into a series of lectures but should be in the nature of discussions in which the counselee is led to participate by his discovering and exploring verbally the various facets of a problem. Between sessions he is encouraged to try out the principles and hypotheses he accepted: reality testing.

Books are also a valuable adjunct to teaching in the counseling program and should be kept on hand to lend. Many of the Public Affairs pamphets are especially helpful.[26] They are also inexpensive and may be available for sale. Many life insurance companies are distributing free pamphets written by experts in the field of psychology and counseling and available to ministers and others.

---

[25] Morris, *Premarital Counseling—A Manual for Ministers,* pp. 51ff.

[26] May be ordered from Public Affairs Committee, 22 E. 38th St., New York, N.Y. Pamphlets are twenty-five cents. They are written by experts in the fields of family relations, social problems, health and science, and intergroup relations.

They are too numerous to list, but an inquiry through a local insurance office should be sufficient to give one an idea as to what is available.

SUMMARY

One of the aims of counseling is to help the counselee to become motivated to carry out his decisions and to achieve self-actualization. To do this the counselor must help the counselee to acquire a new self-image because many who come for counseling see themselves as inferior, disgusting failures. Self-depreciation must be replaced with a new perception of oneself so that behavior which once seemed beyond control comes within the boundaries of conscious control. This is accomplishd by the acceptance of the counselee by the counselor, by changing the emotional environment, and by instruction. The innate potentialities in the individual, when set free, will enhance the personality, because there is in one a basic tendency toward self-actualization.

The internalization of values is also essential to motivation. The external practices of religious ceremonialism do not of themselves mean that the values they represent have been internalized. Moral and spiritual values can be internalized by a couple's reevaluating the course they have been following, by their changing to another group because the group usually sets the moral standards of its members, by their consciously living the Christian life, and by their having a Christian marriage as their goal.

Christian family ideals have been clearly defined by most churches, e.g., the Anglican Communion, the Methodist Church, and the Presbyterian Church in the United States.

Failures and frustrations in reaching one's goal can be very discouraging, but if one gains insight into and understands the dynamics of one's failures, then one may be motivated to make a new effort. Kurt Lewin's analysis of conflict situations is of help to couples in understanding their frustrations.

Teaching must never be overlooked as a function of counseling. Goals must be clearly defined, chosen, and desired; only then can one be strongly motivated to achieve the goals of a happy and successful marriage.

SUGGESTED READING

Allport, G. W., *The Nature of Personality*. Cambridge, Mass.: Addison-Wesley Publishing Company, Inc., 1950.

Asch, S. E., *Social Psychology*. Englewood Cliffs, N.J.: Prentice-Hall, Inc., 1952.

Becker, Howard and Reuben Hill, *Family, Marriage, and Parenthood*. Boston: D. C. Heath & Company, 1955.

Garrett, Henry E., *General Psychology*. New York: American Book Company, 1955.

Johnson, Paul E., *Christian Love*. Nashville: Abingdon Press, 1951.

King, Richard A., *Readings for an Introduction to Psychology*. New York: McGraw-Hill Book Company, 1961.

Mace, David R., *Marriage: The Art of Lasting Love*. Garden City, N.Y.: Doubleday & Company, Inc., 1952.

Maslow, A. H., *Motivation and Personality*. New York: Harper & Row, Publishers, 1954.

Munn, Normal L., *Psychology* (4th ed.). Boston: Houghton Mifflin Company, 1961.

Oates, Wayne E., *Religious Factors in Mental Illness*. New York: Association Press, 1955.

Roberts, David E., *The Grandeur and Misery of Man*. New York: Oxford University Press, Inc., 1955.

Conclusion

13 The minister may see himself in several roles as preacher, administrator, teacher, or pastor. In whatever role he thinks of himself as being most effective, he will be in contact with people who are troubled about problems of personality adjustment. Foremost among these problems will be those involving relationships within the family, and more often than not, between husband and wife. Many of these people will consult him believing that because of his calling to be a pastor, he will be able to help them solve their problems in such a manner as to result in happiness and peace of mind and heart.

Many people who have moved across the preceding pages were on a quest for a fullness of life they had not been able to achieve because of some breakdown in the marital relationship. They began their marriage for the most part with high hopes of success, only to find in a few months or years that it had eluded them. Selfishness due to immaturity or crises which they were unprepared to handle cast dark shadows over their union causing them to lose sight of their goals and to become frustrated, angry, and bewildered.

Counseling with people whose marriages are "sick" and falling apart cannot be done effectively without scientific knowledge of the dynamics of human behavior as revealed by psychology and related sciences. "Commonsense psychology" belongs to the past—it is not sufficient to meet the needs of modern man. The minister must take advantage of every opportunity to read and study in the field of human behavior and counseling. Whatever he may learn will enrich his own personality, his preaching, and his pastoral care.

But, lest someone feel that mere knowledge of psychology will make one a good counselor, it must be added that along with knowledge there must go love—a sincere love which reaches out toward the counselee in empathic understanding, holding forth hope and encouragement. The pastor who has no time to prepare couples for marriage and no time to spend with those whose marriages are threatened with dissolution has lost sight of two great privileges of his ministry; namely, to share in the joy of expectancy with those preparing for marriage, and to walk through the valley of the shadow of death with those pursued by fear of failure in marriage.

Marriage counseling is rapidly developing as a profession. Excellent courses are being offered in several universities and institutes. The American Association of Marriage Counselors, Inc., is seeking to set high standards of counseling proficiency and to promote ethical standards of the highest order. Ministers should be familiar with this organization and its requirements for membership in order to evaluate their own limitations and to seek to prepare themselves for membership.

It is gratifying to see that pastoral counseling by well-trained ministers is becoming more and more a part of the church's program. The American Association of Pastoral Counselors lists 161 church counseling centers in the Association's 1964 directory.[1] Seminaries are aware of the need for this training and some are requiring it under the Council for Clinical Training [2] during the summer months. Other ministers are enrolled in colleges and universities offering courses in counseling. Older ministers are finding it necessary to read and study in this field so that they may be more effective in helping their people with their personal, marital, and family problems. One evidence of this new interest is the number of books being published in this field for the minister's library.

The hope of the author is that this present book may not only help pastors in the practical work of marriage counseling but will also stimulate their interest both to pursue the subject further and to become even more proficient as a reconciler between God and man, and between man and his fellows.

---

[1] This is a recently formed organization. Information may be obtained by writing The Service Department, 100 Maryland Ave., N.E., Washington, D.C.

[2] Address: 475 Riverside Drive, New York, New York, 10027.

1 Declaration of Intention

In the Name of the Father, and of the
Son, and of the Holy Ghost. Amen.

Declaration of Intention

We,

_____

and

_____

desiring to receive the blessing of Holy Matrimony
in the Church, do solemnly declare that we hold
marriage to be a lifelong union of husband and wife
as it is set forth in the Form of Solemnization of
Holy Matrimony in the Book of Common Prayer.

We believe it is for the purpose of mutual
fellowship, encouragement, and understanding, for
the procreation (if it may be) of children, and their
physical and spiritual nurture, for the safeguarding
and benefit of society.

And we do engage ourselves, so far as in us lies,
to make our utmost effort to establish this relationship and to seek God's help thereto.

_____

SIGNATURE OF GROOM

_____

MAIDEN NAME SIGNATURE OF BRIDE

Dated _____ *A.D.* _____

313

// Schedule 1A

Marriage Council OF PHILADELPHIA, INC.

3828 LOCUST STREET • PHILADELPHIA 4 • PENNSYLVANIA

Serial No. ....

Before .... interviewer

Partner's Code ....

MARRIAGE ADJUSTMENT SCHEDULE 1A

NAME .... DATE SCHEDULE IS FILLED IN ....
    (Surname)   (First name)   (Maiden name)

AGE .... Years .... Months   PARTNER'S AGE .... Years .... Months

PERMANENT ADDRESS ....

Place where you are while filling in this schedule (Marriage Council office, class, elsewhere) ....

Please be sure to answer every question.* In answering them, DRAW A CIRCLE AROUND THE <u>NUMBER</u> IN FRONT OF THE APPROPRIATE RESPONSE, or put a check mark where called for. Do not circle more than one alternative unless asked to do so.

1 How long have you been married to your spouse, as of present time? .... months or .... years
(If less than 1 month, give time in weeks ....)

2 How long was it between the date you became formally engaged and the date of your marriage? .... months or .... years
(If less than 1 month, give time in weeks ....)
If you were not formally engaged, check here ....

3 Give your marital status at time of filling schedule:
1—Married
2—Separated (because of marital friction) for
.... months or .... years
3—Divorced .... months or .... years ago
4—Widowed .... months or .... years ago
5—Other (Common law marriage, etc.) ....
Date of separation, divorce, or death of spouse ....

4 What has your marital history been?
1—Married once (circle here if present marriage is your only marriage)
2—Married twice—first marriage ended in divorce
3—Married twice—first partner died
4—Married more than twice
5—Status other than the above (specify) ....

Date previous marriage ended ....

5 What has your partner's marital history been?
1—Married once (circle here if present marriage is partner's only marriage)
2—Married twice—first marriage ended in divorce
3—Married twice—first partner died
4—Married more than twice
5—Status other than the above (specify) ....

6—Do not know

6 What are the living arrangements of you and your partner?
1—Living in own quarters
2—Living with parents or parents-in-law
3—Other (specify) ....

*If separated, answer all questions on the basis of what was current when you lived with your partner, except when asked to answer as of the present time.

7 If you or your partner were or are in military service during your marriage, has it involved separation from each other?
1—Yes
2—No
3—Not applicable

8a How do you feel military service during your marriage affected your relationship with your partner?
1—Not applicable
2—Helped relationship
3—Interfered with the relationship
4—Did not affect the relationship

8b How does your partner feel that military service during the marriage affected your relationship with each other?
1—Not applicable
2—Helped relationship
3—Interfered with the relationship
4—Did not affect the relationship
5—Do not know

9 What are the occupational classifications of yourself and your partner? If you or your partner are either unemployed or temporarily in the armed forces, answer this question about the former occupation.
Yourself Partner

Yourself	Partner	
1	1	Not employed for compensation (circle here for housewife, student, etc.)
2	2	Unskilled worker
3	3	Semi-skilled worker (garage attendant, bench hand, farm hand, etc.)
4	4	Skilled worker (automobile mechanic, toolmaker, draftsman, police, fireman, engineman, etc.)
5	5	White-collar worker (file clerk, typist, salesman, secretary, bookkeeper, etc.)
6	6	Small business man (retailer, garage operator, etc.)
7	7	Professional worker (teacher, minister, doctor, lawyer, artist, musician, regular army or navy officer, etc.)
8	8	Business executive or professional administrator
9	9	Farmer

10 Approximately how long during your married life together has or did the wife work for compensation?

....................................months or ....years

(If less than 1 month, give time in weeks....................)
If wife has not worked for compensation since marriage,

check here....................................

11 Is wife working for compensation at present?
1—Yes
2—No

12 What are the reasons for wife's working for compensation during your married life together? (Circle only the most important reason, even if more than one reason exists)
1—Wife has not worked for compensation since marriage
2—Wife has worked **mainly** in order to continue a career
3—Wife has worked **mainly** in order to provide necessities
4—Wife has worked **mainly** to provide a higher standard of living for the family
5—Wife has worked **mainly** because she preferred it to staying home
6—Other (specify) ....
7—Do not know

13 Whether you are the husband or the wife, do you approve of the wife's working for compensation since marriage? (If wife has not worked, check only alternative No. 1)
1—Wife has not worked for compensation since marriage
2—Yes, approve
3—Do not approve
4—Indifferent

14 To what extent are you satisfied with your husband's occupation or your occupation if you are the husband? (If unemployed or in the armed services answer this question about your former occupation)
1—Extremely satisfied
2—Satisfied
3—Somewhat dissatisfied
4—Extremely dissatisfied

15 Is your income (whatever is earned by you and/or your partner) supplemented regularly by other resources?
1—No regular supplementation
2—Yes, by parents (own or in-laws)
3—Other (specify) ....

16 Do you confide in your spouse?
1—About most things
2—About a few things
3—Not at all

17 Does your spouse confide in you?
1—About most things
2—About a few things
3—Not at all
4—Do not know

18 Are you satisfied with the amount of demonstration of affection in your marriage?
1—Yes
2—Desire less
3—Desire more

19 Do you think your spouse is satisfied with the amount of demonstration of affection in your marriage?
1—Yes
2—Desires less
3—Desires more
4—Do not know

20 When you and your partner have spare time simultaneously, do you spend it together or separately?
1—Most of it together
2—Some of it together
3—Little or none of it together
4—Have no spare time that occurs simultaneously

21 How do you feel about the situation described in your answer to the previous question?
1—Satisfied
2—Dissatisfied (Comment....................)
3—Indifferent
4—Do not know

22 How do you and your spouse take part in the following activities? (Put a check mark in the appropriate space for each type of activity)

	Both participate together	Both participate but not together	One partner participates, other does not	Neither participates
Motion pictures				
Dances				
Competitive sports (playing tennis, etc.)				
Spectator sports				
Outdoor activities (riding, walking, fishing, etc.)				
Social gatherings with friends (to play cards, talk, etc.)				
Reading				
Art appreciation (listening to music, visting museums, etc.)				
Creative and interpretive art (writing, drawing, music, acting, etc.)				
Politics				
Hobbies (collecting, mechanics, woodwork, needlework, etc.)				
Membership in clubs and organizations				
Business or professional activities or interests (beyond office hours)				

23a. How do you get along with each of the following? (Put a check mark in the appropriate space for each person)

	Very well	Fairly well	Poorly	Not applicable (not living, etc.)
Your mother (or her substitute)				
Your father (or his substitute)				
Your mother-in-law				
Your father-in-law				

23b. How does your partner get along with:

	Very well	Fairly well	Poorly	Not applicable (not living, etc.)
Your mother (or her substitute)				
Your father (or his substitute)				
Your mother-in-law				
Your father-in-law				

24 Since your marriage, has there been any disagreement between you and your spouse over any of the following matters? (Put a check mark in the appropriate space for each area of disagreement)

	None because the matter has not arisen	None because the matter arose and you found that you and your partner agreed	A little	Some	Considerable
Household management					
Financial matters					
Mother					
Father					
Mother-in-law					
Father-in-law					
Other relatives					
Personal habits (smoking, drinking, etc.)					
Health					
Wife working					
Husband's work					
Religious matters					
Education					
Social background					
Friends					
Sharing of household tasks					
Matters of recreation					
Sexual adjustment					
Jealousy					
Infidelity					
Personality disagreement					
Children					
Other					

25 When disagreements arise between you and your spouse do they usually result in:

1—Your giving in
2—Your spouse giving in
3—Agreement by mutual give and take
4—Neither giving in
5—No disagreements

26 Do you like doing household tasks? (Answer this if you have had any experience with domestic activities. If you have not had any, circle alternative No. 5)

1—Like very much
2—Like somewhat
3—Slight dislike
4—Considerable dislike
5—Does not apply

27 How do you and your spouse divide responsibility for home activities? (Put a check mark in the appropriate space for **each** type of activity.

	Entire responsibility of wife	Primarily wife's responsibility with husband's help	Shared responsibility	Primarily husband's responsibility with wife's help	Entire responsibility of husband	Does not apply
Daily household tasks (beds, dishes)						
Buying of supplies (food, equipment)						
Handling the money (paying bills and budgeting, etc.)						
Maintenance activities (furnace, lawn, etc.)						
Child care						
Supervision of household employees or any paid outside help						
Other (specify)						

28 Rate the personality traits of your spouse and yourself on the scale which follows. Write W for wife, H for husband. In the last pair of columns check if either of the spouses' traits cause difficulty in the marriage.

	Considerably	A little	Not at all	Husband's traits cause difficulty	Wife's traits cause difficulty
Angers easily					
Gets over anger quickly					
Takes responsibility willingly					
Stubborn					
Selfish					
Dominating					
Sense of humor					
Easily hurt					
Makes friends easily					
Likes belonging to organizations					
Easily influenced by others					
Acts impulsively					
Easily depressed					
Easygoing					
Easily excited					
Jealous					
Punctual					

29 Everything considered, how happy has your marriage been for you?

    1—Very happy
    2—Happy
    3—Unhappy
    4—Very unhappy

30 Everything considered, how happy do you think your marriage has been for your spouse?

    1—Very happy
    2—Happy
    3—Unhappy
    4—Very unhappy
    5—Do not know

31 If your marriage is now at all unhappy, for how long has it been so? .... months or .... years

32 What do you feel are the main causes of difficulty?

....

....

33 How do you and your partner get along together at the present time?

    1—Very well
    2—Fairly well
    3—Poorly

34 How do you feel that your present love for your spouse compares with your love for her/him before marriage?

    1—Much stronger
    2—A little stronger
    3—The same
    4—A little weaker
    5—Much weaker

Index

Index